COMMUNICATION
An Overview

COMMUNICATION
An Overview

Suraj Singh

CENTRUM PRESS
NEW DELHI-110002 (INDIA)

CENTRUM PRESS
H.O.: 4360/4, Ansari Road, Daryaganj,
New Delhi-110002 (India)
Tel: 23278000, 23261597, 23255577, 23286875

B.O.: No. 1015, Ist Main Road, BSK IIIrd Stage,
IIIrd Phase, IIIrd Block, Bangalore-560085 (INDIA)
Tel: 080-41723429

Email: centrumpress@gmail.com
Visit us at: www.centrumpress.com

Communication: An Overview

First Edition, 2010

ISBN 978-93-80836-11-9

PRINTED IN INDIA

Printed at Mehra Offset Press, Delhi

Contents

Preface

Communication is a process of transferring information from one entity to another. Communication processes are sign-mediated interactions between at least two agents which share a repertoire of signs and semiotic rules. Communication is commonly defined as "the imparting or interchange of thoughts, opinions, or information by speech, writing, or signs". Media stands as an attractive career prospect to the youth of today. So, we have introduced this section so that an individual can become familiar with the various streams that make up Mass Communication and also become aware of what Mass Communication has to offer him in terms of career.

Although there is such a thing as one-way communication, communication can be perceived better as a two-way process in which there is an exchange and progression of thoughts, feelings or ideas (energy) towards a mutually accepted goal or direction (information). Communication is a process whereby information is enclosed in a package and is channeled and imparted by a sender to a receiver via some medium. The receiver then decodes the message and gives the sender a feedback.

All forms of communication require a sender, a message, and a receiver. Communication requires that all parties have an area of communicative commonality. There are auditory means, such as speech, song, and tone of voice, and there are nonverbal means, such as body language, sign language, paralanguage, touch, eye contact, and writing. Visual communication as the name suggests is communication through visual aid. It is the conveyance of ideas and information in forms that can be read or looked upon.

Primarily associated with two dimensional images, it includes: signs, typography, drawing, graphic design, illustration, colour and electronic resources. It solely relies on vision. It is form of communication with visual effect. It explores the idea that a visual message with text has a greater power to inform, educate or persuade a person. It is communication by presenting information through visual form. The evaluation of a good visual design is based on measuring comprehension by the audience, not on aesthetic or artistic preference.

There are no universally agreed-upon principles of beauty and ugliness. There exists a variety of ways to present information visually, like gestures, body languages, video and TV. Here, focus is on the presentation of text, pictures, diagrams, photos, et cetera, integrated on a computer display. The term visual presentation is used to refer to the actual presentation of information. Recent research in the field has focused on web design and graphically oriented usability. Graphic designers use methods of visual communication in their professional practice.

Chapter 1

The Importance of Communication

Although the Internet may be portrayed as a communication technology unique to the 1990s, this depiction is somewhat misleading. The Internet's origins are in fact traceable to the 1960s development of the military-funded communication network, ARPANET, with the Internet officially making its debut as a civilian tool for communication in 1983.

However, widespread public awareness of the Internet's existence did not occur within the United States until the early 1990s when it was privatized and online services such as America Online (AOL) were developed to serve the general public. Hence, there is a tendency to think of it as a turn-of-the-twenty-first-century phenomenon.

Prior to the 1990s, early public access to the Internet was limited mostly to government agencies, universities, and computer-related organizations, such as hardware and software developers. Initially, users experienced the Internet in the form of text-based communication applications such as e-mail and navigation systems such as Telnet.

In 1992, the World Wide Web (WWW) became publicly available in the United States and began to diffuse widely in 1993 with the release of the iconbased web browser Mosaic, which made web navigation more "user friendly" and visually appealing. Subsequently, use of the Web helped to popularize the Internet in general. As use of the Internet has shifted from a small community of researchers and government employees to a worldwide community, researchers recognize the Internet as an important area in need of study. The widespread diffusion and adoption of the Internet in the United States and abroad provides scholars with numerous research opportunities. Because the Internet functions as a channel for communication, this is especially true for the field of communication. However, as with any innovation, it can be difficult at first to know how to approach the investigation of an innovation's contribution to and effects on the society into which it is introduced.

With regard to the Internet, communication researchers, as well as others, must grapple with numerous decisions, such as determining how applicable existing theories and methods of inquiry are to this newest communication technology.

While the arguments for why and how to study the Internet vary, a common theme to arise within our discipline concerns the unique opportunity that today's communication scholars have to witness and record, first hand, the introduction of a major communication technology.

Scholarly journals are one forum where communication researchers record the results of their research for the benefit of current and future generations of scholars. Published articles inform other researchers of the types of approaches being used to study a wide variety of topics, including the Internet.

A number of disciplines are conducting Internet research as is evident when searching electronic databases. For example, a simple keyword search conducted in December 1999 in the Social Sciences Abstracts database on the term "Internet" yielded a return of 969 articles published across a diversity of disciplines, most notably in the areas of business, demographics, law, and policy studies.

Each discipline, including communication, typically contains a core set of journals considered to be "leaders" among all others in terms of their coverage of subject matter, length of publication, and quality of published articles. The question asked in this study concerns how leading journals in the field represent Internet-based research conducted by communication scholars, because an important goal of scholarly journals is to document a field's evolution over time.

This study examines the content, frequency, and pattern of published Internet-based research articles-studies that focus on some aspect of the Internet-in leading communication journals for the purpose of assessing how these journals are keeping pace with the Internet's influence on the communication process. It also considers how these journals represent our response to these changes to other disciplines in the social sciences.

THE IMPORTANCE OF COMMUNICATION SCHOLARS RESEARCHING THE INTERNET

Within the discipline, a handful of articles has addressed the importance of communication scholars studying the Internet. The reasons for study as well as the ways in which the Internet should be studied are varied. For example, in 1996, the Journal of Communication devoted the majority of its winter issue to "The Net."

Within this issue, in a dialogue between Newhagen & Rafaeli, Rafeali pointed out that the development of the Internet, in part, is rooted in academe and, as such, "this alone behooves our involvement" in its study. Beyond this statement Rafeali suggested that researchers focus on what he called the "five defining qualities of communication" on the Internet which, although somewhat abstract, included "multimedia, hypertextuality, packet switching, synchronicity, and interactivity."

Newhagen argued that communication researchers must take a more active role in understanding the Internet by first understanding computer architecture, an area often left to engineers. A bridge must be constructed between the worlds of communication and engineering so that communication researchers no longer find themselves in the position "where the engineers roll out a new technology, and we hold up numbers from 1 to 10, rating it."

Concerning the benefits of studying virtual reality, Biocca stated, "Communication researchers rarely have had the chance to observe the introduction, diffusion, and sociocultural presence of what may become the next dominant communication medium." However, he cautioned against viewing new communication technologies as a revolutionary by stating that many "new" technologies build upon, and borrow from, existing ones.

As such, researchers are likely to start out using existing theories and methods to study a new technology. He suggested focusing on questions such as the shape the medium is taking, and how the medium shapes and is shaped by the user-areas well suited to communication research. In a 1993 article, writing more broadly about humancomputer interface design, Biocca, as Newhagen was to do later in 1996, called for communication scholars to be more proactive in researching computer-mediated communication (CMC) by taking part in the design and development of new communication technologies.

Although, both of Biocca's articles were written just prior to the Internet's widespread public diffusion, his ideas, as if in anticipation of its introduction, are very applicable to the Internet and have been echoed in the later writing of Newhagen and Rafaeli.

Other communication scholars assuming the importance of studying the Internet have suggested additional approaches to its study. December argued for the need to define specific units of analysis for Internet research that would act as guideposts for researchers, helping to facilitate cross study comparisons.

These four units were defined as media space, media class, media object, and media instance. He also proposed a definition of Internet-based computer-mediated communication as that which involves information exchange that takes place on the global, cooperative collection of networks using the TCP/IP protocol suite and the client-server model for data communication. Messages may undergo a range of time and distribution manipulations and encode a variety of media types. The resulting information content exchanged can involve a wide range of symbols people use for communication.

As such, he argued that the Internet is not a single

medium but is instead made up of several media. Additionally, he cautioned that researchers studying on-line services such as Prodigy or America OnLine (AOL) should be aware that they were not actually conducting Internet-based research because these access providers offer proprietary services not available on the Internet.

While this caveat is technically correct, it is perhaps overly restrictive. In addition to offering proprietary services to its users, on-line vendors such as AOL also function as Internet Service Providers (ISPs), allowing for communications to be exchanged via the global network.

In contrast to December, Morris and Ogan viewed the Internet as a single flexible mass medium capable of the synchronous and asynchronous transmission of text, audio, and video communication.They argued that the Internet provides the opportunity for communication researchers to rethink rather than abandon traditional views on mass media and to adopt a more flexible perspective on communication models.

Additionally, they suggested that researchers study the Internet using a variety of existing frameworks, such as network analysis, and theories, such as social presence. In summary, these scholars essentially argue that communication in relation to other disciplines should be a leader, if not the leader, in researching the Internet because it is a communication phenomenon.

Communication scholars need to be proactive and creative in their research designs in order to reach this goal. To do this, they must possess a thorough understanding of how the technology works by taking an active role in the design and evaluation of future Internet applications.

RATIONALE

Knowledge of the extent to which Internet-related topics have been addressed and what methods of inquiry have been applied can assist communication researchers in placing their work within a broader range of studies. This information also identifies over- and under-emphasized topics and methods.

Lastly, knowledge of the degree to which the Internet is represented within a discipline can provide researchers with a sense of the area's development and relative importance to the field as a whole. It is not uncommon for communication researchers to analyse articles within an individual journal or a range of journals in order to assess the status of the discipline as a whole with respect to a particular issue.

Examples of these studies include analyzing the frequency with which qualitative research is published, investigating the content and quality of published content analyses, and assessing the status of published mass communication articles by women across eight journals. Continuing this type of inquiry, this study examines the publication history of Internet research among five leading journals in the field.

JOURNAL SELECTION CRITERIA

While acknowledging the presence of newer electronic Internet and new technology-specific publications such as Internet Research and Journal of Computer-Mediated Communication, this study purposely focuses on mainstream, established communication journals. The reasons for this emphasis are threefold.

First, and most obvious, the Internet is a channel for communication and as such it falls within the realm for study by communication researchers and, in turn, publication in our leading, established communication journals. Second, established journals-those in existence for a period of decades-have the distinct advantage of having built both a reputation and a following over time.

These journals are widely read within the discipline, contributing to scholars' perceptions of and currency with changes in the field. A third reason, closely related to the second, is that established journals can be viewed as historical records that document the field's evolution. Ideally, these journals reflect trends in the development of a discipline and the segments of society with which it deals as accurately as possible for the benefit of current and future scholars.

Selection of the five journals examined in this study employed two criteria: previous research identifying leading journals in the field and the reputation of Social Sciences Abstracts as a valid resource for communication research. In a content analysis of women's published research in mass communication, Dupagne, Potter, and Cooper identified eight leading communication journals, defined according to high circulation counts and low acceptance rates.

The journals identified in their study included: Communication Monographs, Communication Research, Critical Studies in Mass Communication, Human Communication Research, Journal of Broadcasting and Electronic Media, Journal of Communication, Journalism Quarterly, and Quarterly Journal of Speech.

These journals functioned as a starting point for this study; however, application of the second criterion, communication research indexed in Social Sciences Abstracts, resulted in the omission of four titles from the original list.

The decision to further limit the journals examined was based on a twofold rationale. First, electronic databases are increasingly used by scholars to conduct literature searches because of their ease of use and convenience in comparison to print indexes. Within the vast realm of electronic indexes available for searching, Social Sciences Abstracts is a widely used leading index published by the highly reputable indexing service, H. W. Wilson Company.

Second, subject-specific indexes, such as Social Sciences Abstracts, are typically more useful to and more likely to be used by scholars than general indexes, such as Expanded Academic Index, because they cover indexed journals in more detail, are more likely to index all articles in a journal rather than a chosen few, and they provide longer, more detailed abstracts.

By restricting the focus to leading communication journals indexed in Social Sciences Abstracts, this study attempts to take into consideration a broader view concerning how scholars in other disciplines might perceive the role of our discipline in the area of Internet research based on the presence of communication journal articles contained in the index. With the application of this second criterion, the final list of journals examined in this study include: Communication Research, Human Communication Research, Journal of Broadcasting & Electronic Media, Journal of Communication, and Journalism & Mass Communication Quarterly. Measures. This study uses December's definition of Internet-based communication but with a slightly more liberal view on what constituted Internet-based communication.

An article was considered Internetbased if it focused on computer-mediated communication technologies requiring access to an ISP, including services such as AOL or Prodigy, or closely simulated an Internet-based communication environment (e.g., intranets, e-mail exchange between AOL members).

This definition broadly included the Internet in general, intranets, World Wide Web (WWW), e-mail, mailing lists, bulletin boards, newsgroups, chat, virtual reality games such as multi-user domains (MUDs), and video/audio/text computer conferencing. From the interfaces specified above, it can be seen that in most instances Internet access was necessary for communication to occur.

As with any area of research, certain information is useful in providing scholars with an overall sense of an area's progress or current status. For the purpose of this study, the concept of current status is operationalized into nine measures-author name, authorship, author rank, affiliation, topic, interface, method, total number of Internet-based articles per issue, and total number of research articles per issue.

Identification of an area's primary researchers provides scholars with a sense of which perspectives may be dominant in an area of study. While quantity of publication by an author does not necessarily equate with quality of research, it can provide scholars, especially those new to an area, with a starting point in the literature. The same can be said for the order of authorship on an article.

Distinguishing between primary and secondary authors can indicate, but not necessarily guarantee, which researchers are initiating studies, taking primary responsibility for the studies, and acting as primary contacts or "experts" in an area. Knowledge of which universities or organizations are conducting research in a particular area is benefi'.ial for those interested in matters such as networking, educational, and employment opportunities.

The rank (e.g., faculty, staff, student) of an author provides information on the diversity or homogeneity of the contributors to an area of research. This study attempts to answer two basic questions. First, what is the frequency and pattern, if any, of published Internet-based research articles in five of the leading communication journals?

Second, what do the contents of these articles reveal about the status of Internet research within and outside of the communication discipline?

METHOD

UNIT OF ANALYSIS

The unit of analysis for this study was the scholarly communication research article that focused on Internet-based communication. This included "research in brief" articles but excluded editorials, rejoinders, and book reviews.

Coders primarily read titles and abstracts to determine if an article fit this study's definition of Internetbased research. In instances where article titles and abstracts did not provide sufficient information, coders skimmed the articles for details.

POPULATION DATA

All research articles were examined in four major communication journals between the years 1994-1999. Because frequency of publication over time was one question asked by this study, population data were used instead of sample data in an effort to obtain a more accurate depiction of publishing trends across time by these journals.

The four journals selected for the main study included

Communication Research, Human Communication Research, Journal of Broadcasting & Electronic Media, and Journal of Communication. A fifth journal, Journalism fa Mass Communication Quarterly, was selected for a pilot study to test the codebook.

To identify leading communication journals publishing Internet-related articles, a basic keyword search was conducted using the term "Internet" in the Social Sciences Abstracts electronic database; four journals were consistently referenced in the search results and thus selected for closer examination. One limitation of this selection process concerns the exclusion of some communication journal titles from the Social Sciences Abstracts index. However, this limitation was considered acceptable given the broader focus of the study discussed earlier.

Despite this limitation, the five journals selected for this study are examples of the mainstream publication outlets available through most of the field's major associations: the Association for Education in Journalism and Mass Communication, Broadcast Education Association, and International Communication Association.

The starting year for the study, 1994, was selected because, based on the Social Sciences Abstracts search results, in general, Internet publications did not begin to increase until that point in time. The first recorded Internet article in the database occurred in 1992; one article was referenced in 1993. However, in each year thereafter, the number of articles increased steadily. This pattern is consistent with the growing popularity of the Internet with the general public in the United States. The communication journals selected for study during this time frame contained a total of 961 research articles (323 from the pilot study and 638 from the main study). Each article was examined to determine if it met the definition of Internet-based research. Those articles that qualified were then coded.

OPERATIONAL DEFINITIONS

To answer the questions proposed in this study, nine

measures were recorded for each Internet-based research article: author name, authorship, author rank, affiliation, topic, interface, method, total number of Internet-based articles per issue, and total number of research articles per issue. For each article the last name and initials of all authors were recorded.

Authorship was coded as primary (first author) or secondary (all additional authors). The rank of each author was coded as faculty, student, staff (university affiliated, nonfaculty/non-student employees), government employee, business employee, or other. Author affiliation was recorded as the name of the university or organization with which the author was identified at the time of publication.

Rather than attempt to anticipate the range in subject matter, article topic was recorded as open text by each coder and then later grouped into six broad categories: access, adoption/diffusion, policy, research/theory, social interaction, and other.

Interface, the application used to communicate via a computer, was divided into eight categories: World Wide Web, e-mail, mailing lists/newsgroups/bulletin boards, chat rooms, virtual reality game sites (e.g., MUDs, MOOs), video/audio/text-based conferencing, Internet in general (no specific interface identified), and other (coders recorded the specific interface).

Method of inquiry was coded as policy study, critique/essay (non-policy studies), interview/case study, content analysis (qualitative and quantitative), experiment, survey, other (coders recorded the specific method) and combination for multiple methods used within a single study (each method was recorded and then weighted).

Lastly, for each journal issue, coders recorded the total number of Internet-based articles and overall total number of research articles.

CODING PROCEDURES

The author and another communication researcher acted as coders. The codebook was created by the author and reviewed for clarity by the second coder. A pilot test to check for intercoder reliability was conducted on all issues of Journalism & Mass Communication Quarterly, 1994-1999, resulting in a 100% overlap of 323 articles.

Discrepancies in coding were discussed, and slight modifications for the purpose of clarification were made to the codebook before proceeding to the four journals selected for the main study.

Reliabilities for the number of Internet-based research articles and total number of articles for the pilot test were at the acceptable levels allowing for the inclusion of these articles in the study, under separate reporting.

Intercoder reliability for the main study was calculated using a 20% overlap. Issues for the reliability check were selected using a stratified random sample. The total overlap between the coders contained 128 articles.

INTERCODER RELIABILITY

For the main study, the level of agreement concerning which articles qualified as Internet-based research was 98.4%. Percentages of agreement and Scott's pi corrections for chance (where applicable) were as follows for the measures: author name, 97.9%; authorship, 97.9%,.96; author rank, 97.9%,.97; affiliation, 97.9%; topic, 94.3%; interface, 96.9%,.96; method, 97.7%,.97; and total number of research articles per issue, 96.9%.

For the pilot study, percentage of agreement for Internet-based research articles was 84.6% and 99.7% for total number of articles per issue. Frequency analyses are reported for each measure. With the exception of overall trends in publishing, all other measures report data collected from the four journals in the main study.

This is because intercoder reliability for the pilot study was only reached on the two measures: Internet-based articles per issue and total articles per issue.

TRENDS IN PUBLISHING

Of the 961 research articles analysed, 37 (3.9%) were Internet-based. Among the four journals in the main study,

4.1% (26 of 638 articles) were Internet-based. Trends in the publication of Internet-based articles across the five journals revealed no distinct pattern of increase, decrease, or stabilization during the six-year time period. This finding was also the case within each of the five journals.

Overall, the Journal of Communication (32%) published Internet research articles the most frequently followed by Journalism & Mass Communication Quarterly (30%), Journal of Broadcasting & Electronic Media (24%), Human Communication Research (8%), and Communication Research (6%).

The percentage of published Internet-based research articles varied widely by year; however, a trend line reflecting a moving average suggests that the number of articles has increased over time.

TOPIC, INTERFACE, AND METHOD

Social interaction (31%) was the topic most often researched. This was followed by research/theory (23%); other (15%), which included the topics of competition among local news web sites, digital art on the WWW, TV audience feedback via email, and portrayals of the Internet in magazines; access (12%) and adoption/diffusion (12%); and policy issues (7%).

The interface studied most often was the Internet in general (42%) followed by mailing lists/newsgroups/bulletin boards (19%), WWW (15%), email (12%), and chat rooms (4%), video/audio/text conferencing (4%), and other (4%) which included an Internet-based interactive health programme. The two most frequently used methods of inquiry were content analysis (27%) and critique/essay (27%).

These were followed by experiment (11%) and survey (11%), and, lastly, policy study (8%), interview/case study (8%), and combination (8%), which included groupings such as network analysis and content analysis, and surveys and content analysis. The results of this study present a somewhat vague picture as to where this newest area of study is positioned within the selected journals.

In part, this is due to the low number of Internet articles available for examination and thus discussion. The results also indicate that scholars searching the Social Sciences Abstracts would find a scarcity of Internet-related research in our leading journals. It may be that the infrequent and uneven publication of Internet research in the journals examined is simply a typical reflection of any field's initial attempts to come to terms with a new area of study.

This finding suggests that Internet research is an area within the field that is clearly open for study. Within the four journals analysed, only two authors stood out in total number of publications potentially providing greater opportunity for other scholars to become better known through their research in comparison to more established areas in communication.

Not surprisingly, faculty are the dominant group publishing Internet research articles, but, again, because of the newness of the area student authors may have more opportunities to publish than in more established areas. While certain universities are represented more than others, it remains to be seen which programs will eventually come to the fore regarding Internet-based communication research.

In the areas of topic, interface, and methods, similar opportunities for growth exist. However, as speculated by Biocca and Morris and Ogan, thus far, communication researchers primarily are using traditional methods to study the Internet (e.g., content analysis, essays/critiques) with a few studies employing network analysis, as suggested by Morris and Ogan.

Additionally, research has tended to focus largely on the Internet in general, leaving specific interfaces such as mailing lists and e-mail in need of attention. Topics also seem to follow widely used categories (e.g., adoption/diffusion, social interaction) in communication research. This trend may be useful for making comparisons across different types of media; however, it also risks overlooking effects that may be unique to the Internet.

The low number of Internet-based research articles (3.9%) and the sporadic publication of the articles within the five communication journals examined may be attributed to several factors. To begin with, the Internet, despite nearly a three-decade history, is still a relatively new area of study. Although the World Wide Web, which helped make the Internet popular, became publicly available in 1992, it was not until 1995 that awareness of the Internet by the media and the general public began to increase.

With this increased awareness among the populace, researchers are realizing the importance of researching the Internet, but this can be a slow process. In 1995, Dennis Davis, the editor of Journal of Broadcasting & Electronic Media, wrote in his annual summary, "One of my editorial priorities is to increase the number of articles dealing with new technologies.

To do this, the number of submissions will need to be increased. This past year 10 submissions (4.9%) dealt with new industries or new technologies. Three times as many manuscripts dealt with existing industries (30 papers, 14.8%). I would like to see a more even balance between submissions dealing with old and new industries."

To its credit, the Journal of Communication published a symposium on "The Net" in its 1996 winter issue. Factoring in the timeframe necessary for the review, decision, and printing process, the calls to action contained within this issue may partially explain the noticeable increase in the publication of articles during 1998.

The drop off in 1999 may be a reflection of this cycle as well, or possibly a reflection of changes in editors' interests. Still, it seems clear that some of these journals are demonstrating a desire to publish Internet-based research articles; however, as Davis indicates, perhaps few studies are being submitted.

Alternatively, it may be that a number of studies are being submitted; however, because of the relative newness of Internet-based research some of these studies may lack the theoretical grounding often desired in published works by our leading journals. A review of the literature reveals that communication researchers are attempting to unveil the parallels and distinctions between new and traditional technology theories and methodologies, but the research waters are still murky in this area.

Additionally, the emergence of new technology journals such as Internet Research and New Media and Society, may serve as alternative outlets for these studies, thus siphoning off submissions to the mainstream, established communication journals. As well, given the crossdisciplinary nature of the Internet (e.g., computing, communication, human factors), depending on the topic, communication researchers may be submitting their works to journals in other fields.

If this is the case, then the communication journals examined might more actively solicit Internet research submissions in an attempt to better represent the amount and type of research being conducted in this area. While this author does not advocate the lowering of acceptance standards for research articles, communication journals could potentially foster increased publication of Internet research, following the lead of the Journal of Communication, by dedicating issues to symposia on the topic.

These symposia could be viewed as debuts of Internet research that, while possibly less theoretically rigorous, would be considered valuable contributors to the development of future, more theoretically based studies. The main point to be emphasized is that the communication research community is widely dispersed across numerous universities and organizations worldwide.

Scholarly journals function, in part, as a communication link between researchers. Communication scholars interested in studying the Internet benefit most by knowing who else is researching in the area and what results have been found. Leading journals play an important role in conveying this information, but only if that information is being published.

If it is the case, which remains to be seen, that Internet research is not being published because of a lack of strong theoretical foundations, then an important question needs to be addressed. Namely, how are scholars to build theory if they do not have access, which these journals can provide, to studies on which to build a foundation? The answer may lie in the emergence of topic-specific journals such as New Media and Society.

In 1996, Morris and Ogan, commenting on the Internet's growth (25 million at the time), asked, "Why, then, have communication researchers, historically concerned with exploring the effects of mass media, nearly ignored the Internet?" This is a question still in need of an answer, or possibly reformulation. We might also ask why our leading journals appear to be slow on the uptake.

Notably, Wartella and Reeves, in a 1985 study that examined historical trends in publishing about children and the media, observed "that the relationship between research activity and media popularity is not simultaneous." Their findings illustrated that research related to a communication technology (e.g., film, radio, television) often lags behind the diffusion rate of the technology, a pattern confirmed in this study.

Nevertheless, Internet research appears to be an area of study with which communication researchers must become more comfortable and skilled at conducting. Unlike television, radio, or print media, the computer requires certain knowledge and skills to operate-and ultimately to study.

As Biocca and Newhagen and Rafaeli argue, communication scholars are being called upon to take a more active role in the understanding and design of new communication technologies. These challenges, as well as knowledge and skills requirements, may act as barriers for some researchers who are less technically oriented.

This particular barrier may be offset over time as communication programs develop tracks of study in new technologies on both the graduate and undergraduate levels that emphasize familiarity with and understanding of computer communication technologies.

Additionally, the Internet can simultaneously function as an interpersonal and mass channel for communication. This hybrid nature tends to blur the traditional lines used to distinguish different types of communication from one another. Is the Internet really a form of mass communication? Questions such as this one make it difficult for communication scholars to identify perspectives from which to study the Internet.

Finally, because Internet research is more or less in its infancy and as such lacks a strong history of research on which to build, communication researchers must be especially thoughtful about and creative in their approach to its study. They must also make the effort to network, outside of journal publications, with other Internet researchers to share research strategies and results.

Certainly, not every communication researcher is interested in studying the Internet nor, given the numerous areas available for study within the field, should it be the focus of every communication scholar or the sole topic of our leading publications. However, in general, to overlook the Internet as an area for study is to be remiss as a discipline.

Before concluding, two limitations must be addressed regarding the narrow focus of the research. First, the conclusions drawn from this study are primarily limited to the five journals examined.

It should be noted, though, that these journals have historically attempted to keep pace with changes in the discipline so that cautious speculations of a more general nature about the discipline's response to the Internet might be made. However, additional research examining a broader range of communication journals is necessary to confirm these speculations.

Second, the definition used to identify Internet-based research excluded articles examining computer-mediated communication more generally. Future studies may wish to examine this broader category of research as well. This study makes two primary contributions to the field. First, it informs communication scholars of the content and amount of published Internet research in leading journals that represent our research efforts both within and outside of the discipline.

Second, it generates discussion concerning why the

numbers are relatively low in light of earlier calls to action regarding the importance of studying the Internet. Both communication journals and communication scholars play important roles in determining where Internet research will be positioned within the discipline, as well as where the discipline will be placed relative to other fields investigating the technology.

Despite the small number of Internetbased articles published by five of our leading journals during the sixyear time period examined, communication scholars studying the Internet should be encouraged in that, overall, the number of articles published appears to be increasing.

However, to more accurately reflect the Internet's importance as a research topic within the discipline, it is hoped that the findings in this study will encourage communication scholars to submit more of their Internet-based research to our leading journals while current and future editors of these journals will be encouraged to include more of these articles in their publications.

As a discipline we possess the potential be a leader in Internet research, and our core journals can, and should, reflect this potential not only to scholars within the field but also to the larger academic community.

Chapter 2

Communication: An Interactive Model of Political Development

The role of communication in political socialization has been recognized for several decades. Early research on political socialization was implicitly founded on a transmission model of communication of knowledge, partisanship, and attitudes from parents to children.

Research then began to examine the role of different patterns of communication within the family in political socialization, and revealed significant effects? Other research, conducted primarily in the 1970s, posited a role for mass communication, particularly television news, in the socialization of young adults.

Another paradigm in political socialization research focused on the role of age as a developmental factor determining political socialization. Much of the research in the 1960s attempted to describe differences in socialization criteria (e.g., political knowledge and attitudes) based on the age of the child being observed. It became clear that attitudes and knowledge varied with age.

Much of the early research seemed to be based on the implicit assumption that age was a measure of cognitive capacity in the Piagetian sense. However, in the past decade the strict stages of development proposed by Piaget have been questioned and significantly modified to conform to more recent theories of development that do not propose distinct stages occurring at specific ages.

The study of political socialization waned between the

early 1970s and the mid-1990s, and much of the recent work has focused on adults instead of children. There has been little work published that takes advantage of developments in the study of children's cognitive capacities, or in improvements in the study of media effects.

However, in the past few years there has been renewed enthusiasm in political socialization research. The purpose of the present study was to build upon the two traditional paradigms of political socialization research described above and to elucidate a revised model, the "interactive model of political development."

Specifically, we focused on the acquisition of political knowledge by middle and high school students. Although research on political socialization has used countless criteria, the present study focuses on political knowledge as the primary criterion to represent political socialization.

We have done this because research has shown that there are high levels of instability in attitude measures for children as well as other serious problems,lo leading to current concerns about the reliability and validity of measurement of attitudes in pre-adults.

Literature Review and Theoretical Development

Communication and Political Socialization. Beginning in the late 1960s and early 1970s, research on political socialization began to emerge in the field of communication. Early work examined the role of family communication patterns in influencing the knowledge and attitudes of children.

Later research began to evaluate the use and influence of news media among children and adolescents, finding that news use (especially television news) was relatively prevalent among children and that it had some impact on their political knowledge.'

Early in the study of mass communication and political socialization, Chaffee and his associates found that high school students from Wisconsin rated mass media higher than teachers, parents, and friends as sources of information about current affairs. Then, using cross-lagged correlation to analyse their panel data, they found that attention to media public affairs was positively related to political knowledge, implying a causal relationship.

A sample of third- through sixth-graders from Michigan were shown to have high levels of exposure to both political advertisements and viewing of television news.There were relationships between political knowledge and advertisement exposure, campaign news viewing, and general news viewing, with the strongest relationship being for campaign news viewing.

Similarly, a sample of 9-year-olds, 13-year-olds, and 17-year-olds interviewed by Rubin demonstrated a significant relationship between television public affairs viewing and two different measures of knowledge.' More sophisticated analyses of the effects of news media use on political knowledge have revealed reciprocal effects of news media use and political knowledge for children in fifth and sixth grades. The primary causal link, however, was from news media use to political knowledge, not from political knowledge to news media use.

This finding bolsters the initial Chaffee, Ward, and Tipton finding of causal effects among Wisconsin students. The literature thus supports the conclusion that, even across disparate age groups, media use has some causal influence on political knowledge.

Other research has also demonstrated that news media use (particularly television news) can lead to some form of knowledge for pre-adults. Evidence has been based on both cross-sectional and panel survey data as well as experimental studies comparing recall of experimental news stories or broadcasts across groups.

Interpersonal discussion is also important in childhood political socialization. McLeod and Chaffee have repeatedly demonstrated the importance of family communication patterns for many dependent variables, including political socialization. Other research has also demonstrated effects of interpersonal discussion on the political knowledge of children, although sometimes it has been found to be less important than mass mediated communication. Based on the communication literature, then, the following hypothesis was offered:

HI: High levels of political communication (both mass mediated and interpersonal) will be positively related to political knowledge.

Age and Political Socialization. Much of the initial research on political socialization was primarily descriptive-it focused on determining the knowledge level and attitudes of children at different ages. However, it is important to focus on exactly what age means in this particular programme of research. Wartella points out that simply describing changes in a dependent variable across age groups is not an explanation in itself.

In the early political socialization research there seems to be an implicit assumption that age (or grade in school) is a measure of cognitive development and that as children develop cognitively there will be qualitative changes as well as quantitative increases in their political knowledge. Indeed, Sigel states that "the ability to reason logically, to think abstractly, and to apply such thought to concrete situations-all prerequisites for meaningful political thoughtare age-dependent."

The notion that cognitive development is a function of age is based on studies conducted during the early years of socialization research. This early research generally followed Piaget's claim that children progressed through two major distinct stages of cognitive development during their primary school years: concrete operations (from about ages 7-11) and formal operations (from about 12 years of age on).

Since it is not until the stage of formal operations that children are able to (mentally) manipulate abstract concepts and ideas that serve as the fundamental bases of politics, their ability to think about political matters as "adults" should begin at about this time.

Unfortunately for research on socialization, however, "age is only a rough locator for these concepts"and "is confounded with temporal sequence concepts of all kinds, both personal (developmental or life cycle) and historical."

Other prominent scholars of political socialization agree to a greater or lesser extent with the inherent limitations of age as a precise measure.

The difficulty of discerning what age measures is highlighted by Bar-Tal and Saxe's argument that changes in political knowledge are the result of both cognitive developmental changes and a continuous build-up of political information over time-two effects inexorably combined in a measure of age. Even Piaget himself was not certain about the actual validity of the age norms specified for the different stages of cognitive development because of large individual differences."

In socialization research, age has been viewed as a primary determinant of levels of political knowledge. Most recent research has been able to demonstrate that older children score higher on political knowledge quizzes or provide better answers to open-ended questions about the political environment than do younger children.

However, the relative dearth of research on childhood political socialization in the late 1980s and 1990s has meant that the early descriptive studies have rarely been elaborated on and examined within a modern theoretical foundation. Thus, if anything, much of the research continues to use the traditional Piagetian stages of development framework. It is rare when these studies address the fundamental question of where the knowledge comes from, since it seems obvious that the capacity to process information, not the content of knowledge itself, is the real product of cognitive development.

Based on the conceptualization of age as a rough indicator of increased cognitive capacity and a greater store of general information (which serves to facilitate integration of new information into an overall cognitive framework), but not as a measure of qualitative shifts in mental ability (as Piaget has proposed), the following hypothesis is offered:

H2: Age will be positively and linearly related to political knowledge.

An Interactive Model of Political Development. The literature clearly demonstrates that levels of political knowledge vary by age. In addition to traditional direct effects models of how age impacts political knowledge, two additional, more complex models of the role of age in political socialization are also important: mediating models and moderating models.

A mediating model would examine the relationship of chronological age with some other variable that may be what directly causes greater knowledge. For example, age may bring with it higher verbal functioning, which would encourage greater levels of discussion of politics between parents and children.

This discussion in turn could lead to the greater knowledge of politics found in older children. In this example, then, the effect of age (as a measure of verbal functioning) is indirect, through political discussion.

McLeod, Eveland, and Horowitz tested a mediating relationship between age and political knowledge through the primary agents of political socialization (that is, family, peers, schools, and media) and found that age did indeed influence political knowledge both directly and indirectly through newspaper reading and television news use.

Another possibility is a moderating model, what we will here call an interactive model of political development. Scarr-Salapatek and Salapatek see socialization as "an interaction between socio-cultural and organismic factors." Political socialization researchers have also noted the importance of moderating variables: "It would appear that innate characteristics such as levels of basic intelligence and rates of cognitive maturation set the broad parameters within which political learning takes place.

As these inner forces develop they permit more fruitful interaction with environmental stimuli provided by parents, teachers, peers, and the public media." O'Keefe and Reid-Nash similarly note that socialization occurs at each level of analysis from individual through societal, pointing to the importance of studying the process at each level.

Taking this notion quite literally, socialization may occur through biological characteristics of the individual (e.g., cognitive capacity as represented by a measure of age) and social factors such as the level of information available in the child's environment (e.g., communication via mass media or interpersonal sources). That is, the level of information available through the social-level process of communication has some impact on knowledge levels, but the child's cognitive capacity to deal with this information moderates the effect.

Thus, socialization is a process that is dependent on the interaction of several factors, including cognitive capacity and information levels in the environment. Although this model seems quite obvious, and many political science and communication theorists have stated it implicitly or explicitly, few studies have directly tested this model, and even fewer have tested it using the appropriate statistical methods.

This perspective on political socialization predicts that when the capacity is clearly present (such as in later adolescence and adulthood) but information unavailable, there will be low levels of knowledge. As Bar-Tal and Saxe argue, the study of knowledge must be connected to the information that is available in the environment.

Similarly, if the cognitive capacity is not present (such as in early childhood), even great amounts of information may lead to only slight gains in knowledge. This effect is similar to that predicted by the knowledge gap hypothesis, albeit research on the knowledge gap typically uses the education level of adults as the indicator of capacity to deal with mediated information.

Statistically speaking, cognitive capacity is a moderator of political communication (either interpersonal or mass-mediated) effects on knowledge.This formulation of socialization effects can explain the finding that during adolescence media use is more important than age for political socialization; that is, once the cognitive capacity has been developed, it is the level of information available in the environment that will lead to knowledge gain.

There is some evidence for this hypothesis in the literature on the socializing effects of mass communication.

For example, Rubin found that the relationship between public affairs television use and issue specificity (one of his measures of knowledge) was significant only for the oldest age group in his sample, 17-year-olds.

Atkin demonstrated that the effects of both television news use and campaign advertising on knowledge were greater for fifth- and sixth-graders than for third- and fourth-graders. Similarly, Atkin and Gantz detected a correlation between national news exposure (as well as exposure to Saturday morning kids' news programs) and political knowledge for fifth- and sixth-graders but not for kindergarten through third-graders.

However, direct comparisons could not be made in this case because knowledge was measured differently for the two age groups. Not all of the evidence in the literature has supported this hypothesis, however. Garramone and Atkin expected greater effects of newspaper reading on knowledge for older children than younger children, but hypothesized no difference by age for television news viewing.?

Using data from 149 seventh- and tenth-grade students, they found no support for their expectation of different effects of newspaper use by age. The main effect of television news was greater than for newspapers for current events knowledge, however, which was consistent with their hypotheses. Despite this limited contradictory evidence, the logic of the interactive model of political development and the bulk of the literature suggest the following hypothesis:

H3: The impact of political communication on political knowledge will be greater for older children than for younger children.

METHODS

Sample

The data for the present study were collected by telephone interview from San Jose, California, during the two weeks directly after the 1994 midterm election. The 290 children in this sample were in grades five through twelve of both public and private schools, and ranged in age from 9 to 18 years. One parent of each child was also interviewed separately to provide additional information.

The data were collected as part of an evaluation study of Kids Voting San Jose. Initially, 457 sampled parent-child pairs were separately interviewed in order to evaluate a school-based programme called Kids Voting designed to encourage political socialization and parental voting turnout. Of these 457 parent-child pairs, those who served as the experimental group for the evaluation (that is, those who received the Kids Voting stimulus) were excluded from this analysis, leaving the sample size for the present analysis at 290.

Although it would have been possible to use the full sample and include a variable for experimental vs. control group as an initial covariate in the analysis, possible interactions between this covariate and the other control and independent variables would make this approach cumbersome and potentially statistically inappropriate. Measures. Twenty-three questionnaire items were used to measure communication in the present study.

From these twenty-three items, six indices were built-four pertaining to media use, one to interpersonal discussion, and one to a form of media information processing. News media use was measured using twelve indicators to represent both general and campaign specific media use. These items were factor analysed (principal components with oblique rotation) and produced four distinct factors with Eigenvalues greater than one (total variance accounted for = 53.6%) which were used to compute factor score variables.

The first factor represents campaign media attention (Eigenvalue = 2.93) and has three items as primary loaders-attention to news about candidates for office, attention to news about ballot propositions, and attention to news about the national government in Washington, D.C. The second factor represents general newspaper exposure (Eigenvalue = 1.32) and has four primary loaders-days per week reading the newspaper, reading the front page of the newspaper, reading letters to the editor, and reading opinion columns and the editorial page. The third factor was general television news use (Eigenvalue = 1.14), on which days per week watching a television news programme and agreement that news is something the child tries to watch on television were primary loaders. The fourth and final factor was non-traditional media use (Eigenvalue = 1.05), with three primary loaders-listening to talk radio, attention to candidate advertisements on television, and watching the candidate debates on television.

Interpersonal political discussion was measured using a seven-item additive index (alpha =.75). This index combined items included in both the parent and child questionnaires. Children were asked about their political discussions with their friends, who initiated these discussions, the level of discussion of the campaign in their school classes, the level of discussion of the campaign and election in their family, and the level of this type of discussion between the child and the parent that was interviewed.

The parent interviewed was asked only about the level of campaign and election discussion in the family and the level of discussion between themselves and the child interviewed. The final communication variable is actually a hybrid measure which is at once linked to media use and cognitive processes. Research has demonstrated that the way people cognitively use the information they are exposed to in the mass media has important implications for the effects of that information.

Specifically, those who think about, elaborate on, question, and make use of information they encounter in the media (both print and broadcast) are more likely to learn from the media content they encounter Active reflection is a four-item factor that represents this form of information processing.

The criterion used for political socialization in the present study was current political knowledge, an additive index (KR20 =.80) of fourteen multiple choice questions (coded as either correct or incorrect, with "don't know" responses coded as incorrect).

Among these were questions asking the child to identify the winners of the gubernatorial and U.S. Senate races in the child's state, along with other highly publicized national races, such as the race for Ted Kennedy's U.S. Senate seat and the race for the Texas governorship. Other questions asked the child to identify candidates from the child's own state based on well-publicized information about their campaigns, accomplishments, or personal background.

Stage models of development (e.g., Piagetian models) suggest that qualitative changes in a child's thinking would occur when he or she shifted from one stage of development to the next. The only stage shift that would occur on average in the age group in the present study (according to Piagetian theory) would be between the concrete operational and formal operational stages, which is believed to occur around age 11 or 12.

The nature of a qualitative shift (as opposed to a quantitative shift) is inherently non-linear; that is, if children truly go through stages and these stages are similar for most children, we should expect that the relationship between age and political knowledge should change dramatically around the age of the stage shift.

Although the knowledge measure used in the present study is not designed to be sensitive to such a qualitative shift, it is important to verify that no such shift took place for our measure in order to satisfy the statistical assumptions of our later regression analyses. In order to do so, quadratic and cubic functions were fitted to the data in order to see if they provided a better fit to the data than a linear regression line.

However, in no case did these nonlinear functions significantly improve on the linear prediction. Once we established that linear regression analyses were appropriate, we could proceed to test the hypotheses of the study.

Age and all forms of communication except nontraditional media use seem to have substantial influence on political knowledge, providing general support for Hypotheses 1 and 2.

Research on political socialization using communication as a dependent variable has demonstrated that in many cases communication itself is a function of age-that is, as children age, they become more likely to use mass media news and to engage in political discussions.

To test whether or not the relationship between communication or age and knowledge is spurious, the unique contribution of age controlling for communication, and conversely the unique contribution of communication controlling for age, were computed via partial correlations.

However, these reductions were in no case large enough to be considered significant. There was an interesting increase in the strength of relationship between non-traditional media use and knowledge after age controls, indicating that age had a weak suppressing effect on the relationship between non-traditional media use and political knowledge, in part due to a negative relationship between age and non-traditional media use.

The implications of controlling for communication (all six communication variables simultaneously) when examining age effects are similar-although there was some reduction in the size of the correlation between age and political knowledge, the change is not significant. Clearly there were substantial unique contributions of both age and communication to political knowledge.

The shared variance, on the other hand, is minimal. Hypotheses 1 and 2 seem to have received strong support. The zero-order relationship between each variable (except non-traditional media use) and knowledge was substantial, and the contribution of each was sustained after control for the other.

Age was entered alone in the first block and accounted for about 13% of variance. In the second block, the six communication variables were entered simultaneously. The second column, however, reports the coefficients with simultaneous control for all variables in the model. Here, the multicollinearity of the communication variables is revealed-three of the six variables dropped to non-significance, while the impact of the other three was substantially reduced.

However, as a block the six communication variables accounted for over a quarter of the variance in political knowledge, indicating that there was certainly a strong relationship between political communication and political knowledge. The variables accounting for the most unique variance-newspaper exposure, campaign media attention, and active reflection-remained significant predictors of political knowledge.

O'Keefe and Reid-Nash note that "A socialization perspective entails rather sophisticated multivariate designs incorporating indicators of life cycle position, source of influence, type of learning process, and structural variables."To address concerns about the need for incorporation of stringent controls, additional models were run simultaneously controlling for parental education, household income, child's gender, and child's performance in school as a first block in the regression before age and the communication variables were entered into the equation.

These controls did not change the model in any significant way and were theoretically unimportant for the present study, so they were left out of the final model to maintain simplicity.

Hypothesis 3 stated that there would be an interaction between communication variables and age when predicting political knowledge. Specifically, the interactions were expected to take the form of a contingent or contributory condition-communication should have the greatest (or possibly only) effects for older children who have developed cognitive structures to deal with the information to which they are exposed.

Based on recent discussions in both mass communication and psychology noting the substantial likelihood of Type II errors in interaction tests using survey data, we chose to follow a suggested approach and relax our alpha level for the interaction tests to $p < .10$.

It may be noted that the variance accounted for by the multiplicative terms was quite modest-however, statisticians have noted that interactions are more useful for interpreting relationships than in accounting for variance in criterion measures. In general, the interactions were significant for those communication variables that had the greatest effect on political knowledge at the bivariate level.

All of the interactions were of a similar form-the contributory condition expected. Contrary to the findings (but consistent with the prediction of) Garramone and Atkin, the strongest interaction was between general newspaper exposure and age-older children learned more from newspapers than younger children, as expected. Similarly, attention to the campaign also produced greater effects for older than younger children.

Active reflection, which is more cognitive than behavioral (unlike the other communication measures), was still moderated by age level. Younger children were less able to make thinking about and questioning media information translate into greater knowledge of politics. Finally, older children obtained more information from political discussions with family and friends than did younger children. Television news use and non-traditional media use effects were not significantly moderated by age, however.

In both of these tests the effects of communication and age were clearly additive, not multiplicative. Additional controls were added to all these interactive models. Again, simultaneous controls for parental education, household income, child's gender, and child's performance in school did not alter the models substantially, and so were left out to maintain simplicity.

These findings provide many clues about childhood political socialization that can be used to advance and possibly revive a field that has gone through more than a decade of decline,6 and to inform researchers with more practical interests. First, as a preponderance of past research has shown, age does have an effect on political socialization, at least when political knowledge is the criterion. The results of this study also indicate that communication plays an important role in political socialization.

Six communication variables, including both mass and interpersonal communication and a variable measuring processing of mediated information, were found to be significantly related to knowledge either at the bivariate level or after some degree of control. Although controlling for age did reduce the relationships between communication and knowledge in some cases (and increased it in one case), these changes were not large, and therefore we can reject the notion that the effects of communication are spurious due to the relationship between age and communication.

The primary intention of the present study was to offer an alternative model of political development that can be applied across many socialization contexts. The interactive model as proposed here suggests that political socialization is dependent on both cognitive capacity and available information, that is, on characteristics of the individual and characteristics of the environment.

Using age as a rough indicator of cognitive capacity and life experience and communication variables as measures of information available in the environment of the child, it was proposed that effects of the presence of socializing information would be dependent on at least some minimal level of cognitive capacity. In essence, the model proposes a simple, intuitive condition-for children to learn the political information presented to them either interpersonally or through mass media, they must have the cognitive capacity to process and understand this information. Empirically, this relationship would be observed as an interaction between communication and age when predicting knowledge. Few researchers in the field of political communication have explicitly tested for this moderating effect of age.

The results indicated strong support for the interactive model of political development. Evidence for four of six hypothesized interactions was found, and each of these interactions was in the expected direction.

The effects of political discussions, general newspaper readership, attention to news about the campaign, and active reflection on campaign information obtained from the media on political knowledge were all dependent on the age of the child, such that the relationships were greater for older children than for younger children.

Not only are the effects of communication not spurious due to age, they are also not additive with respect to age. It might be questioned, if the interactive model of political development is valid, why was there no interaction observed between age and either television news use or non-traditional media use?

Although we are unable to settle this question sufficiently with the present data, Salomon's research on differences in learning from different symbol systems provides one possible explanation. It may be that communication via television is easier for children in our sample (ages 9 through 18) to learn from because they had already developed the requisite skills for dealing with the visual information from this symbol system.

That is, it may be necessary to examine younger children who do not have as much experience with television news, possibly from preschool to middle school, to find the expected interaction. By the time they move into high school (about half of our sample), most children may be able to deal with the symbols (not to mention the level of information provided) in television news.

Similarly, Neuman, Just, and Crigler found that television news provides context through exciting visuals that is typically unavailable in newspapers. Their results indicate that television was also able to make abstract issues easier to understand for their adult sample.

These findings support the notion that television news (and the debates and advertisements that made up most of our non-traditional media variable) may have been easier to use for our younger respondents and therefore did not require the greater cognitive development and life experience that other communication sources necessitated.

The fact that the strongest interaction found in the present study was for the only print media variable, newspaper exposure, while the weakest significant interaction was found for campaign media attention (which is content but not medium specific), seems to support this explanation.

Despite the theoretically interesting findings produced

by this study, it does have some limitations. First, the small, local sample limits direct generalizability to larger populations. However, it is unlikely that the relationships found here are unique to our sample of San Jose, California. Childhood development is unlikely to vary much from locale to locale, and even if development occurs more quickly among certain subsets of the population than others, it is unlikely that the order of developmental effects vary across subsets of the population.

Second, the criteria for political socialization in the present study was limited to a single variable, political knowledge. Socialization research has focused on countless criteria over the years, and many have not used knowledge as the primary criterion. Often used measures include internalization of norms, attitudes toward political leaders, partisan affiliation, and political participation. Future research should be conducted to discover whether the interactive model applies only to knowledge or whether it applies to attitudes and behaviors as well.

A final potential flaw in this test of the interactive model of political development is one that haunts all research using self-reports by children. Since reliability of measurement is generally lower for younger children than older children and low reliability tends to reduce the size of correlations, there is some possibility that the weaker relationship between communication and political knowledge found for the younger members of our sample was due to greater measurement error among this group.

To examine this possibility we divided our sample into three roughly equally sized groups (912 year olds, 13-15 year olds, and 16-18 year olds) and found that our dependent variable was indeed less reliable among the younger group than among the middle and oldest groups.

However, if this was the sole cause of our interactions, the unreliability of the criterion measure should have affected the relationship between the dependent variable and all independent variables equally. In fact, it did not since, as we have already reported, the interactions did not appear for television news and non-traditional media use independent variables. Thus, the differential measurement error by age is a possible, but unlikely, competing explanation for our results.

The findings supporting our theoretical model can provide valuable information for those interested in media intervention programs designed to actively socialize middle and high school students. Although our data cannot confirm it, since our approach is based on general principles of development there is little reason to suspect that our findings would not apply across socialization content domains (such as health or environmental protection information) and therefore have wide applicability for professional journalists and social action campaigners.

The implications of an interactive model suggest that those who intend to use the mass media to deliver socialization messages must take into account the age or expected level of development of the target audience in order to produce the desired effects and avoid an inducement of the knowledge gap. That is, those who target children in their preteen years (even if these are only a subset of the total target audience) should likely make use of the entertaining visual or auditory media of television and radio, because both younger and older children are able to learn equally well from these media.

If preadolescents are not part of the target audience, newspapers are likely to be more effective tools for socialization. Although both older and younger children seem to learn equally well from television and nontraditional media, this learning is not as substantial as the learning older children do using newspapers.

Therefore, when the target audience has developed enough cognitively to make use of the print media, then print seems to be the most effective media agent of socialization. Further, if programme designers are not concerned with knowledge gaps based on age, they should use print media to reach older children while simultaneously using television to reach younger children.

The choice made will depend on the relative importance

placed on equal distribution of knowledge across age groups versus maximal learning for a particular age group. It should be noted, however, that the present study could not separate the difference between medium effects and content effects. That is, while it may be that younger children inherently have greater difficulty with print media than with television, it may also be that the content carried in newspapers is simply more difficult to understand.

That is, if the content of the newspaper was transferred to television, younger children would still have difficulty understanding it. Therefore, we caution that media differ on at least two dimensions, form and content, and it may be either dimension that leads to the differences in learning between age groups.

Overall, this study has successfully demonstrated support for the proposed interactive model of political development. If the study of political socialization is to again become an important subfield of the larger study of political communication, the current lack of interest and research must be replaced by alternative ideas and new methodological approaches.

The interactive model of political development provides one possible alternative approach to the study of communication in socialization processes, and now there is some initial evidence supporting this model. Future studies of political socialization should attempt to replicate and expand on the findings presented here.

Chapter 3

Gender Role Self-Perception on Communication Style

It has long been argued that men and women differ greatly in the way they communicate and interact with others. Despite apparent differences, however, considerable research suggests that sex differences may play only a small role in the cognitive and behavioral processes that underlie communication. This investigation explores the possibility that gender role selfperception, not biological sex, serves as the predominant referent for how people see themselves interacting with others.

Researchers often argue that language is not sex-neutral: it seems to divide, separate, and differentiate women from men. The separation between male and female as a simple dichotomy prevails in many cultures as evidenced, for example, by the Chinese Yang and Yin, the Hindu Lingam (Shiva) and Yoni (Shakti), and the Tantric Buddhist Jewel and Lotus.

In Western cultures, in particular, differences between the communication styles of males and females are often viewed as so divergent they are considered cross-cultural. Tannen, for example, contends that "instead of different dialects, (males and females) speak different genderlects". Indeed, some commentators argue that it's as if males and females have been raised on two different planets (or, at least, two different cultures), with two unique patterns of communicating.

Granted, we all can envision a stereotypical "Barbie Doll"

female and "Marlboro Man" male. Within this stereotypic frame, as numerous scholars have observed "Barbie" characteristically is emotional, passive, sweetly proper, mindless, high-pitched, silly, gentle, vague, euphemistic, endless, highly talkative, enthusiastic, self revealing, gibberish, easily influenced, and shows an abundance of hand and face expressions.

"Marlboro Man," on the other hand, displays characteristics of being a "get things done" leader who is boastful, blunt, militant, aggressive, ambitious, straight to the point, domineering, angry tempered, and independent. Although these "Barbie doll" and "Marlboro man" stereotypes seem to pervade Western culture, considerable research evidence suggests that these perceived differences in sex-typed language may exceed the actual differences. Indeed, studies examining several different attributes suggest that sex differences yield only weak effect sizes at best.

For instance, Maccoby and Jacklin, in a monumental narrative review of the literature, concluded that there are few sex differences and that those that do emerge are small in magnitude and often overshadowed by interactions. Thus, counter to conventional wisdom, the findings of Maccoby and Jacklin suggested that females were not more social than males, were not better at simpler tasks, did not have lower self-esteem, and were not more suggestible than males. Similar research from Zimbardo found no evidence to support the cultural assumption that females are more shy than males.

Application of meta-analytic techniques to quantitatively summarize the sex-differences literature has revealed a similar pattern. Frieze, Whitley, Hanusa, and McHugh, for instance, concluded that sex did not have an impact on how individuals interpret and explain the outcome of why things or events had occurred. Similarly, Eagly and her colleagues have found that differences between males and females in influenceability, leadership style, helping, aggressiveness, and social leadership were quite small.

Focusing specifically on communication styles, Montgomery and Norton proposed that "a large but fragmented body of literature suggests that men and women differ significantly in their interpersonal communication". However, after analysis of data from two samples, Montgomery and Norton concluded that males and females differed little in their perceptions of their own communication style.

Similarly, Hyde and Linn found that no sex differences existed in verbal ability among individuals; Burleson and Samter also found sex differences to be insignificant in social participation and communication skills; and Heiss found that, contrary to stereotypic beliefs, male and female displayed equal power and dominance through their communication styles in intimate relationships. These conclusions are also echoed in more recent work.

Along the same vein, Wheelen and Verdi investigated male and female communication patterns evident in small groups. They found no stereotypic sex differences in the categories of task, maintenance, or verbal participation. Simkins-Bullock and Wildman also found that sex differences did not explain substantial differences in the type of language incorporated in the communication styles of males and females.

Finally, a meta-analysis conducted by Lustig and Andersen found no sex difference in the degree to which males and females are communicatively avoidant or anxious. Viewed together, the body of research suggests that no substantial sex differences emerge across many aspects of communication behaviour. But the question remains: Where do we derive our attitudes and beliefs about sex-differences in communication? It appears that another factor must provide the foundation on which stereotypic attitudes and beliefs about communication style are constructed.

Most of us rarely encounter extremely stereotypical models in our everyday lives. We are socialized under more moderate conditions where sex -and gender- differences are frequently intermingled, if not confounded (i.e., feminine males, masculine females). Given this consideration, how can it be argued that separate sex cultures perpetuate when many of us come from family/social environments where divergent gender roles interact on a continuous basis?

In other words, because all of us were not raised in two separate sex cultures, perhaps it's not maleness and femaleness, as some argue, that makes people behave and communicate differently. Instead, it could be that our gender role self-perception is the key factor underlying our attitudes, beliefs, and behaviors when interacting and communicating with others.

Most people develop an implicit theory, a naive psychology, and/or a cognitive schema of individual gender differences. These cognitive structures are seen as culturally based summaries of a person's experiences. As cognitive structures, gender role conceptions can serve as filters that transform and modify one's own perceptions and behaviors and serve to help explain differences in behaviors evidenced by others.

Research examining gender oriented cognitive structures suggests that two constructs, agency and communion, effectively summarize a broad range of attitudes and beliefs on what is colloquially called maleness and femaleness. The agentic gender role construct includes characteristics such as goal-orientation, assertiveness, protectiveness, self-activation, and having the urge to master. In contrast, the communal construct involves characteristics such as selflessness, openness, caring, affectionate, kindness, helpfulness, sympathy, and having a desire to be at one with others.

Whether an individual embraces an agentic or communal gender role self-perception-or perhaps no particular gender role self-perception at all-is thought to result primarily from socialization. Children encountering predominantly agentic models should be expected to adopt agentic behaviors and characteristics. The opposite result would be expected for children encountering predominantly communal individuals. Within this framework then, a female influenced by a communal role model should exhibit a gender role self-perception consistent with stereotypically feminine characteristics.

A male, on the other hand, influenced by an agentic role model should exhibit a gender role self-perception consistent with stereotypically masculine characteristics. At the same time, others will acquire gender role self-perceptions (i.e. agentic female, communal male) that are incongruent with sex-stereotypic cultural norms. And, some individuals will develop a more flexible gender role self-perception.

These considerations highlight a key weakness of early endeavors exploring for sex-differences alone. Not all males are socialized to be assertive and domineering, and not all females follow the stereotype of being passive and dependent. By leaving sex-differences confounded with gender role self-perceptions, critical information about differences between individuals is lost and the emerging picture of variations in communication styles can become clouded.

The applicability of the gender role self-perception concept in understanding communication phenomenon is suggested by several studies. Leaper explored the influence of gender role self-perception on interactions between unacquainted individuals in dyadic situations. The individuals, whether male or female, who endorsed an agentic gender role self-perception showed more verbal assertiveness and used more direct statements.

Individuals who identified with the communal gender role self-perception, on the other hand, used more personal references and were found more likable. Similarly, Luttrell examined the effect of gender role selfperception on listening preferences, as assessed by the Listener Preference Profile. Communal females were found to prefer people-oriented (emotive) listening more and content-oriented (factual) listening less than agentic females.

Although the pattern of means was less distinctive for male respondents, the impact of gender role self-perception illustrated the same trend: communal males tended to prefer people-oriented listening more than agentic males. Most recently, Weaver et al. explored the impact of agentic versus communal self-perceptions on communication apprehension. They found, independent of sex, that individuals reporting a predominantly agentic gender role orientation displayed mastery and expressed confidence about engaging in public, small group, and interpersonal communication situations.

In contrast, individuals oriented primarily toward the communal gender role expressed distress and apprehension at the possibility of facing such circumstances. In other words, agentic men and women reported experiencing significantly less communication apprehension than their communal counterparts. Interestingly, significant sex differences were also evident. However, the variance explained by sex-differences, especially when compared with the effect size for gender role orientation, proved very small.

Taken together, these findings suggest that substantial differences in our concerns about, listening preferences when, and behaviour during interactions with others can emerge as a function of gender role orientation. Is it possible that this concept might also apply to the more general evaluation of how we see ourselves communicating with others? Specifically, could gender role self-perception also be a predictor of our predominant communication style?

The construct of communication style has long been a topic of interest among scholars. During the Roman times, style was one of the "five canons of rhetoric" and Aristotle's observations and recommendations of speaking style are still found in contemporary college textbooks. Currently, the way people perceive themselves interacting and communicating with others is called communication style.

In perhaps the first research on this topic, Norton initially identified nine different aspects of communication style that were labeled: dominant, dramatic, contentious, animated, impression leaving, relaxed, attentive, open, and friendly. More recently, however, Norton has concluded that these nine components actually reflect a single continuum ranging from nondirective communicative style through directive communicative style. The nondirective style embraces the attentive communicator who encourages, accommodates, and acknowledges others. On the other end of the continuum, the directive style involves the dominant communicator who talks frequently, comes on strong, and takes control in social situations.

Hansford and Hattie have drawn a comparable conclusion. Following a factor analysis of Norton's original inventory they found an underlying structure defined by an attentive/supportive dimension and a dominant/animated dimension that paralleled the nondirective and directive communication styles. Equally important, other researches employing different operationalizations of communication style and methodologies have yielded congruent findings.

The most recently developed tool for exploring variations in the way people perceive of themselves interacting with others is the Communication Style Profile Test. McCallister's conceptualization of communication style, which appears to have evolved from the earlier work of Norton and Hart, Carlson, & Eadie, involves three, rather than two, predominant styles that are labeled noble, reflective, and socratic.

The noble style of communicating is conceptualized as directive and straightforward. Individuals who endorse the noble style are characterized as bottom-line, result-oriented people, who get frustrated when others do not accept the same communication premise. On the other hand, reflective communicators are conceived of as nondirective. Individuals who endorse the reflective style are relational and strive to maintain or advance personal relationships, rather than using an interaction for function and goal attainment. As the label implies, they tend to reflect off situations, avoid confrontations, and are the best listeners.

While the noble and reflective communication styles articulated by McCallister appear consistent with the bifurcated conceptualization proposed by others, the socratic style emerges as uniquely different. The socratic communicator is seen as concerned with rhetoric, the analysis of details, and debate. Individuals who endorse the socratic style are verbose, persuasive, and argumentative. They are believed to see a holistic picture of communication and to have the ability and desire to sort through the gray areas to reduce hostility. In this conceptualization, McCallister argues that communication style is acquired through socialization, but that sex-differences have "absolutely nothing at all to do with communication style". This contention does not, however, appear to have been empirically determined.

At the same time, the potential impact of gender role orientation on communication style has not been addressed. In particular, the striking similarity between the conceptualization of noble (i.e., directive, resultoriented) and reflective (i.e., nondirective, relational-oriented) communication styles versus agentic (i.e., assertive, goal-oriented) and communal (e.g., selfless, social-oriented) gender role self-perceptions has been overlooked.

This investigation was designed to address these possibilities by examining the three communication styles as a function of sex and gender role self-perception. Specifically, the following research questions were advanced:

- Do the communication styles reported by females differ from those reported by males?
- Do the communication styles endorsed by individuals reporting a predominantly communal gender role self-perception differ from those of their agentic counterparts?
- Do respondent sex and gender role self-perception interact to influence self-reported communication styles?

To answer these questions, a large sample of undergraduates was recruited to complete a self-administered questionnaire. Gender role self-perception was assessed using the Bem Sex Role Inventory. The three communication styles were tapped via the Communication Styles Profile Test. Significant links between each communication style and sex and gender role orientation variables were explored using both analysis of variance and regression modeling.

Females (n = 495) and males (n = 599) enrolled in an introductory level professional communication course at a large Southeastern university completed instruments assessing gender role self-perceptions and communication apprehension. These instruments were incorporated with several other communication related inventories into a self-administered questionnaire.

Although the respondents did not receive extra credit for helping in the study, completing the inventory made them eligible to participate in other credit awarded research. The data were collected during the initial meetings of the course in the Fall 1993 and Winter 1994 academic quarters before any discussion of gender role self-perception, communication styles, or related topics.

GENDER ROLE ASSESSMENTS

A shortened version of the Bern Sex-Role Inventory, incorporating forty self-descriptive attributes, was used in this study. Respondents were asked to indicate how well each attribute described herself or himself on a scale ranging from "never" (0) to "always". Incorporated in the inventory were twenty items reflecting our culture's definition of femininity (e.g., tender, understanding) and twenty reflecting masculinity (e.g., assertive, independent). For each respondent, femininity and masculinity scales were computed by summing these responses.

In a manner adapted from previous research, the femininity and masculinity scale scores were used to compute a single gender role self-perception measure that ranged from communal (negative values) to agentic (positive values). Specifically, the femininity and masculinity scores were standardized within each gender, the femininity scale scores were reversed, and then the mean of the two scales was computed for each respondent.

This operationalization is conceptually the same as the "gender schematicity" typology advanced by Bern and her associates, but offers two advantages. First, both a continuous and discrete variable can be computed to operationalize gender role self-perceptions offering greater versatility.

Second, when forming the discrete variable, this approach allows for approximately equal cell sizes within each gender rather than the 25% sextyped, 25% cross-sextyped, and 50%

undifferentiated division resulting from Bern's scheme. The tertile distribution of the gender role type index produced the following distribution: communal, undifferentiated, and agentic.

COMMUNICATION STYLES ASSESSMENT

Respondents completed a shortened version of the Communication Style Profile Test. According to McCallister, the CSPT is designed to assess three predominant communication styles that people may employ when interacting with others in both interpersonal and group settings.

The inventory included 48 statements that explored several aspects of the communication process by asking the individual to reveal self-perceptions of competence during, willingness to engage in, and apprehension about communication. The statements were then organized, as outlined by McCallister, to operationalize three communication styles: noble, socratic, and reflective.

The noble communication style is defined as involving assertiveness, directness, precision, impatience, and domination. Individuals who prefer this communication style are characterized as bottom-line, result-oriented people, who get frustrated when others do not accept the same communication premise. Sixteen items were used to operationalize this concept including, for example, "There is a right and a wrong way to do most things," "I say what I think, and I expect the other person to do the same," and "I do not tell others about my personal feelings."

The socratic style is defined as being concerned with rhetoric, the analysis of details, debate, and evaluative judgment. Individuals who prefer this style are characterized as being verbose, persuasive, argumentative, philosophical, and redundant.

Sixteen items were used to operationalize this concept including "I have an excellent ability to recall details," "I enjoy analyzing all of the various aspects and details in a given situation," and "Sometimes it appears that people tune me out when I am talking." The reflective communication style is defined as being accommodating, non-confrontational, and showing concern for others. Individuals who demonstrate the reflective style tend to be warm, supportive, patient, soft-spoken, and good listeners. Sixteen items were used to operationalize this concept including, for example, "I am polite, supportive and warm when I talk," "I share my personal feelings with others," and "I often feel frustrated because I don't actually say what I really feel."

Respondents were asked to report how well each statement applied to themselves on a scale ranging from "never" (0) to "always". In a fashion detailed by McCallister, three indices were computed by averaging the sixteen items for each communication style for each respondent. The resulting indices-labeled noble, socratic, and reflective-were used in subsequent analyses.

Tests for intercorrelation between the communication style measures were computed. All correlations were weak. A significant positive relationship was evident between the noble and socratic styles. A significant negative relationship between the noble and reflective styles also emerged. No overlap between the socratic and reflective styles was evident.

The three dependent measures (noble, socratic, and reflective communication style) were analysed using both multivariate and univariate analyses of variance. Specifically, a 2 X 3 factorial design was employed with respondent sex (male, female) and gender role type (agentic, undifferentiated, communal) as independent-measures factors.

Approximate F statistics for the multivariate tests were derived using the Hotelling-Lawley algorithm. Mean comparisons following the univariate tests were computed using the Newman-Keuls procedure.

MULTIVARIATE TESTS

The MANOVA revealed that both the respondent sex [F(underscored)(3,1076) = 29.6, p(underscored) <.0001, effect size =.08] and the gender role type [F(underscored)(6,2150) = 78.44, p(underscored) <.0001, effect size =.18] main effects were significant. The respondent sex by gender role type interaction accounted for no significant variation (F(underscored) < 1.0).

UNIVARIATE TESTS

The results of the ANOVA models on each dependent measure proved consistent with the multivariate tests. The univariate tests showed significant sex main effects on noble [F(underscored)(1,1078) = 86.87, p(underscored) <.0001, eta-square =.07] and reflective [F(underscored)(1678) = 5.89, p(underscored) <.01, eta-square <.01] communication style measures. The sex main effect for the socratic measure, on the other hand, was not significant [F(underscored)(1,1078) = 1.361. Examination of the means associated with the respondent sex main effects revealed that males (M(underscored) 37.16) scored higher on the noble measure than did the females (M(underscored) 33.64). For the reflective communication style, on the other hand, females (M(underscored) = 35.35) scored higher than the males (M(underscored) = 34.54).

Univariate tests of the gender role main effects were significant (pv <.001) across all three communication style measures [noble, F(underscored) (2,1078) = 81.96, eta-square =.13; socratic, F(underscored)(2,1078) = 6.50, eta-square =.01; reflective, F(underscored)(2,1078) = 183.25, eta-square =.25]. As can be seen, on the noble communication style scale, the mean for the communal group was less than the undifferentiated which was less than the agentic group. Similarly, on the socratic scale, the mean for the communal group was less than the undifferentiated which was less than the agentic group. Conversely, on the reflective communication style scale, the mean for the communal group was higher than the undifferentiated which was significantly higher than the agentic group mean. Finally, the sex by gender role type interactions was examined for all three communication styles. The amount of variance explained by the interaction was trivial (F(underscored) < 1.0), however.

FURTHER ANALYSIS

Even a cursory review of the questions employed in the

Communication Styles Profile Test highlights the fact that a variety of communication concepts underlay each communication style. Constructs such as communication competence, willingness to communicate, and communication apprehension are all intermingled to compose each communication style.

Within the socratic style, for example, communication competence is assessed by items such as "I enjoy trying to persuade another person to accept a position that I support," willingness to communicate is assessed by items such as "I really like to sit and talk with other people," and communication apprehension is tapped by items such as "Sometimes it appears that people tune me out when I am talking." Similar patterns are evident across the other communication styles.

An element of redundancy also exists in the design of the CSPT. For example, the item "I am direct, straightforward, frank, and spontaneous when I talk" from the noble scale seems to tap the same concept as "I often feel frustrated because I don't actually say what I really feel" from the reflective scale.

While the multidimensional nature of the CSPT may be useful for pragmatic applications, from a research standpoint, vital information may be lost by combining all statements into indices. To overcome this potential problem, we examined the individual statements of the CSPT instead of the cumulative measures, to develop a better understanding of the communication style differences between the sexes and across gender role selfperception.

Specifically, stepwise regression analyses were computed. The forty-eight items of the Communication Style Profile Test were entered individually into separate models for both the sex and gender role variables. To be conservative, the probability for entry and retention in these models was set at p(underscored) <.001.

The sex difference variable was converted to a dummy variable with mates coded as +1 and females coded as -1. The continuous operationalization of the gender role type variable was employed (M(underscored) = 0; SD(underscored) =.69). Values for this variable ranged from a minimum of -2.58 (communal) and a maximum of 2.85 (agentic). For ease of explication, the results for the sex and gender role variables are presented separately.

SEX DIFFERENCES

The regression model for the sex difference measure yielded five regressor variables that explained 19% of the variance. For example, males (+1) scored higher on items such as "There is a right and wrong way to do most things", "I say what I have to say in as few words as possible", and "I enjoy discussing abstract or philosophical concepts".

Females (-1) scored higher on the item measures of "Other people tell me their problems" and "I really like to sit and talk with other people". Gender role differences. The regression model for the gender roles measure yielded eight regressor variables that explained over two-fifths of the variance.

Five items entered the model in a negative relationship with the gender role measure. They were: "I am soft spoken"; "I am polite, supportive, and warm when I talk"; "1 tend to 'give in' more than other people and sometimes this bothers me"; "I share my personal feelings with others"; and "I will laugh at an unfunny joke to make the joke teller feel better" all yielded negative links.

This negative relationship shows that those who see themselves as communal individuals tended to endorse these items. Three predictor variables entered the equation in a positive relationship with the gender role measure. For example, "I give my opinions on issues openly", "I get irritated with people who are not decisive", and "I am very exact and detailed when I tell someone how to go about doing something" all were positively related to the gender role measure.

This positive relationship shows that those who see themselves as agentic individuals tended to endorse these items. Consistent with earlier research, the findings show that gender role self-perception mediated self-reported communication styles. Specifically, the findings reveal that, independent of biological sex, the communal respondents reported a preference for a selflessness, caring, expressive communication style.

Conversely, the agentic respondents reported a preference for a goal-oriented, assertive, dominant communication style. Counter to McCallister's projections, significant sex-differences were also evident in communication style preference. Females, on average, reported a relational, socially-oriented style of communicating; whereas males, on average, reported a more direct and results-oriented style of communicating. Further, there was no interaction between the sex and gender role variables.

Given the previous research, perhaps the most provocative finding of this study is that gender role differences appear to provide a better explanation for variations in communication styles than sex differences. Tannen, along with others, has argued that females speak and hear a language of negotiating relationships, connection, and rapport; whereas males speak and hear a language of status and independence.

The data at hand suggest, alternatively, that because such conceptualizations cast communication styles in terms congruent with sexual stereotypes that pervade Western culture while ignoring the diversity of gender role socialization, the reasoning may suffer from a confounding of sex and gender role differences. The findings do, however, reveal sex differences in communication style. Exploratory regression modeling revealed that females showed a greater desire to be social, talkative, and to involve others when communicating.

In contrast, males emerged as preferring dogmatic, pragmatic, and cerebral aspects of communication. This pattern of communicating is consistent with other research. Berryman-Fink and Wilcox, for example, found females to use communication as a socio-emotional function: for males, they found that communication fulfilled the task or instrumental function. Similarly, Doyle and Paludi found the female speech was indirect, while mate speech was direct and powerful. However, the origin of these sex differences remains unclear. What is it about human biology that would explain these differences in communication styles?

One possible explanation is that these findings reflect a response bias due to cultural expectations. That is, a look at the distribution of two specific items from the sex-difference regression model suggests that the responses of males and females were compressed in sex specific ways.

For example, male responses to the item "There is a fight and a wrong way to do most things" exhibit a negative skew, whereas female responses are positively skewed. The opposite tendency is evident for the item "I really like to sit and talk with other people." Responses of females evidence a negative skew while those of males are positively skewed. These trends, which suggest the possibility that the observed sex differences reflect a "cultural stigma" response bias, highlight the need for additional research.

One aspect of these findings that differs from many conceptualizations of the impact of sex and gender roles on communication behaviour is that respondents provided self-perceptions rather than evaluations of others. It must be recognized that the criteria we use when forming perceptions of ourselves may be distinctively different from how we perceive others.

When we evaluate ourselves, biology is generally not a question: sex is implicit. But when we encounter other people, their physical and sexual attributes are often the first characteristics we scrutinize. Assessment of their gender roles may occur much later. When meeting people for the first time, for example, a first step is assessing their sex to decide what role they could play in our lives (i.e. friend, mate, lover). A second step is deciding if their gender role orientation is appropriate for our tastes, wants, or desires, which can take more time and effort.

Thus, although essentially unimportant in self-perceptions, it's the interaction between sex and gender roles that may be critical in how we perceive others. An example of this situation occurs in the skit "Pat, the Androgynous Person" from the television programme Saturday Night Live. Pat, to the consternation of colleagues, exhibits no clear indication of either biological sex or gender role orientation. None of the colleagues, as portrayed in the skit, can figure out Pat's sex, and their apparent cognitive inconsistency and discomfort provides the backdrop for humour.

The skit suggests that if only the colleagues could figure out Pat's sex, they could handle the rest. Again, this portrayal highlights the proposition that both sex and gender role orientation are critically intertwined when we perceive others. The findings of this study, however, suggest that these two factors are independent of each other in reporting self-perceptions. Clearly more research should focus on this apparent discrepancy in the perceptions of self and others.

Understanding the communication styles of individuals reporting undifferentiated gender role self-perceptions remains an intriguing issue. Recent research, for example, by Dion and Notarantonio suggests that individuals evidencing agentic or communal tendencies alone were much less effective as salespeople than were those who displayed a combination of agency and communion (i.e. a precise but friendly presentation).

Unfortunately, the operationalization of gender role selfperceptions employed in this study does not allow for isolation of those individuals who blend communion and agency from those whose selfreports on the Bern Sex Role Inventory suffered from response sets. In other words, it is impossible to distinguish the responses of "yeah sayers" and "nay sayers" from those of individuals who exhibit equal quantities of both gender roles. But, the potential that these individuals are particularly effective communicators suggests that this should be a fruitful avenue for further research.

While the findings of this investigation are informative, some caveats must be acknowledged. The cultural diversity of the sample was limited. Ninety-five per cent of the respondents were Caucasian; diverse ethnic groups were under-represented. Since gender roles are socialized, unique variations in family structures often associated with different ethnic groups could result in differing patterns of gender role stereotypes. Also, the Southern university sampling of the volunteers could be a limitation.

These students tend to have more conservative values and attitudes and, perhaps, endorse more strongly traditional gender role stereotypes. And, perhaps the higher education level enabled them to be more aware of gender role differences and the importance of effective communication. Thus, they could have presented image management biases in their responses. However, this type of process would only inflate the error variance, which ultimately leads to more conservative statistical tests.

Another weakness lies in the fact that the multidimensional concept of communication style may not have been adequately assessed by the operationalization in this study. Since this was an attempt to identify self-perceptions of a predominant communication style, context and situation were not addressed systematically.

Future research might assess communication style in a variety of situations; with, for instance, sex-differences and gender role differences systematically varied across informal or formal, familiar or unacquainted, and dyadic or small group settings. It should be recognized that these findings could be beneficial to the training and consulting fields.

When conducting seminars on communication skills, trainers might stress that effective communication is not sex-based. Instead, it's gender role based. Consequently, although how we communicate with others may be deeply rooted within our self-image, we can learn new, more effective techniques when giving presentations, writing memos, and conducting meetings.

These findings may also prove useful within interpersonal contexts. In discussing why couples have problems communicating, for example, Tannen said that "the real problem is conversational style.

Women and men have different ways of talking". Perhaps this reasoning needs to be reconsidered. In the counseling setting, for instance, if sex-difference stereotypes were set aside when assessing communication style, and attention was focused instead on gender role based differences, more effective therapy could result.

In summary, the findings show that gender role self-perceptions impact self reported communication styles. Independent of biological sex, the findings reveal that the communal respondents preferred a sharing, expressive communication style; whereas the agentic respondents preferred a dominating, assertive communication style. Although a less distinctive pattern, significant sex-differences are also evident in communication style preference. Females reported a more socially-oriented style of communicating and males reported a more direct and results-oriented style of communicating. Further, no interaction was evident between sex and gender role differences.

Chapter 4

The Core Elements of Management in a Communication Context

Research into the managerial role of communication/public relations practitioners represents a major strand in public relations research and theory development. However, much of this research has focused either on how female gender discrimination affects career advancement, salary, and status, or on arguments about practitioner involvement or exclusion from participation in management decision making and strategic planning, rather than focusing on questioning what is understood by the concept of "management" in the communication/public relations context. Although public relations researchers have advanced a number of role typologies to help explicate the key dimensions of practitioners' roles within organizations, most notably, Broom and Smith's four role-typology framework and Dozier's manager-technician dichotomy, neither conceptual framework explains effectively what it is that public relations managers actually do.

The manager-technician role dichotomy has been the most widely used framework in roles research over the past two decades, but this typology has come under both ideological and methodological criticism. The former centers primarily around the vociferous liberal feminist critique of the manager-technician dichotomy (in the work of Creedon; Choi and Hon; Toth and Grunig; and Toth, Serini, Wright, and Emig) which maintains that this typology tends to trivialize the technical dimension of the practitioner's role that tends to be performed more frequently by female than male practitioners.

However, it is the methodological criticisms of how the manager's role has been conceptualized and measured in the public relations context that is this chapter's focus. These criticisms, focused on the limitations of the role measures used to identify manager role enactment, and on the argument that the manager-technician dichotomy oversimplifies the complexities of role enactment, are drawn from work by Leichty and Springston, and by Moss, Warnaby, and Newman.

This chapter responds to these methodological criticisms by presenting results drawn from an ongoing international collaborative research programme into the nature of communications/public relations management and managerial work.

The principal aim of this research, begun with an earlier phase of qualitative research into work patterns of practitioners operating at managerial levels in U.K. and U.S. organizations, is to develop a more comprehensive and empirically-based understanding of management and managerial work performed by communication/public relations practitioners-one that reflects what it is that public relations practitioners actually do.

By extending the research across a range of countries, the aim is to eventually establish whether any generic elements or components of managerial work can be identified in the communication/public relations context that might transcend national and cultural boundaries.

Broom and Dozier's pioneering work in practitioner roles research and in advancing the principal role typologies widely used by other roles researchers is well documented. In addition to the emphasis on identifying and classifying the main elements of work activity associated with the enactment of different role typologies, research has examined the relationship between roles and a number of other variables, including gender and role enactment, gender salary inequalities, and practitioner career advancement.

Other themes emerging from roles research include the relationship between role enactment and the status and power of public relations units in organizations;" practitioner involvement in strategic decision making; practitioner use of and involvement in evaluation research and environmental scanning; and practitioner involvement in issues management.

Roles research has come under increasing criticism during the past five to ten years on ideological and methodological grounds, including the strong feminist critique of roles research highlighted earlier. Other criticisms have focused on the rather static perspective of role enactment often provided by roles research, which has tended to treat roles as static categories into which practitioners are "pigeon-holed."

One of the most significant criticisms has been the call for a re-examination of how the managerial dimension of practitioners' work is understood. Leichty and Springston challenged the value of the manager-technician typology, suggesting that meaningful information may be lost by categorizing practitioners as either simply managers or technicians.

They suggest that the public relations manager scale "lacks a coherent theoretical justification," and the eighteen items comprising the management role scale might be labeled "the everything other than technical activities scale." Moss, Warnaby, and Newman also questioned the appropriateness of the way the managerial dimension of practitioners' work has been defined, pointing to the failure of most roles studies to distinguish between "managerial tasks and responsibilities" and "managerial behaviors."

Although roles researchers have developed some alternative role measurement scales, in most cases these are variations on Broom's original role inventory derived mainly from reviews of the public relations consulting and/or boundary spanning literatures, rather than being empirically based.

Wright's research is one of the few studies that focused on more senior communication practitioner roles, using survey, interview, and focus group research to identify a "communication executive" role comprising corporate senior vice presidents who appeared to report directly to CEOs.

Reviewing these research and role measurement strategies, Grunig, Grunig, and Dozier pointed out there is no simple answer to the question of which approach to measuring practitioner roles is best, since roles are essentially abstractions of reality, making their measurement inherently problematic.

They acknowledged that the ongoing evolution of the communication profession suggests that Broom's "original twenty-four item role set needs constant reinvention through intensive observation of what communicators do." It is here that some comparison with the work of management scholars who investigated the nature of managerial work and behaviour may prove informative.

THEORETICAL PERSPECTIVES ON MANAGEMENT

Our previous research pointed to the contrast between the broad consensus view of "management" and the practitioner's managerial role found in the public relations literature, and the ongoing and often-contested debate about the nature and practice of management found within the management literature. From the management theory perspective, two main schools of thought about the nature of managerial work emerge.

On one hand, the classical view of management, normally associated with the seminal work of Fayol, is of a rational profession in which managers perform a set of activities designed to enable them to plan, organize, command, coordinate, and control.

This technocratic model of management as a rational profession has been challenged by a series of studies conducted during the past thirty to forty years that sought to identify what managers actually do. The general picture suggests that the image of managers as rational analytical planners, decision makers, and issuers of commands does not stand up to scrutiny. Rather, as Stewart has suggested, a manager appears to be someone who often: lives in a whirl of activity, in which attention must be switched every few minutes from one subject, problem, and person to another. It is a picture not of a manager who sits quietly controlling but who is dependent on many people, other than subordinates, with whom reciprocating relationships should be created; who need to learn how to trade, bargain and compromise.

Although on the surface these two views of management may appear irreconcilable, as Hales and others have suggested, these differing management perspectives can be attributed, in part, to the different foci and methods adopted by management researchers. While some studies have examined the substantive "elements" of managerial work (what managers do), others have examined the distribution of managerial time between work elements (how managers work), managerial interactions with others at work, or the informal elements of managerial work (what else do managers do).

Perhaps the most significant distinction that emerges across these studies is how scholars have conceptualized the constituent features of managerial work in terms of the difference between the "observable activities that constitute the performance of the job, and the implied or reported tasks, which represent expected or intended outcomes."

This distinction has not been recognized in public relations roles research, where the focus appears be placed primarily on identifying the reported tasks that constitute the "manager's role" rather than investigating how managers work-in terms of observing or recording what activities they undertake.

As Culbertson and others highlighted, most roles studies essentially offer a "snapshot view" of practitioner role enactment, rather than attempting to reflect the dynamism of role behaviour, particularly in terms of capturing the fluidity of managerial work in its different guises.

Two further observations about the work of managers

emerging from management research might also be relevant to understanding the manager's role in the public relations context. First, management scholars broadly agree that managerial work is contingent upon inter alia function, level, organization (type, structure, size) and environment second, managerial jobs appear to be sufficiently loosely defined to be highly negotiable and susceptible to choice in terms of style and content.

Not only do managers appear to make choices about the job content (which aspects of a job a manager chooses to emphasize), but also about the methods (how the work is done). Dalton suggested that negotiation over job content is not only part of what managers do, but also a motif running through all managerial activity.

Turning to the treatment of the manager's role in public relations roles research, with one or two exceptions, there appears little explicit recognition that the content of the manager's job might vary with functional level as well as from organization to organization.

Despite the fact that roles theory suggests an individual's role is determined through an interactive process of "role sending and role taking," there seems to be little explicit acknowledgment that practitioners might "negotiate" their role's content other than in terms of demonstrating a preference for the retention of a craft or creative element in their work.

There are clearly some significant differences between management and public relations scholars in terms of their understanding of the potential complexity and variation in managerial work and practice. Public relations roles research has offered a relatively simplistic onedimensional view of management, focusing largely on the reported "tasks" performed by public relations managers, and largely ignoring the "how" and "why" dimensions of management.

Even in examining what public relations managers reportedly do, questions arise about the adequacy of the role inventory measures used to try to capture what it is that public relations managers actually do.

Only in more recent research have public relations scholars begun to consider how management work and management expertise might vary in scope both within and across organizations. Grunig, Grunig, and Dozier suggested managerial expertise can be usefully segmented into two empirically and conceptually distinct components-strategic and administrative managerial expertise.

However, even here there appears to be some incongruity in terms of the elements of expertise that the authors designate as "administrative," and "strategic," tying the latter to elements of stakeholder environmental and evaluation research-what they suggest arc the strategic tools a communication department needs to use with the two symmetrical and asymmetrical models.

More controversially, Grunig, Grunig, and Dozier suggested activities such as "developing strategies," "managing issues," and "developing goals and objectives" should be recognized as elements of "administrative" rather that "strategic" managerial expertise. Such questions about what constitutes "strategic" or "administrative expertise" in the communication/public relations context represent a further example of the lack of integration of management and public relations theory building with respect to the concept of management and managerial work.

These limitations in the understanding and treatment of "management" within the public relations context surfaced clearly in our earlier qualitative study of senior practitioner role enactment.

We recognized that a comprehensive reconceptualization of management in the communication/public relations context would require a re-examination of not only the key elements of managerial work (what communication/public relations managers do), but also of managerial processes (how practitioners perform their managerial roles), and the influences on managerial role enactment (why they behave in the way they do).

To conduct such a single multi-dimensional study would prove highly complex and difficult, so for this study the emphasis was placed on identifying the key elements of managerial work performed by communication/public relations practitioners to develop a more effective and empirically grounded conceptualization of the communication/public relations manager's role.

The literature reveals a variety of qualitative and quantitative approaches and methods used to measure constructs such as management roles. In the case of public relations roles research, the majority of studies take a quantitative approach, primarily using surveys based on Broom and Smith's traditional twenty-four-item role inventory.

This study also uses a survey instrument focusing on the type of work activities performed by practitioners operating at a managerial level, but rather than drawing on Broom and Smith's role inventory, it uses an inventory of practitioner managerial work activities derived from the public relations' practitioner role literature, management literature, and our previous research.

This exploratory research is unique, as it departs theoretically from Broom's role inventories to measure practitioner role enactment, and instead develops a survey design that explores empirically the public relations practitioners' work activities.

Survey items were constructed and measured using a series of seven-point semantic differential scales, common in studies of this kind. These are used to rate a specific variable depending on the relative importance it possesses.

The instrument was a self-administered mailed questionnaire, with fifty-seven items covering eight operational dimensions of managerial responsibility or work: (1) counseling and advisory responsibilities; (2) issues management; (3) policy and strategy making; (4) trouble shooting and problem solving; (5) administration; (6) monitoring and evaluation; (7) negotiation; and (8) technical responsibilities. A later section of the instrument contained the classification and demographic sections.

At item level, question development drew on the content

analyses of the managerial public relations practitioners' narratives from earlier qualitative work. In this phase, the elicitation of statements drew substantially on the analyses of subjects' accounts of their daily tasks and work activities across eight dimensions.

This stage focused on identifying the core elements and relative importance of the work performed by managerial-level practitioners, rather than attempting to investigate how they might perform their roles and the distribution of time spent on activities. To improve reliability and eliminate reverse coded items, the questionnaire was pilot tested with a small sample of public relations practitioners accustomed to specifying role definitions.

The characteristics of this study's sampling frame embraced two important criteria: (1) respondents reflected as many industry sectors as possible, including government, corporate, and not-forprofit practice; and (2) all respondents held managerial-level positions within their respective departments or organizations. The authors first developed a comprehensive typology of U.K. sectors and then, using these sampling criteria, randomly drew more than 1,000 names and address of suitable candidates from the U.K.'s Institute of Public Relations (IPR) online database.

From this initial trawl, relocated members and educators or student categories were eliminated from the sample, which comprised 900 surveyed respondents. To boost response rates a postal survey with a return envelope was chosen in place of e-mail and electronic attachments. The mail survey, which took place in March and April 2004, achieved a 25% response rate. After adjustments for spoiled questionnaires, 218 cases were analysed.

FINDINGS

Factor analysis has been widely employed within roles research as a method of reduction to simplify data and facilitate analysis of variables, as exemplified in studies such as Kelleher and Dozier and Broom. However, exploratory factor analysis was the chosen approach for this study rather than confirmatory factor analysis, as this work sought to uncover knowledge beyond the established two-factor (manager-technician) theoretical dichotomy.

Exploratory factor analysis explores the field to uncover new dimensions and constructs, and was therefore suited to this exploration of what might constitute the managerial dimension of practitioners' work, particularly given the relatively large number of variables that needed to be analysed. The ultimate objective of the analysis was to reduce and summarize these variables with minimum loss of information, while a relatively small number of latent factors represented relationships among interrelated variables.

The forty work activity scales were subjected to Principal Components Factor Analysis, with the remaining variables retained for later analysis. This revealed the presence of nine components, all of which achieved eigenvalues greater than one. These nine components explained a total of 66% of the variance, which suggested the salience of these components. However, it was recognized that PCA can overestimate the number of factors to draw on and that the variance accounted for is also a function of the instrument's scale item wording.

As this exploratory research design necessitated the isolation of a relatively small number of dimensions on which relevant items loaded, two further methods were chosen as confirmation of the number of factors to rotate: the computation of total variance explained and a Scree test as verification of this cut-off point (the point at which the slope of the line changes). Based on these observations, a five-factor model was identified.

An orthogonal Varimax rotation facilitated the identification of a simplified factor structure. The five key factors that emerged suggest the core dimensions of the role performed by communication/public relations practitioners operating at the managerial level and, by implication, represent the core dimensions of what can be termed the communication/public relations manager's role.

These five dimensions or core areas of practitioner work comprise four areas of what is identified as being essentially managerial responsibility: monitor and evaluator; key policy and strategy advisor, trouble shooter/problem solver: and issues management expert; as well as a further technical dimension labeled communication technician dimension.

The second stage of the analysis, an Oblimin or oblique rotation procedure, provided the theoretically important underlying dimensions and, because factors were correlated, represented the relatively large number of variables more accurately. Basing initial judgements on Hair et al.., and given the sample size (n=218), it was determined that a factor loading of.32 and below was poor,.40 was significant, and loadings of.60 or greater were very significant.

Items with secondary loading lower than.40 were disregarded. Factor loadings on the monitor and evaluator, key policy and strategy advisor, trouble shooter/problem solver, issues management expert, and communication technician dimensions ranged from.41 to.89.

Cronbach alpha scores were computed on the items to indicate the level of internal consistency and reliability. The five key factors (with alpha scores) or core dimensions of the communication/public relations manager's role are now discussed within the context of factor loadings by drawing on the pattern matrix.

The first dimension (Factor 1), labeled the Monitor and Evaluator dimension, consisted of ten items, seven (primary) and one (secondary) (alpha =.87), and two secondary loadings on Key Policy and Strategy Advisor dimension.

This dimension captures the important managerial responsibility managerial-level practitioners often have for "organizing, controlling, and monitoring" the work of communication/public relations departments from both an internal and external standpoint; in the former case, being responsible for setting targets, operating within budget, monitoring performance against targets, and preparing departmental reports.

In the latter case, the manager's role involves coordinating with other organizational management units, including top management, to set targets for the public relations function, negotiating for organizational resources, and commissioning external agencies.

The secondary loadings on items in the Key Policy and Strategy Advisor dimension suggest how the work of target and goal setting along with reporting on results embraces elements of close working with senior management in planning communication strategies and ensuring senior management appreciate the communication implications of their decisions.

The second factor (Factor 2), the Key Policy and Strategy Advisor dimension, focuses on the relationship public relations practitioners have with the senior management function (dominant coalition) within organizations, and comprised eight items, five primary (alpha =.83), and one secondary item that loaded on the Issues Management Expert dimension.

Items here were indicative of the type and level of policy advice and contribution that at least normatively public relations practitioners operating at a managerial might expect to offer to senior management. The negative loading on this factor's items suggests that for most of the U.K. practitioners surveyed, this type of involvement in the work of senior management teams (dominant coalitions) within their organizations remains largely the exception rather than the rule.

The third factor, the Issues Management Expert dimension, consisted of six primary and three secondary items related to the public relations practitioner's role in diagnosing and responding to external threats from major or minor issues. Working in this issues management mode sees practitioners acting not only as the organization's "eyes and ears," but also as an information processor and interpreter adding meaning to information.

The primary and secondary loadings on the Trouble-Shooter/Problem-Solver dimension suggest a degree of ambiguity experienced by practitioners in terms of how they might distinguish between what is "trouble shooting" and what is "issues management."

This dimension also embraced some degree of involvement in providing support for other organizational departments, although the relatively low secondary loadings of less than 0.50 for some activities suggest that such involvement may be infrequent or at least not a regular job element.

The Trouble-Shooting/Problem-Solver dimension (Factor 4) focuses on the practitioner's role in responding to and dealing with a range of internal or external challenges, threats, and/or crises confronting the organization. In this sense, public relations/communication practitioners are generally acknowledged to be the organization's designated "fire-fighters." The dimension encompassed six primary items (alpha =.83), three of which loaded on the Issues Management Expert dimension and three on the Trouble-Shooting/ Problem-Solver dimension.

Two secondary items also loaded on the Issues Management Expert dimension. The existence of the primary loadings across two dimensions again suggests there may be a degree of ambiguity in the minds of U.K. practitioners about their understanding of what constitutes "trouble-shooting/ problem solving" as opposed to "issues management."

The negative loading on three of the primary items relating to practitioners' involvement in regular intelligence gathering and analysis, monitoring external trends, and making recommendations about handling a range of internal and external challenges that might potentially threaten the organization suggests that the majority of U.K. practitioners surveyed did not engage in this type of work.

While the previous four dimensions of the senior practitioner's role in organizations relate to what can be defined as managerial elements of their work, this study found a further fifth factor or dimension of the senior practitioner's role, labeled the Communication Technician dimension. Although it produced the lowest alpha scores (alpha =.60) on three primary items, this dimension was retained because this research is exploratory and thus an alpha of.60 is acceptable.

The strong loadings on two of these items relating to the handling and/or overseeing of technical work suggests many of the U.K. practitioners surveyed retain responsibility for at least overseeing technical communication within their departments, which may also include some direct involvement in this type of work. One interesting finding is the media relations variable negative and positive loading of -.46 and.41.

This dual loading has been interpreted as suggesting that, although operating at a managerial level, some practitioners appear to continue to engage in media relations work, while others do not. The retention of some media relations work by some of the practitioners surveyed might reflect differences in department size and resources available to delegate such work, but equally, may reflect a preference on the part of some practitioners to retain a degree of involvement in media relations even though they may have moved up the organizational hierarchy.

In this sense, the findings here reflect those of previous roles research that has pointed to the tendency for practitioners to enact elements of both the manager and technician roles. The sample's characteristics helped ensure that the study captured the dimensions of the public relations manager's role across a range of the U.K. sectors (e.g. government, corporate, not-for-profit).

On the surface, this interpretation of the key dimensions of the role performed by public relations practitioners operating at a managerial level in organizations might appear to display some similarities to the main elements comprising Dozier's manager-technician role typology. However, we believe the five-dimensional model advanced here offers a more robust and empirically grounded representation of the key responsibilities that practitioners have identified as of central importance in their managerial jobs.

This study focuses only on the U.K. phase of an international programme of comparative research into management and managerial work performed by communication/public relations practitioners.

It is suggested that this five-dimensional model of the managerial level communication/public relations practitioner's role will provide a useful framework for explicating the managerial dimension of the role performed by communication professionals in organizations operating in other national, regional, and/or cultural settings across the world.

By focusing on communication/public relations professionals identified as holding managerial-level positions within U.K.-based organizations, this study uncovered what appeared to be the major elements of "managerial responsibility" and "managerial tasks" performed by practitioners operating at managerial levels.

Moreover, the five-dimensional model advanced here offers a more comprehensive and empirically grounded explication of the managerial dimension of practitioner role enactment in organizations than is provided by the traditional definition of the "manager-technician" role dichotomy used by public relations roles researchers. The authors believe this five-dimensional model of practitioner role enactment provides a more effective representation of the increasing complexity and sophistication of the work performed by communication/public relations professionals in many of today's organizations.

In one respect, however, this study does appear to confirm the findings of previous roles research in that even practitioners operating at relatively senior levels within their organizations appeared to retain some elements of technical work alongside their "managerial" responsibilities.

Albeit true for many of the more senior-level practitioners in the United Kingdom, this involvement in technical work appeared to be confined to overseeing the work of more junior colleagues. It is important to acknowledge this research has focused on identifying the reported tasks or responsibilities that comprise the main elements of the "manager's role" in the communication/public relations context; the study did not attempt to investigate how managers work-in terms of recording the day-to-day pattern of practitioner activities.

Uncovering the latter would have required a far more intensive, essentially qualitative investigation using observation or diary techniques similar to the approach taken by management scholars such as Kotter, or in the public relations field, by Moss, Warnaby, and Newman, and DeSanto and Moss.

It is also important to re-emphasize that this present study is based on responses from a U.K. sample of practitioners only, so it would be inappropriate to attempt to generalize about the wider applicability of the five-dimensional model until further research has been completed in other regions/countries of the world to test the validity and reliability of the dimensions of communication/public relations management advanced here.

This study found that although elements of the work performed by those practitioners studied such as monitoring and evaluation, issues management, policy and strategy advice, and trouble shooting/problem-solving might figure more prominently, most practitioners acknowledged that they continued to retain personal responsibility for what they saw as those more important elements of technical work.

In some sense, this finding reaffirms the findings of other roles researchers who argued that, in practice, all practitioners "enact activities of both the manager and technician roles." Our earlier qualitative research phase also found evidence of many managerial-level practitioners continuing to engage to some degree in elements of technical/craft work, particularly those elements deemed to be highly important or sensitive.

The retention of some technical/craft responsibilities by public relations/communications practitioners might also simply reflect the relatively small size of the communication departments found increasingly in organizations today. Toth et al. noted the impact of this trend toward smaller-sized communication/public relations departments in the United States and suggested that this trend resulted in many experienced managerial-level practitioners spending more time looking after day-to-day operational matters at the expense of performing more significant "managerial tasks" such as advising and counselling. The expectation and even preference of some practitioners to retain some involvement in technical work irrespective of their seniority was noted by Dozier and Broom who acknowledged that for many practitioners the task of "creating and disseminating communication, especially mediated communication, is core to the public relations function."

Reflecting on what have been identified as the other core dimensions of the communication/public relations manager's role, two further important observations warrant consideration. First, one obvious inference is that practitioners operating at a managerial level appear to have a strong external focus in their work, emphasizing the importance of issues management, policy and strategy advice, trouble-shooting/problem solving, and the evaluatory elements of the manager's role.

Much less emphasis was placed on day-to-day administrative and organizing tasks as well as on human resource/team management responsibilities. This particular characteristic of the managerial dimension of practitioner work might be explained in terms of Hales's observation that: "managerial work is contingent on inter alia: function, level, organization (type, structure size) and environment."

For the public relations function, the expectation may well be that practitioners will focus their efforts on maintaining effective organizational-stakeholder relationships, particularly with external stakeholders, and handling events and issues that might impinge on or threaten such relationships. This is not to suggest that dayto-day team management and administration tasks are or can be ignored; rather, it may be a matter of priorities and the relative importance assigned to them.

Thus, we believe the five-dimensional model of communication/public relations practitioner responsibilities/work described here represents a significant advance in terms of developing a more comprehensive framework for analyzing and understanding what can be identified as the "managerial dimension" of the work performed by communication/public relations practitioners and the contribution they can make to the overall strategic management of organizations.

This remains an essentially exploratory model and is based only on data collected from a cross section of U.K.-based practitioners. However, further international comparative studies in collaboration with researchers from other countries are being conducted, which should not only enable the robustness and reliability of the dimensions of public relations management identified here to be tested further, but will allow the generalizability of these dimensions of communication/public relations management to be tested across different cultural settings.

Chapter 5

Non-Assertive Communication in Harassment Situations

Researchers examining educational settings and communication practices have focused largely on behaviors inside the formal classroom. For example, Nussbaum's review of effective teacher behaviors limited the review to in-class behaviors of teachers and found over 1000 studies in this area published since 1970. In comparison, relatively little research has focused on out-of-class (OOC) communication, yet what has been conducted consistently supports the importance of this kind of faculty— student interaction.

OOC communication certainly is considered important by the vast majority of universities that require faculty to maintain office hours for this purpose, and it is generally considered to be a part of the area of teaching for faculty. The body of research that has been conducted on OOC contact between faculty and students, however, has not examined the role that communication plays in these interactions, nor has it examined OOC contact as an important part of the climate in higher education.

As Hall and Sandler point out, a "chilly" climate for women has existed both in and out of the classroom in post-secondary education. They assert that this climate may result in less in-class and out-of-class involvement by women, damaged confidence, and dampened aspirations. While the climate faced by women in the classroom has been examined, the OOC experiences students have with instructors can play a central role in the nature of the climate women face and also affect their learning experiences, aspirations, and confidence levels.

Sandler has also argued that there is a chilly climate for women faculty at the college level, and has called for research examining the way students perceive and treat female versus male faculty. Relatively little research in this area exists currently, and there is a particular lack regarding the role of out-of-class communication.

Research is needed to explore the role of communication and sex of the communicators in OOC interaction settings (e.g., seeing instructors out of class, advising) from both the point of view of the students and faculty involved. This study deals with students' reports of and perceptions about their out-of-class communication experiences at the college level. Specifically, student sex, instructor sex, and students' perceptions of instructors' empathy and credibility are linked to OOC communication.

BENEFITS OF OOC COMMUNICATION

OOC communication between faculty and students refers to interactions outside the formal classroom and may be initiated by students or faculty. It includes advising, students seeking out faculty to ask questions about class content, faculty involvement in student organizations, and/or student-faculty discussions about non-class related issues.

These interactions may only be a few minutes before or after classes, may take place in faculty offices, or may take place in other contexts. This would not include a casual greeting while crossing paths in hallways, but OOC communication topics, lengths, and contexts vary widely.

Most of the research on student-faculty OOC contact has been published in the education literature, with a central focus on its importance in student retention. Generally, students who stayed in college reported significantly more contacts with faculty outside the classroom than did students who dropped out. At a time when higher education is facing increased public criticism and more competition for a declining number of students, student retention is becoming a high priority at most institutions. There are other important benefits associated with student-faculty interaction outside the traditional classroom. Some researchers have found that this OOC contact has a direct influence on students' academic performance. This research has supported the concept that greater OOC contact leads to greater educational aspirations as well as improved GPAs and better GRE scores.

Other benefits for students from greater OOC contact found in prior literature have included better developed career plans, higher educational aspirations, more satisfaction with college experiences, and better intellectual and personal development. Thus, there exists considerable support for the value of OOC contact with faculty for students, and what helps students may benefit educational institutions as well.

Certainly educational institutions seek to improve student performance and student satisfaction, and OOC communication is considered by some to be an integral part of liberal education. As Theophilides and Terenzini suggest " a sound undergraduate liberal arts education is gained in a holistic academic context, one grounded in faculty-student interaction not confined by the physical boundaries of the formal classroom".

There are also, however, reports by prior researchers of benefits for faculty from OOC contact with students. Several studies have noted that there are positive correlations between OOC contact with students and higher course evaluations. Theophilides and Terenzini note that this is particularly true for OOC discussions of intellectual or course-related matters and for discussing campus issues or problems.

Wilson, Woods and Gaff also found that faculty with more OOC contact with students were more likely to be satisfied with the stimulation they receive from students, more often include teaching among the major satisfactions in their lives, were more knowledgeable about their students, and received more nominations from colleagues and college seniors for teaching awards.

Thus, there is considerable support for the importance of OOC contact between faculty and students for students, faculty, and institutions of higher education. However, little recent research has examined the frequency and nature of these interactions, and still less has examined the role of communication variables in this context.

FREQUENCY OF OOC COMMUNICATION

Past research that has examined the frequency of out-of-class communication has shown a pattern of relatively infrequent contact. As Wilson, Woods and Gaff point out, relatively little is known about the nature and frequency of faculty-student interaction on college campuses. Most of the research in this area, however, suggests that OOC interaction is at least in most institutions fairly infrequent and superficial.

For example, in a study of Columbia University undergraduates, Thielens found that less than half of the students had "visited at least three instructors to talk about studies, one or more times during the year." Data from faculty during this time period were consistent in suggesting OOC contact with students is relatively infrequent.

In their own study, Wilson, Woods and Gaff concluded that "the majority [of faculty] do not see each of their students for a fairly extended talk even once during a term to discuss intellectual or course-related matters".

In a review of the literature, Pascarella concluded "intense informal contact with faculty is experienced by only a minority of students at the majority of academic institutions student-faculty contact in most colleges and universities is largely restricted to formalized, somewhat structured situations such as the lecture, laboratory, or discussion section".

The most recent study of OOC contact focused on a community college sample where the author argued that increased access to OOC contact between faculty and students should exist. Even in this setting, Fusani reported that 23% of students had " neither visited nor informally chatted with the instructor while 50%Io of respondents had experienced two or [fewer] contacts".

Fusani also collected data from faculty and found that

the two groups did not differ significantly in their reports of OOC contact. Since most students have about five instructors each semester, the conclusion from this research still seems to be that OOC contact is not a frequent occurrence for most students. While much of the data collected on OOC contact is fairly old, the most recent data reinforces those prior patterns. There is no reason to believe OOC contact has become more frequent, but the level of occurrence needs to be studied more broadly.

One variable that could influence the occurrence of OOC contact is the sex of the student. As noted earlier, Sandler has suggested that the instructional climate faced by men and women in higher education is different, and those differences can affect learning experiences, educational and professional aspirations, and personal confidence levels.

Most of this climate research has focused on the formal classroom, which accounts for only a small percentage of the average college student's waking hours. Since the OOC interaction research that exists has documented its significance on many levels, it is important to examine whether student sex plays a role in OOC communication as it does in in-class interactions.

There has been little research examining the role of student sex in OOC communication. When sex has been studied, researchers have suggested that male and female students do not approach OOC communication with faculty the same way, and they may be seeking different outcomes.

For example, in an investigation of the role of OOC contact, Pascarella and Terenzini found that academic integration was more important than social integration as a factor influencing student retention for men, but the reverse pattern existed for women. They also found that both frequency and interpersonal quality of OOC contact with faculty were important, but that the quality of faculty contacts was more important for women. Fusani found that female students experienced more immediacy (i.e., warmth, caring) in OOC contact. Gadzella, Tomcala, Fullwood, Channon, and Benton found that women students in particular valued instructor accessibility outside the classroom. This research has been quite limited, but it does suggest that student sex may affect the amount of and the nature of OOC contact with faculty. This is an area that warrants further exploration.

There has been a limited amount of research examining differential treatment of male and female faculty by students, but the general conclusion is that students have different expectations of male and female faculty. For example, Fusani reported that women faculty were visited more often out of class and received more immediacy from students during those contacts.

Some of these differential expectations reflect generalized societal stereotypes about appropriate behaviors for the sexes and may be relevant to OOC settings. For example, Bennett found that both male and female students expected female faculty to be more supportive and personal with students. This may translate into greater expectations for out-of-class communication availability and different expectations about the kinds of communication that occur in those settings.

However, Zigmund argued that women faculty complying with these expectations may be evaluated less positively by students who perceive the caring behaviour as a weakness, while women faculty who do not display such warmth are penalized for engaging in sex role incongruent behaviour.

Additionally, Bennett found that students expected and received more time and attention from female faculty, yet female faculty were not rated as more accessible than male faculty. Thus, the time female faculty spend with students may be overlooked as an expected part of their role, while male faculty may be perceived as busier and valued more for being willing to spend even a lesser amount of time with students.

These time expectations may place a greater student contact demand on female faculty with little or no reward for that time. Time spent with students is time that is not available for other duties that are considered important in overall faculty evaluation (e.g., research, class preparation).

If there are differential pressures for faculty in this area based on their sex alone, then this can carry over into issues affecting promotion and/or tenure.

These expectations of faculty can also affect student evaluations. While some research has found no real difference, other research has concluded that students rate female faculty less favorably overall than they rate male faculty. This may be related partly to the sex role congruency issue raised above.

Several researchers reported that the ratings of how sociable faculty were affected female faculty ratings more than male faculty ratings, yet Hall and Sandler argued that women who complied with more traditional feminine qualities were evaluated as less competent. This may also be applicable in OOC settings, and the communication that occurs out-of-class may play a role in perceptions of faculty that influence faculty evaluations. Even without overt behavioral differences between male and female faculty, there may still be differences in perception and evaluation. Research conducted outside the educational environment has suggested that the work of women in general is often devalued whether it is articles, art, or resumes.

When the same items were attributed to men, they were rated higher than when they were attributed to women. This aspect can easily carry over into the college environment. Thus, faculty sex is a factor in OOC contact with students that warrants investigation. As a result, the following research questions are posed: RQ1 - Is there a difference in the frequency with which students meet with their instructors outside of class and the length of those meetings based on student sex and/or instructor sex? RQ2 - Is there a difference in student satisfaction with, evaluation of, and/or behavioral intentions toward out-of-class communication with instructors based on student sex and/or instructor sex?

STUDENT PERCEPTIONS OF INSTRUCTORS' SOURCE CREDIBILITY

In addition, a variety of instructor characteristics may relate to student willingness to see instructors out of the classroom. A broad variety of communication factors have been studied in many contexts. Two that would be particularly relevant in the OOC faculty-student interaction setting are source credibility and empathy.

Source credibility has been consistently found to be composed of two major dimensions: competence and trustworthiness. Perceived trustworthiness of faculty could easily affect student willingness to approach faculty outside the formal classroom, and it could also affect the kinds of topics that would be discussed.

Perceptions of faculty competence would certainly be relevant to student interest in pursuing further information outside the classroom. Additional information would only be sought from sources students expected to be competent. In addition, research above has indicated that students perceive male and female faculty differently across multiple dimensions, so it is quite possible that credibility dimensions may vary based on student sex and/or instructor sex.

Thus, the following research questions are posed:

- *RQ3*: Is there a difference in student evaluations of instructor credibility based on student sex and/or instructor sex?
- *RQ4:* Is there a relationship between perceived instructor credibility and the frequency with which students meet with instructors out of class and/or the length of those visits?
- *RQ5:* Is there a relationship between perceived instructor credibility and student satisfaction with, evaluation of, and/or behavioral intentions toward out-of-class communication?

Student Perceptions of Instructors' Empathy

Another faculty characteristic that may play a role in OOC interactions with students is empathy. While empathy was cast originally as a psychological construct, Miller and Steinberg asserted that it should be viewed as a communication variable. They introduced their transactional perspective in depicting empathy as the ability to determine another individual's motivational/attitudinal posture and the capacity to engage in communication behaviors toward the individual which are desirable/rewarding.

More recently, Stiff, Dillard, Somera, Kim, and Sleight concluded that empathy is multi-dimensional as it includes cognitive (i.e., perspective taking), affective (i.e., empathic concern and emotional contagion), and behavioral (i.e., communicative responsiveness) components.

In OOC communication, a student's perceptions of an instructor's empathy may relate to the student's comfort with, likelihood of meeting with, and the nature of topics discussed with the instructor out of class.

In particular, the empathic dimensions of empathic concern (i.e., showing compassion/caring for the other person's welfare), perspective taking (i.e., adapting the other person's viewpoint), and communicative responsiveness (i.e., listening and responding effectively to the other person's viewpoint) may correlate with the frequency of OOC interactions as well as the topics discussed.

As a result, the following research questions are advanced:

- RQ6 - Is there a difference in student evaluations of instructor empathy based on student sex and/or instructor sex?
- RQ7 - Is there a relationship between perceived instructor empathy and the frequency with which students meet with instructors out of class and/or the length of those visits?
- RQ8 - Is there a relationship between perceived instructor empathy and student satisfaction with, evaluation of, and/or behavioral intentions toward out-of-class communication?

METHOD

Sample

The sample consisted of 149 undergraduate students enrolled in the basic communication class at a medium-sized (15,000 undergraduate students) Midwestern university. The respondents included all levels from first year students to seniors and represented a broad cross section of majors. The sample included 67 males and 82 females.

Data was collected from subjects for each of their instructors that semester individually, so the N for male subjects became 263 and the N for female subjects became 316. Subjects were instructed not to include their basic communication class instructors. There was data reported about 579 instructors with 420 male instructors and 159 female instructors (a degree of duplication was possible if two respondents had the same instructor).

Procedures

Students in basic communication classes were solicited to sign up outside of class time toward the end of the semester in order to meet a research participation requirement. Participants were told that the researchers were interested in studying student perceptions of and experiences with their OOC communication with instructors.

Respondents were told that no instructors' names would be requested, and that no attempts would be made to discover who their instructors were. They were asked to complete a questionnaire and were then completely debriefed. Students were asked not to discuss the research with their classmates.

Questionnaire

Respondents were asked to fill out a questionnaire about each instructor they had that semester. The cover section to the packet of questionnaires gathered student data including sex, year in college, and major. For each instructor questionnaire, the sex of the instructor was requested. The next section included seven semantic differential items designed to measure instructor credibility along the dimensions of competence and trustworthiness drawn from McCroskey, Jensen and Todd and Mehrley and McCroskey.

The competence items included informed-uninformed, trained-untrained, and intelligent-unintelligent. The trustworthiness items included honest-dishonest, friendly-unfriendly, good-bad, and reliable— unreliable. Each item was measured on a seven point scale, with one representing the negative end and seven representing the positive end of the scale.

The third section of the questionnaire included Stiff, Dillard, Somera, Kim, and Sleight's Empathy Scale, which is composed of 17 statements that represent the dimensions of empathic concern, communicative responsiveness, and perspective taking. Each statement was followed by a five point scale ranging from strongly agree (scaled as a 5) to strongly disagree (scaled as a 1).

The fourth section of the questionnaire included six evaluation questions about the likelihood of student behaviors regarding the instructor rated on a seven point scale from very likely (7) to not at all likely (1).

The questions included the likelihood of recommending the instructor as an instructor to a friend, recommending the instructor as an adviser to a friend, seeing the instructor out of class about class-related matters, seeing the instructor out of class about general academic matters, seeing the instructor out of class about personal matters, and taking another class from the instructor.

These items were combined with a seventh item seeking an overall rating of the instructor on a seven point very good (7) to very bad (1) scale to comprise an evaluation rating ranging from 7 (low) to 49 (high).

The final section of the questionnaire collected information about how many times the subject had met with each instructor out of class, the average length of those interactions, and the student's satisfaction with the out-of-class interactions.

Reliability of the Measures

Reliability indices were computed for the two credibility dimensions, the three empathy dimensions, and the seven instructor evaluation items combined. For the three items representing the competence dimension of credibility, the Cronbach coefficient alpha was.78. For the four items representing the trustworthiness dimension of credibility, an alpha of.80 was obtained. For the empathic concern dimension of empathy, alpha was.86. For the communicative responsiveness dimension of empathy, an alpha of.89 was obtained. For the perspective taking dimension of empathy, alpha was.88. For the seven items evaluating the instructor, an alpha of.92 was obtained. Overall, the reliability estimates lent support to the use of these measures in answering the research questions.

Data Analysis

Analysis of variance procedures were employed to examine the first four research questions. Pearson Product Moment Correlations were employed to examine the last four research questions. For all the ANOVAs, two tailed tests with an alpha of.05 were employed to determine statistical significance of results. Since several correlations were computed, an alpha of.01 was utilized to determine the statistical significance of these results.

Results

Research question one examined the frequency and length of OOC contact between students and instructors based on student sex and/or instructor sex. Here, a main effect was found for student sex such that male students reported a greater frequency of OOC communication with instructors than female students. No significant differences resulted for instructor sex and/or the length of interactions.

Research question two focused on student satisfaction with and evaluation of OOC communication with faculty. An interaction effect was obtained for the overall evaluation scale for student sex and instructor sex.

Female instructors were rated most positively by female students and least positively by male students, while male instructors' evaluation varied less between male students and female students. Thus, there was a same-sex preference, with female instructors experiencing the most variation based on student sex.

Since this is an exploratory study, follow up on this

overall significant pattern found for the evaluation items is warranted. The evaluation items focusing on behavioral intentions toward instructors were analysed individually. Students' likelihood of talking with instructors OOC about class-related matters yielded an interaction effect based on student and instructor sex.

Male students were less likely to intend such interactions with female instructors than with male instructors, while female students were more likely to intend this kind of interaction with female instructors than with male instructors. Thus, a same-sex preference emerged for male and female students.

Behavioral intentions dealing with OOC communication concerning personal matters yielded both a main effect for sex of instructor and an interaction effect for student and instructor sex. Female instructors were more likely to be visited about personal matters than were male instructors.

The interaction effect suggested female students were least likely to see male instructors about personal matters and most likely to see female instructors while male students reported less variation between male instructors and female instructors. Thus, there was a same-sex preference for intentions to discuss personal matters, with female students expressing the most variation.

There was also an interaction effect for student and instructor sex for behavioral intentions to talk to instructors OOC about general academic matters. Male students were less likely to intend this interaction with female instructors versus male instructors while female students were more likely to intend this interaction with female instructors versus male instructors. Again, a same-sex preference resulted.

A similar interaction effect between student and instructor sex resulted for behavioral intentions to recommend the faculty member as an instructor to a friend. Male students were more likely to recommend a male instructor than a female instructor while female students were more likely to recommend a female instructor than a male instructor. Thus, a same-sex preference again resulted with female instructors experiencing the most variation. This pattern was repeated for behavioral intentions to take another class from the instructor. Male students were less likely to intend to take another class from female instructors versus male instructors, while females were more likely to intend to take another class from female instructors rather than male instructors. Thus, another same-sex preference existed with female instructors experiencing the most variation.

Finally, this pattern also occurred for the item measuring overall instructor rating. Female instructors were rated most negatively by male students and most positively by female students while male instructors received less variation in ratings between male and female students. Again, a pattern of same-sex preference existed with more pronounced variation for female faculty.

Research question three explored student perceptions of credibility based on student and instructor sex. The competence dimension yielded both a main effect for instructor sex and an interaction effect for student and instructor sex. Male instructors were perceived as more competent than female instructors. Female instructors were perceived as more competent by female students and less competent by male students, while male instructors experienced less variation between male. Again, a same-sex pattern of preference existed with female instructors experiencing more variation.

An interaction effect for student and instructor sex resulted for the trustworthiness dimension. Female faculty were viewed as more trustworthy by female students and less trustworthy by male students, while male faculty experienced less variation between male and female students.

Research question four studied the relationship between perceived instructor credibility and the frequency and length of OOC visits by students. A significant correlation was found between the trustworthiness dimension and number of OOC visits, but no significant correlation was found between perceived instructor competence and number of OOC visits. There were no significant results for correlations between either credibility dimension or the length of OOC visits. Research question five focused on the relationship between perceived instructor credibility and student satisfaction with, evaluation of, and/or behavioral intentions toward OOC communication with faculty. A number of significant correlations were found. Both dimensions of credibility yielded significant results for the overall set of instructor evaluation items as well as student satisfaction with OOC communication.

There were also a number of significant correlations found between perceived instructor credibility ratings and behavioral intentions about types of OOC communication. Both credibility dimensions correlated significantly with student likelihood to visit the instructor OOC about class-related matters, about personal matters, and about general academic matters. Similarly, both credibility dimensions were significantly correlated with student likelihood of recommending the instructor to a friend, recommending the instructor as an advisor to a friend, taking a future class from the instructor, and the overall rating of the instructor.

Research question six examined student perceptions of instructor empathy based on student and instructor sex. For the three dimensions of empathy explored in this study, only empathic concern (EC) yielded a main effect for instructor sex. Female instructors were perceived to express more empathic concern in OOC communication than did male instructors. There were no significant results found for communicative responsiveness (CR) or perspective taking (PT).

Research question seven examined the relationship between perceived instructor empathy and the frequency and length of OOC visits by students. A significant correlation between the number of OOC visits and perceived instructor empathy was found for all three dimensions of empathy explored in this study. However, no statistically significant correlations were found between the length of those visits and any of the empathy dimensions.

Research question eight examined the relationship

between perceived instructor empathy and student satisfaction with, evaluation of, and/or behavioral intentions toward OOC communication with faculty. A number of significant correlations resulted.

All three dimensions of empathy yielded significant results for the overall set of instructor evaluation items. A similar pattern resulted for student satisfaction with OOC communication with faculty for all three empathy dimensions.

There were several significant correlations found between perceived empathy ratings and behavioral intentions about types of OOC communication. All three empathy dimensions correlated significantly with student likelihood to visit the instructor OOC about class-related matters, about personal matters, and about general academic matters.

Similarly, all three empathy dimensions were significantly correlated with student likelihood of recommending the instructor to a friend, recommending the instructor as an advisor to a friend, taking a future class from the instructor, and the overall rating of the instructor.

Prior and somewhat older research had indicated that OOC faculty— student interactions were relatively infrequent, and the data from this study support that claim. Students in our sample reported no OOC contacts with approximately 40 per cent of their instructors late in the semester, and reported more than two contacts during the semester with less than 20 per cent of their instructors.

Wilson, Woods and Gaff referred to a "fairly extended talk" with faculty as being 10-15 minutes. Less than 45 per cent of those with OOC contact reported OOC interactions which were estimated to have lasted 10 minutes or longer. Thus, despite its benefits, faculty-student OOC contact is not as extensive as might be expected.

Even though the OOC contacts were relatively infrequent, this study found that male students engaged in significantly more OOC interactions with faculty than did female students. Since research consistently supports a positive relationship between OOC interactions and improved academic aspirations, educational outcomes, personal development, and other benefits, this gap suggests an area of concern for female students.

Some of the data offer a basis for speculation about this gap. Students of both sexes seemed to be more comfortable with OOC communication with same-sex instructors, yet same-sex faculty are more available to male students. At the institution studied, faculty are more than two-thirds male. Thus, male students have more choices among faculty to find same-sex instructors than do female students.

Indeed, cell sizes indicated that male students reported far fewer female instructors (22 per cent) than did female students (32 per cent). Student selection of faculty may play a role in student comfort levels for seeking OOC interactions with faculty, and male students have more options for comfortable choices in this sense.

The data from this study did not show different frequency in OOC visits to male versus female faculty. This may be an accurate reflection of what occurred, but it may also reflect less student values for and awareness of OOC interactions with female faculty. Other researchers have found that female faculty spend more time and/or have more OOC contact than male faculty.

Bennett found that female faculty were not recognized or given credit for these interactions. Data from faculty as well as a more objective form of data collection (e.g., sign in logs of OOC contact) and a broader sample (e.g., other colleges/universities in various geographical locations) might reveal a different pattern of results.

The results showed a consistent pattern of same-sex preference for students, and it also showed that female instructors consistently experienced the greatest variation in results. Female instructors tended to have both the highest and lowest mean ratings in each group of ANOVA cells, while male faculty ratings varied less based on student sex/faculty sex interactions.

Female instructors may have wider variation in course evaluations based on the composition of their classes. This raises an equity issue for female faculty since course evaluations play a role in most institutions' promotion, tenure, and merit raise evaluations. Thus, OOC interactions are a part of the climate for both female students and faculty, which warrants further investigation.

Behavioral intentions regarding the content of OOC interactions also provided interesting results. As might be expected, students were most likely to engage in OOC interactions with faculty about course-related matters and least likely to discuss personal matters. While students overall were most likely to discuss personal matters with female faculty, a same-sex preference also existed here.

It would seem likely that personal matters are probably discussed with faculty in cases where they affect a student's performance in the course. This also raises equity issues for both female faculty and female students. The results of this study and prior research suggest that students expect more in the affective and/or relational domain from female faculty, but they do not value it in evaluating faculty.

This feeds into the double bind Sandler referred to and supports Bennett's conclusions. In addition, female students can suffer from experiencing less comfortable environments for discussion of personal matters that may be affecting academic performance since most faculty are male. Both students and faculty can benefit from these kinds of interactions where faculty can better understand student needs and assist students in meeting educational goals.

The results of this study also reinforce the importance of studying communication variables in OOC contexts. Only one of the three empathy dimensions (empathic concern) showed up as a main effect for instructor sex, but all three dimensions of empathy produced significant correlations with visits to instructors OOC, student satisfaction with OOC communication, evaluations of instructors, and behavioral intentions regarding OOC interactions. The correlations between perceived instructor empathy and number of visits were significant, but relatively low.

The correlations between perceived instructor empathy and the other measures (student satisfaction with OOC communication, student evaluation of instructors, student behavioral intentions toward OOC interactions) were moderately high. Thus, this suggests important advice for all faculties regarding the importance of empathy in providing a climate supportive of faculty— student OOC communication. This OOC interaction can help students attain their goals while benefiting faculty evaluations at the same time.

A similar pattern of results emerged for credibility. Male faculty was perceived as more competent than female faculty. This pattern reflects a bias against female instructors that deserves exploration. This finding can also have a negative effect for important outcomes (e.g., promotion, tenure, raises) for women. Both competence and trustworthiness yielded moderately high correlations for student satisfaction with OOC communication, instructor evaluations, and behavioral intentions toward OOC contact.

In all cases, trustworthiness entailed stronger correlations. This focus on the importance of the affective dimension in combination with the empathy results reinforces the value of interpersonal communication concepts in supporting OOC interaction.

DIRECTIONS FOR FUTURE RESEARCH

This exploration into OOC communication between faculty and students has several key implications that point to directions for future research. First, OOC communication is important, yet it is underutilized. An understanding of why OOC communication is so infrequent deserves exploration. Certainly multiple demands on faculty time may lead to limitations in availability for OOC interactions and may lead faculty to express less openness to it. Demands on time as students become more involved in extra-curricular activities and/or jobs to support rising college expenses may also influence student preferences.

These data suggest that the climate that is reflected by communication variables, as well as sex role expectations, also plays a role in this process. Certainly additional investigation of factors affecting the amount of OOC contact is warranted, and this is particularly true for female students. For example, it would be valuable to focus on the 40 per cent of instructors who had no OOC interactions and study what is different between them and the faculty who did have OOC interactions with students.

In addition, it is important to study faculty perspectives about OOC interaction as well. A focus on student perceptions is an important part of the process, but it offers only part of the picture. Faculty perceptions and more tangible data on OOC visits (e.g., logs of visits as they occur) would offer useful information.

This study focused on credibility and empathy as important communication variables in the OOC context. Additional research into other communication variables that have emerged as important in the classroom and/or in interpersonal relations (e.g., relational perceptions, immediacy) would be important in exploring OOC communication.

Finally, an exploration of the different forms of OOC contact that take place would be useful. For example, more faculties are experimenting with e-mail, electronic bulletin boards, and other technological innovations which can take the place of face-to-face OOC contact. Research into the implications of format for student comfort, climate, and key communication variables is needed in order to understand the potential value of these options.

This research supports the conclusion that OOC communication is linked to the communication variables of empathy and credibility, and that OOC interaction is affected by student and instructor sex. This aspect of the higher education climate holds many potential benefits for students, faculty, and educational institutions, and it warrants a greater research focus-particularly from communication scholars.

Sexual harassment is a problem in academia that has been documented to occur to close to half of the female professors working at U. S. universities. In a mail survey conducted by the Affirmative Action office at the University of

Pennsylvania, between 14% and 46% of female professors reported experiences with sexual harassment.' A similar survey conducted at the University of Minnesota concluded that between 18% and 47% of female professors surveyed had experienced some form of sexual harassment.

At Harvard University, 32% of tenured female faculty and 49% of untenured female faculty reported experiences with sexual harassment. These studies demonstrate that women faculty clearly experience sexual harassment and that the problem is pervasive. Women in academia incur psychological, physical, and economic costs due to the prevalence of sexual harassment.

Psychological costs include a wide range of emotional reactions such as self-doubt, selfblame, and depression. Thoughts like "Is it me?", "If I just worked hard enough," "Maybe I don't teach well enough," and feelings of humiliation are typical psychological reactions to sexual harassment. According to Bravo and Cassedy, "humiliation is a word sexual harassment victims commonly use to describe their experiences.

They feel demeaned and devalued. They go to work to do a job, and instead, they're seen as sexual playthings". Psychological terror associated with fear of reprisal or lack of physical safety also occurs. As a result, women may avoid teaching late night classes, fear walking alone, or fear staying alone late in their offices.

Physical and economic effects of sexual harassment create additional burdens. Headaches, backaches, eating disorders, and fatigue are all common symptoms associated with sexual harassment. The most common economic costs include increased sick days, job loss, lack of promotion and tenure, lack of appropriate recognition, and failure to generate adequate professional outcomes in the form of scholarly papers and presentations.

Bravo and Cassedy indicate that sexual harassment also influences other women in the university setting who may go out of their way to avoid the harasser. For universities to create fertile and open learning environments, academic excellence, equality, and life-long learning, sexual harassment must be publicly addressed and eliminated.

These are difficult goals to accomplish, however, because women overwhelmingly prefer not to report sexual harassment. Research by Bravo and Cassedy demonstrated that women fear not being believed, being further humiliated, and being ostracized. Reporting sexual harassment can mean describing "offensive events repeatedly, in detail, in the presence of company officials, lawyers, agency staff, court personneland the harasser himself.

To many women, the reporting is fully as embarrassing as the abuse itself". Ostracism and damaging or losing one's job are two other fears women confront. As Dr. Frances Conley, a Stanford neurosurgeon reports, "The only reason I put up with it for as long as I did is I really wanted to advance". Thus, women have legitimate and powerful reasons not to report sexual harassment.

Ironically, considerable research points to the importance of women telling harassers about the inappropriateness of their behaviour. For example, the Commission of the European Communities states that "Employees who are themselves recipients of harassment should, where practicable, tell the harasser that the behaviour is unwanted and unacceptable". Friedman et al. recommend to "Tell the harasser in no uncertain terms that his behaviour is not welcome and should stop immediately".

Further, they argue, "facing one's fear and expressing outrage are the most effective ways to stop the controlling and threatening behaviour". While the importance of communication in sexual harassment situations is well documented, little is known about women's forms of communication in those situations. The purpose of this research was to examine women's communication patterns in situations that they defined as sexual harassment. Specifically, this study addressed the degree to which women faculty use assertive-empathic and non-assertive communication in sexual harassment situations.

An emphasis on assertive-empathic and non-assertive

communication is justified because they exemplify the mixed messages that women in this culture often receive about sexual harassment. Whereas the literature on sexual harassment and communication encourages women professors to use assertive communication, these predominantly white, middle-class women's culturally constructed gender identity encourages them to be non-assertive.

Because of this inconsistency, it is unclear how women are likely to respond when confronted by a sexual harasser. Therefore, this study posed two research questions:

- RQ1: To what extent do women professors say they use assertive-empathic communication to respond to sexual harassment?
- RQ2: To what extent do women professors say they use non-assertive communication to respond to sexual harassment?

An overview of research on sexual harassment reveals that most research on this topic uses survey research techniques. According to Gruber, "While such approaches have yielded excellent 'snapshots' of the forms and the correlates of harassment, they have provided little understanding of [its] contextual aspects".

Reinharz argues that contextual research is best retrieved through interviews. She believes that interviewing offers researchers access to people's memories in their own words rather than in the words of the researcher, which is especially important when research includes neglected, marginalized, or manipulated voices.

According to Reinharz, "This asset is particularly important for the study of women because learning from women is an antidote to centuries of ignoring women's ideas altogether or having men speak for women". Hearing women's voices through interviews is one way to validate the seriousness of their stories.

PARTICIPANTS

The participants in this project were 30 self-selected

faculty women in post-secondary teaching and research positions at three U.S. universities. Although this self-selective process was less desirable than a random sample, it was undertaken for several reasons.

First, each woman's contributions were richly informative about largely unknown aspects of sexual harassment. Second, this study was exploratory in nature, designed to provide a framework for future studies. Third, because trust was a critical factor to facilitate disclosure, legitimizing women's stories emerged as the most important goal of the interviews.

Following informed consent, a loosely structured interview was conducted in a private environment chosen by the respondents. Each interview was 45-60 minutes in length during which time the interviewees were asked a series of probes concerning their sexual harassment experiences and their actual responses to such experiences. Interviewees were free to discuss any aspects of these experiences and their communication. Research probes were used to guide the interviews.

VARIABLES

Recurrent patterns in women's verbatim responses constituted the data for this analysis. The themes that emerged related to communicative styles, interactional goals, and definitions of sexual harassment.

Assertive-empathic communication. This communication strategy was defined as standing up for one's own rights in such a way that the rights of others are not violated. Word choices include "I think..", "I want...", "I feel...". Assertive-empathic communication also includes some element of empathy such as: "I don't mean to hurt your feelings, but it bothers me when you make comments about my body"; "I enjoy working with you, but I'd appreciate if you would stop making sexual jokes". When women, in this study, pointed out that they communicated in the above manner, it was seen as assertive-empathic communication.

Non-assertive communication. Unlike assertive-empathic communication, non-assertive communication was defined as insecure statements, justifications for one's actions, profuse apologies, and statements seeking permission such as "I wouldn't normally mention this only ", "I'm terribly sorry, I really didn't mean to", "I'm sorry to bother you ", "I hope you don't mind but would it be all right if ", "I'm hopeless at this ", "You know me, I seem to be useless at", "I can't seem to".

When women pointed out that they looked away, ignored a comment, or apologized for bringing up the sexual harassment issue, their communication strategy was called a non-assertive communication style. Communication goals. Communication goals were divided into instrumental, relational, and self-identity goals. According to Bingham, women who focus on instrumental communication goals are primarily concerned with ending the harassment.

They also were concerned with their own career opportunities, raises, promotions, and tenure. In comparison, relational communication goals involve a woman's relationship to the harasser, others in the organization, family members and/or a relational partner.

Self-identity communication goals refer to a woman's psychological, emotional, and physical well-being, as well as her self-image and self-respect. Reasons that women provided for using assertiveempathic and non-assertive communication were divided into these three communication goals categories. Sexual harassment. For the purpose of this study, sexual harassment was individually defined by each informant. Analysis

ASSERTIVE-EMPATHIC COMMUNICATION

Assertive-empathic communication was often used by subjects to respond to fellow faculty members. The following example from one woman professor illustrates that some women used this communication strategy not only to stop the harassment, but also to clarify boundaries with an harasser. I tell people they are making me uncomfortable. And I ask them not to do whatever they are doing, if it seems wrong to me or it seems inappropriate. I also will bring out what I think is going on. Usually they do it in a joking way using humour. But I do kind of use humour back, but I also am direct and I use eye contact to say "hey let's don't do that." Women used an assertive-empathic style to communicate their dissatisfaction in a gentle yet strong manner.

Although they said they would be direct with the harasser, that directness also incorporated their own discomfort with the situation. These women seemed comfortable using assertive nonverbal communication combined with humour to convey their disapproval. Why women professors chose an assertive-empathic communication style varied.

For some, instrumental goals dominated: they clearly wanted to end the harassment and climb the academic ladder. As one women stated: I think [my] immediate [reaction] was "get away from me, leave me alone." And I don't think I thought a lot about the fact that some of these people were senior to me. I just didn't care, I wanted them to leave me alone. And then later the goal became more to document incidences because that's what OEO told me to do, and I kept intensive notes. I mean, I kept a daily log that's how bad it was for six months.

Other women were concerned about relationships with colleagues since collegial relationships were critical to their future advancement opportunities. Assertive-empathic communication, thus, helped them maintain a professional if not cordial relationship with the harasser. One woman said, "It doesn't damage our relationship usually, you know, unless someone pushes too much. And sometimes they have and that's really uncomfortable.

But I will say what the issue is, and I will say you are making me uncomfortable, that's how I will start". In contrast, some women expressed concern about their own self-identities and the harasser's identity when they addressed why they used assertive-empathic communication. For example, one woman, whose account was based on previous experiences with men, explained that "there are several reasons that I responded some of them personal. When my father was angry, I had been beaten by my dad, and I swore I never let anyone beat me again". Another, however, did not wish to undermine her harasser's own selfrespect: My goal in those situations was to make it clear that there were no possibilities of anything sexual or romantic between us and, at the same time, respect the other person, and try to do it in as respectful a way as possible, so they can have their self-respect too..

In general, women professors were largely satisfied with their choice of assertive-empathic communication. While admitting to being scared, they also felt quite "proud" that they "stood up" to their harasser. Assertive-empathic communication enabled some of the women to reconcile instrumental communication goals with relational and self-identity goals. Perhaps due to this reconciliation, more of the women professors reported that they were not currently using such a style but they would like to learn to use this communication strategy. As one conceded, I just think that I'm not handling it very well, so if I could learn maybe to.. confront, but in a positive way, and ask the person to be aware of it, that might actually help. I might try to do that, if it comes up again.

Non-Assertive Communication

Despite the desirability of assertive-empathic communication, the most frequently use style was non-assertive communication. This often took the forms of nonverbally avoiding the harasser, being indirect with the harasser, and using humour to deflect the harasser's inappropriate behaviour.

It was more like.. avoidance, actually removing myself physically to get away from him. If I knew he would be sitting downstairs, I sometimes would just not go down. [One] thing that I have used in the past is simply humour. Simply laugh it off with the person, so that they feel a little foolish, and usually they take the hint and go away. I think I didn't know how to respond, so I probably responded, when I look back, not the way I would have liked, but didn't want to cause a scene, and didn't want to make them feel like I was uncomfortable, so I just tried to laugh even though I didn't want to. I can remember at other institutions innuendoes about your personal life, your attractiveness or whatever, like little jives that, that I knew if I didn't just laugh off and walked away from that person, then I would be labeled.

Needing to fit in and be liked were the major reasons women professors cited for their non-assertive responses. None of the women mentioned instrumental goals that would end the harassment. Yet, some women pointed to relationships that were important to them for career advancement opportunities.

In this sense, not being cast as an outsider and being viewed as a good team player were two important instrumental goals. I've seen people who have pursued harassment cases or just gender discrimination cases. I've seen them made into icons by both the feminist side and the chauvinist side of the field.

And people have become nationally famous for pursuing these matters. They tend to get very polarized. And I don't like that kind of thing. And I really guard my privacy. I don't want to threaten power in a way that casts me as a bad team member or a person who doesn't understand her place in the hierarchy, which [itself] is denied on the surface. Non-assertiveness is non-threatening and this was critical to these women to accomplish their career goals.

Several women explained that they desired to be liked, wanted to engage in supportive conversations, and enjoyed being nurturers. These accounted for their non-assertive choices. As one woman put it: It's an issue of being liked wanting the person to feel liked. I tend to be a real nurturer and so much of it is to forgive and to nurture and set up the dimensions of the friendship.

Another felt that ignoring the harassing remarks would de-value them and, thus, make them go away. But, additionally, "deep down inside to get along with people" is important, "and there's a feeling that that is somehow necessary in my department". Prioritizing one's life also influenced the degree to which one chose to be nonassertive. Interviewee, for example, noted that "When you get older, you can't fight every battle.

You've got to have some peace in your personal life, you've got to raise your children." These professors' accounts demonstrate that their communicative choices were strongly influenced by a concern for others either inside or outside of the academic setting. Even when women recognized that such a relational focus was unhealthy they still were inclined to be non-assertive to protect their collegial or familial relationships.

Women's perceptions of themselves and their own self-identity goals also led them to choose a non-assertive style. Interviewee #13, for example, observed that she had "a very hard time, in virtually any kind of situation, coming up with calling it as I see it straightforward I'm much more assertive than I used to be, but I try to sort of dance around things, that's my initial strategy."

Whereas nonconfrontation characterized her overall style, physical safety motivated Interviewee's behaviour. She explains:

I remember being actually quite scared of him. I remember my basic fear was really being terrified, and I think this was probably all wrong, but I think I acted as if I hadn't noticed [the harassment] which might have been because I was alone in the building. Self-identity goals explained many of women professors' communicative choices. They used non-assertive communication because it helped them avoid polarization, did not threaten the power hierarchy, maintained their relationships with others, fit their non-confrontative personalities, and provided them with a sense of physical safety.

Women professors who were non-assertive were generally dissatisfied with their responses. However, they also recognized that their choices were based on very good reasons. For example, several women pointed out that their experiences with sexual harassment took place at a time when they-and other women-were unsure about what behaviors constituted sexual harassment. Additionally, some women acknowledged their own personal preferences for a non-assertive communication style. Three examples are illustrative.

You have to give yourself some slack. This was in 1972, [and] I was a parttime instructor out there. It wouldn't have done me much good in that position to have made an issue out of it. But I felt belittled, and I let it affect how I felt about my teaching, and that was a bad thing.

I think it was a terrible way to handle it the first time. I mean [this was] the only real time that it happened to me, and it didn't work. But that was a long time ago, before we even heard of the phrase [sexual harassment] and I was working for him, and I just needed the money.

I'm happy that they take the hint, but I also recognize that it's a way of avoiding. I'm not a confrontational person. I would never sit him down and say "okay, I don't like this, leave me alone." So yes I'm happy and I'm not happy. When it works, it's fine, because it doesn't involve much emotional investment on my part; on the other hand, I feel like I'm avoiding.

Although women were not happy with their non-assertiveness, they did prefer this communication strategy and had legitimate reasons for enacting the style. Still, they conceded that the harassment affected them in a number of ways, including encouraging them to quit, and becoming less enthused about their teaching.

Although women professors used both assertive-empathic and non-assertiveness they preferred non-assertive communication in sexual harassment situations. Non-assertive communication included avoiding the harasser, being indirect with the harasser, and using humour to minimize the seriousness of the behaviour.

Many communication goals guided women in their communicative choices, but women professors seemed especially concerned with relational communication goals. They wanted to be liked and accepted professionally; thus, they engaged in supportive communication.

Several reasons may explain women's penchant for engaging in non-assertive communication. In a culture where white, middle-class women's feminine gender identity encompasses a concern for the other and an acceptance of negative treatment, non-assertive communication is a stereotypical feminine discourse expected of women.

At the same time, it is not surprising that women would be dissatisfied with their non-assertive patterns because this very same culture values assertiveness over non-assertiveness. In a patriarchal and masculine society, assertiveness is powerful communication form while non-assertiveness is perceived as much weaker. Women are left with feelings of dissatisfaction no matter how they respond.

One critical factor that influenced women's communicative choices in sexual harassment situations was their status in the university hierarchy. Women professors who were already tenured were much more likely to be comfortable with assertive-empathic communication. In many cases, these women had trouble even imagining that they, at this point in their careers, would encounter sexual harassment. However, when they imagined confronting inappropriate and unwanted behaviors, they maintained that they would end it immediately. In sharp contrast to tenured women's responses, junior faculty women pointed to the lack of safety they feel still exists in academic settings. One woman stated, "I still regret that there is not enough safety in situations for women to be able to directly confront these things without thinking is this going to come back to haunt me in some other form?". No tenured women expressed this concern.

Because the goal for many women was to end the harassment and feel some measure of satisfaction, communication strategies are needed that go beyond non-assertiveness. Those that empower women include ensuring that more women enter the tenure and promotion tracks. Clearly, women who were full professors were more comfortable communicating assertively; this means that success can engender assertiveness.

Other strategies include committee participation,

networking with other women, and mentoring. Committee work and networks provide women with supportive and collaborative forums for discussion of private and professional issues. Mentoring provides women with guidance and support to succeed in the promotion and tenure process.

All of these strategies can be empowering for they will help women feel comfortable challenging prescribed gender roles, and communicating more assertively to any harasser. Women faculty must be able to communicate in ways that facilitate their personal and professional development.

These thirty women's accounts open a window into sexual harassment experiences that women professors have faced in academic settings. They reveal that women still encounter inappropriate behaviors from their male colleagues. And they demonstrate the complexity with which women approach communication in sexual harassment situations with other faculty members. Decisions about how to communicate become careful attempts to reconcile the instrumental goals of stopping the harassment with career-oriented goals, relationships with others, and women's own preferred modes of communication. In the end, these women reaffirm the complexity and ambiguity of communication in sexual harassment situations.

Chapter 6

Out of Class Communication

Out-of-class communication (OCC) refers to student-faculty communication in the instructor's office, informally on campus, or before and after class. The importance of student-faculty out-of-class interactions became evident in work on student retention nearly 25 years ago. Only recently, however, have communication scholars begun to address student-faculty out-of class interactions and to analyse the communication variables that are related to these interactions. The present study focuses on the relationship between student perceptions of instructor immediacy and OCC, particularly as these perceptions pertain to female and male students and faculty.

OUT OF CLASS COMMUNICATION

Research on out-of-class communication indicates that OCC is valuable for students' educational development, relationships with faculty, and retention in the university. Students engaging in OCC with faculty have greater academic and cognitive development, higher educational aspirations, greater levels of academic integration into the university, and increased feelings of confidence and self-worth.

Furthermore, faculty benefit from OCC in that students' relationships with faculty members are the best predictor of faculty evaluations.

Finally, universities benefit from OCC in the area of student retention because OCC is one factor contributing to students remaining in college. Although the study of OCC is in its infancy, investigation into the nature of out-of-class communication has focused on its frequency, length, and content, as well as on student satisfaction with OCC.

The few studies that have been conducted on student-faculty OCC indicate that student faculty contact outside of the classroom is fairly infrequent and superficial and is predominantly course-related. Communication behaviors that have been found to be positively correlated with student satisfaction with OCC are verbal immediacy and student perceptions of instructor empathy and credibility (i.e., competence and trust).

The research on OCC has also begun to address sex differences between female and male students and faculty. Female and male students may have different expectations about the behaviors of female and male faculty, and female and male faculty may have different expectations about the behaviors of female and male students. The research on gender identity development, socialization, modes of learning, and classroom interaction patterns would seem to suggest that such differences might occur and thus might influence OCC.

GENDER IDENTITY DEVELOPMENT

According to Chodorow, gender socialization begins early in life through the development of gender identity. She posits that the gender identity of girls and boys develops differently because of the influence of the primary caregiver, who is usually the mother.

Daughters tend to develop their gender identities in relationship to their mothers, whereas sons differentiate themselves and define themselves as independent from their mothers. Through differing paths of development, males are likely to come to value independence or autonomy, and females are likely to come to value relationships.

The value of autonomy for males and relationships for females is further substantiated by Gilligan's research on the moral development of females and males. She found that females often come to view their relationships as a web with themselves at the centre of connection, whereas males tend to prefer a hierarchy with themselves at the top.

The valuing of relationships and independence is also suggested by the types of linguistic styles preferred by females and males. Mulac found that males appear to prefer a direct, succinct, personal, and instrumental linguistic style and females appear to prefer an indirect, elaborate, and affective linguistic style. The affective linguistic style preferred by females is likely to facilitate relationship development.

SOCIALIZATION

Socialization in play groups that are usually sex segregated also influences the communication patterns of females and males. Boys, playing in large hierarchical groups, tend to learn to use language to assert positions of dominance, whereas girls, playing in leaderless groups, learn to maintain cooperative relationships through the use of language.

These differences also appear in the conversational objectives of adults. Clark found that in conversations, females and males both had the objectives of showing interest in their conversation partner and in making the conversation pleasant. Females, however, placed more emphasis on feeling-centered objectives, and males placed more emphasis on the entertainment function of conversation.

MODES OF LEARNING

The research on socialization of females and males highlights the importance of autonomy for males and relationships for females, a difference that is further reinforced by the research on how women and men appear to learn. Belenky, Clinchy, Goldberger, and Tarule indicate that women learn in the context of connection, with learning growing out of relationships, life crises, and community involvement. Belenky et al. refer to this as "connected knowing." The style more prevalent among males, "separate knowing," is the acceptance of the standards of impersonal authority and the construction of arguments based on these standards.

CLASSROOM INTERACTION PATTERNS

Another area that may contribute to sex differences in

OCC involves the differences between female and male students and instructors in class. A number of studies have documented the ways in which female and male students receive differential treatment in the classroom.

In addition, a variety of studies have found that male students participate more in the college classroom than do female students. Furthermore, the sex of the instructor may make a difference as to student behaviour in the classroom. Female students appear to participate more in classes taught by female instructors, and female professors tend to encourage more participatory classroom climates.

Karp and Yoels explain that female participation in the classroom, although it rarely reaches the degree of male participation, is maximized in classes taught by female instructors. It is possible that the different interaction patterns in the classroom influence OCC differently for female and male students and instructors.

Studies on the content and nature of OCC further suggest the importance of studying sex differences and OCC. Although both female and male students benefit from informal contact that extends and reinforces formal academic experiences, male students appear to benefit more from instrumental discussions (discussions of courses and academic programs), and females appear to benefit more from intrinsic discussions (informal socializing and discussions of campus issues). In addition, female and male students appear to value different factors in OCC. Dallimore, in identifying what female and male students viewed as "quality" relationships with faculty, found that female students especially valued accessibility of instructors, and male students more often reported valuing the creation of a safe and comfortable class environment.

This chapter will review the literature on OCC as it is related to immediacy and sex differences and report a study that extends previous research on the nature of OCC. Student perceptions of instructor verbal and nonverbal immediacy will be examined as they relate to OCC between female and male students and faculty.

IMMEDIACY

Immediacy has been widely studied for its influence in the classroom. Immediacy behaviors are those that promote physical and psychological closeness between interactants. Immediacy is important to student-faculty relationships because students tend to perceive immediate instructors as accessible, involved, and effective.

Seemingly, if students find their instructors accessible, they may seek them out for OCC, reflecting a positive relationship between OCC and perceived immediacy. Furthermore, immediate instructors may encourage OCC by engaging in conversations with students before and after class.

Two studies that examined verbal immediacy and OCC found that verbal immediacy is correlated positively with student satisfaction with OCC. Fusani extended the research on the relationship between immediacy and OCC to include sex of student and sex of instructor.

On questions of immediacy, such as "I feel comfortable approaching my instructor outside of class" (student questionnaire) and "I feel comfortable when approached by students outside of class" (faculty questionnaire), female students and instructors averaged higher immediacy scores than did male students and instructors.

Jaasma and Koper investigated the relationship between nonverbal immediacy and OCC. They found it correlated positively with student motivation, the frequency of informal contact between students and faculty, the length of visits students made to the instructor's office, and the amount of time spent socializing during these office visits. Immediacy addresses issues of closeness and distance between students and faculty. By analyzing the relationship between student perceptions of instructor verbal and nonverbal immediacy and OCC for female and male students and faculty, this study contributes to an understanding of how sex differences relate to the closeness/ distance dimension of student-faculty relationships.

SEX DIFFERENCES

Communication scholars have begun to examine the

kinds of student and faculty behaviors that contribute to OCC with a few studies addressing sex differences of students and faculty. The studies analyzing the frequency of OCC for female and male students and instructors have generated conflicting results. Bennett found that female instructors received more OCC than male instructors but found no differences for sex of student.

Nadler and Nadler found no significant difference for instructor sex but found that male students reported a greater frequency of OCC than did female students. The current study will seek to clarify this issue of frequency of OCC by addressing student perceptions of the frequency of OCC in relationship to student perceptions of instructor immediacy for female and male students and faculty.

Although a few studies have addressed the length of OCC, only Nadler and Nadler addressed sex differences and the length of OCC. They found no significant sex differences for length of informal interactions. The current study complements Nadler and Nadler's study by determining whether student perceptions of instructor immediacy behaviors have an influence on the length of OCC for female and male students and faculty.

The limited research on the content of OCC has found it to be predominantly course-related. For example, Fusani found that, for the 282 students studied, 84.90% of interactions were course-related, whereas only 7.49% were about personal problems and 8.57% were about social topics. Nadler and Nadler found that female students were more likely to visit female instructors than male instructors to discuss personal matters.

The current study adds to this knowledge by examining whether student perceptions of instructor immediacy are related to the content of out-of-class interactions for female and male students and faculty. If students perceive their instructors to be immediate, perhaps they would be more likely to discuss personal problems and social topics with them as well as course-related issues.

In research on student satisfaction with OCC, Nadler and

Nadler found that verbal immediacy and students' perceptions of instructor empathy and credibility were positively correlated with student satisfaction with OCC.

Although female and male students rated male instructors similarly, female students rated female instructors more positively, and male students rated female instructors less positively, The current study will extend this research to determine how student perceptions of verbal and nonverbal immediacy for female and male instructors are related to satisfaction with OCC for female and male students.

Because females and males typically come to their sense of gender identity differently, are socialized differently in the home and in play groups, appear to prefer different "ways of knowing," and demonstrate different interaction patterns in the classroom, OCC will likely function differently for them.

The greater valuing of relationships by females, as seen in other contexts, may also appear in OCC. The scant research that is available on the nature of student-faculty OCC does point to the importance of relationships for females. For example, female students value accessibility in faculty more than do male students.

In addition, females have reported gains in interpersonal competence from contact with faculty, whereas males reported gains in cognitive complexity from such interactions. Finally, female interactions with faculty influenced their intrinsic occupational values (e.g., autonomy, job challenge), whereas interactions with faculty did not influence such values for males.

The relationship female students have with faculty members appears to be particularly important for, and influential to, them.

Socialization patterns that influence what female and male students prefer in OCC appear to also influence student expectations for female and male faculty members. Female and male instructors appear to be evaluated somewhat differently by sex of student.

Bennett, for example, found that students reported spending a greater amount of out-of-class time with female instructors yet did not report them as more available. Bennett suggests that generalized cultural stereotypes of feminine behaviour encourage students to expect females to be more accessible, and students evaluate female instructors negatively when they fail to meet this stereotypic expectation.

Similarly, Kierstead, D'Agostino, and Dill found that student ratings of instructors improved for female faculty when they socialized out of class with students, but such socializing did not affect ratings for male instructors.

OCC also appears to function differently for female and male students with respect to persistence patterns that affect the university's enrollment management. Tinto proposed that persistence in college is related to integration of the student into the academic and social life of the university.

Specifically, research shows that academic integration is more important for males, whereas social integration is more important for females. Similar results were found when researchers analysed why students persisted in post-college education. Social integration, accessibility of faculty, and parental support were important influences for female students who attended graduate school, whereas for males an achievement-related factor (i.e., college grades) was more significant.

To summarize, it is clear that OCC is valuable for students, faculty, and universities, but OCC likely functions differently for female and male students. Therefore, sex differences should be a consideration in research on OCC. In the present study, OCC is defined as student-faculty communication in the instructor's office, informally on campus, or before and after class.

In part, the likelihood of OCC is determined by faculty in-class behaviors. Students assess the in-class teaching behaviors of faculty as cues to accessibility for out-of-class discussions. For this reason, this study investigates the relationship of OCC to student perceptions of instructor immediacy, an instructor behaviour that has been shown to be important in the classroom.

To add to this limited research, the relationship between

verbal immediacy and OCC with regard to sex of student and instructor is addressed with the following research question:

RQI: What is the relationship between verbal immediacy and OCC for female and male students with respect to female and male instructors?

To extend the research on OCC and nonverbal immediacy to include sex of student and instructor, the relationship between nonverbal immediacy and OCC for female and male students and instructors is addressed with the following research question:

RQ2: What is the relationship between nonverbal immediacy and OCC for female and male students with respect to female and male instructors?

Participants were 302 students enrolled at two medium-sized Western universities, one public and one private. Participants included 193 females and 106 males (3 provided no data on sex), ranging in age from 18 to 60, with the mean age of 24.6. The students, representing 26 majors, included 85 first-year students, 42 sophomores, 83 juniors, 86 seniors, and 3 graduate students.

The ethnic backgrounds of participants were as follows: 2.0% African American,.3% American Indian, 11.9% Asian, 60.6% Caucasian, 1.0% Filipino,.3% Hispanic, non-Mexican, 14.2% Mexican American,.7% Pacific Islander, and 3.0% other (6.0% provided no data on ethnicity).

In order to obtain data on a variety of instructors from a variety of disciplines, students were asked to respond to the questionnaire based on the instructor's behaviour in the class they had attended most recently before the class in which they were completing the questionnaire. Students filled out the questionnaire anonymously in the last month of the semester, which gave them ample time to interact with the instructor over the course of the semester.

The instructors and classes students evaluated represented 27 content areas. The instructors included 105 females and 193 males (4 participants provided no data on instructor sex) with the following reported ethnic backgrounds for the instructors: 3.3% African American, 7.9%

Asian, 76.8% Caucasian,.7% Hispanic, non-Mexican, 5.0% Mexican American, and.3% other (6.0% provided no data on instructor ethnicity).

INSTRUMENTATION

Frequency, length, content, and satisfaction with OCC. Participants were asked to assess interactions with the instructor in two contexts: (1) in her/his office and (2) outside of formal class time but not in her/his office (i.e., before or after class, at break time, or on campus).

For office and informal OCC interactions, students estimated the number of interactions, average length of interactions, and percentage of time spent on course work, personal problems, and socializing. Students also gave an overall rating of satisfaction with OCC on a scale of 1 (very dissatisfied) to 7 (very satisfied).

VERBAL IMMEDIACY

Verbal immediacy was measured by the Verbal Immediacy Behaviors (VIB) instrument. The 17-item Likert-type response scale assesses students' perceptions of their instructors' verbal behaviors, including using humour, providing personal examples, and addressing students by name, with no context specified. In this study, the reliability for the VIB instrument using Cronbach's alpha was.87.

NONVERBAL IMMEDIACY

Nonverbal immediacy was measured by the Revised Nonverbal Immediacy Measure (RNIM). It is a 10-item Likert-type response scale that assesses students' perceptions of their instructors' nonverbal behaviors, such as gesturing, smiling, and using a variety of vocal expressions, again with no context specified. In this study the reliability of the RNIM using Cronbach's alpha was.81.

DATA ANALYSIS

The two research questions were addressed by a series of ANOVAs (2 X 2 X 2 and 2 X 2 X 5 factorial design). The dependent variables were verbal immediacy and nonverbal immediacy.

For each dependent variable, the 2 X 2 X 2 ANOVAs had three factors: sex of student, sex of instructor, and one of the following: (1) frequency of office visits and informal contact (low, high), (2) time spent discussing course work during office visits and informal contact (low, high), (3) time spent discussing personal problems during office visits and informal contact (low, high), (4) time spent socializing during office visits and informal contact (low, high) and (5) student satisfaction with OCC (lower, higher).

For the variables coded low and high, a median split was used to divide the lowest one-half of the responses from the highest. For student satisfaction, students indicating that they were very satisfied, satisfied, or somewhat satisfied were coded as having higher satisfaction. Students indicating that they were indifferent, somewhat dissatisfied, dissatisfied, or very dissatisfied were coded as having lower satisfaction. For both dependent variables, the 2 X 2 X 5 ANOVAs had the following three factors: sex of student, sex of instructor, and the length of office visits and informal contact (1-5 min; 6-10 min; 11-15 min; 15-30 min; more than 30 min).

VERBAL IMMEDIACY

The first research question explored the relationship between OCC and verbal immediacy. For frequency of office visits, there was a significant main effect for instructor sex. An analysis of cell means for female and male instructors reveals that female instructors were perceived to be higher in verbal immediacy than were male instructors.

For verbal immediacy and the length of contact, a significant main effect was obtained for instructor sex for informal contact. Female instructors were perceived as higher in verbal immediacy than were male instructors.

For verbal immediacy and the discussion of course work, the ANOVA for instructor sex for the discussion of course work during informal contact yielded a significant main effect. An analysis of mean scores reveals that female instructors were perceived to be higher in verbal immediacy than were male instructors.

For verbal immediacy and student satisfaction with OCC, there was a significant main effect for satisfaction. Students who were higher in satisfaction perceived their instructors to be more immediate than did students who were lower in satisfaction.

NONVERBAL IMMEDIACY

The second research question focused on the relationship between nonverbal immediacy and OCC. For length of office visits, a two-way disordinal interaction for student sex and instructor sex was statistically significant. The nonverbal immediacy mean for male instructors as rated by male students was lower than the mean for female instructors as rated by male students.

In contrast, the nonverbal immediacy mean for male instructors as rated by female students was higher than the mean for female instructors as rated by female students. In the ANOVA for length of informal contact, there was a significant main effect for instructor sex. Female instructors were perceived to be higher in nonverbal immediacy than were male instructors.

In the ANOVA for discussion of course work during informal contact, there was a significant main effect for instructor sex. Female instructors were perceived to be higher in nonverbal immediacy than were male instructors. For the discussion of personal problems during informal contact, there was a significant main effect for instructor sex.

Female instructors were perceived to be higher in nonverbal immediacy than were male instructors. Results indicate a significant two-way disordinal interaction between student sex and discussion of personal problems during informal contact. Male students in the high contact group perceived instructors to be higher in nonverbal immediacy than did male students in the low contact group.

Female students in the high contact group perceived instructors to be lower in nonverbal immediacy than did female students in the low contact group. For the ANOVA for socializing during informal contact, there was a significant main effect for sex of instructor. Female instructors were perceived to be higher in nonverbal immediacy than were male instructors.

For nonverbal immediacy and student satisfaction with OCC, there was a significant main effect for satisfaction. Students who were higher in satisfaction perceived their instructors to be higher in nonverbal immediacy than did students who were lower in satisfaction.

Whereas previous research has established that OCC is beneficial for students, faculty, and universities, this study contributes to an understanding of OCC by analyzing female and male students' perceptions of the verbal and nonverbal immediacy behaviors of their female and male instructors. Students were asked to evaluate their instructor's in-class immediacy behaviors because previous research has established that students use instructor in-class behaviors to assess their accessibility for out-of-class interaction.

In this study, the results indicate that students, regardless of sex, have different perceptions of the verbal and nonverbal immediacy behaviors of their female and male instructors. Female instructors were perceived to be more immediate than were male instructors in three areas of verbal immediacy.

First, students who reported visiting an instructor's office more often perceived female instructors to be higher in verbal immediacy than were male instructors.

Second, students who engaged in informal contact for longer amounts of time perceived their female instructors as more immediate than were their male instructors. Finally, students who reported spending a greater percentage of time discussing course work during informal contact perceived their female instructors to be more immediate than were their male instructors.

Female instructors were also perceived to be higher in nonverbal immediacy than were male instructors in four areas. First, students who spent longer periods of time in informal interactions with their instructors perceived female instructors to be more immediate than male instructors. Female instructors were also perceived as more immediate for all types of discussions during informal contact: course work, personal problems, and socializing.

Students who reported spending a greater proportion of time conversing informally with faculty about course work and personal problems or socializing with faculty perceived their female instructors to be more immediate than their male instructors. Female instructors tend to be perceived as higher in immediacy and thus are more likely to be seen as promoting closeness with students through their behaviors.

One possible explanation as to why students perceive that their female instructors promote closeness more than do male instructors is suggested in research of female and male faculty differences by Macke et al. (1980) and Statham et al. (1991). These researchers suggest that female instructors may experience more status inconsistency than do male instructors (i.e., they are in a high status occupation [college professor] but are themselves regarded as subordinate status [female] in a society that is based on the male hierarchy).

To reduce the status inconsistency, female professors engage in behaviors that may place students and faculty on a more equal footing, such as giving students more class participation time, soliciting more original contributions from students, and making more personal statements about themselves and their students than do male professors.

Students may perceive these behaviors as more immediate in that they reduce psychological distance between the students and professor. This may account for some of the differences in instructor behaviour as perceived by students in this study that suggest that female instructors are perceived as more immediate.

The differences between female and male instructors were more evident during informal contact than during office visits. It would seem that both female and male instructors are perceived to treat students similarly during office visits. One possible explanation for this similar treatment by female and male instructors in the instructor's office is that the instructor's office may be viewed as the instructor's domain where the role of faculty member is salient.

The office visit may also be more rule-governed in terms of what is discussed, how it is discussed, and the time frame of the discussion. Students are likely to go to the instructor's office when they have a problem or question or when the instructor asks them to come for an office visit. Regardless of who initiates the office visit, an academic— related agenda most likely governs the interaction.

For informal contacts (before or after class or informally on campus), the reasons for initiating contact and the topic of the discussion may be different for the student and/or the faculty member than for office visits. The interaction could range from small talk to a discussion of a problem the student is having.

Female instructors appear to indicate nonverbally that they are open to such contact perhaps because students evaluate them as more nonverbally immediate in discussion of course work, personal problems, and socializing. Furthermore, in a study of faculty perceptions of OCC, Nadler and Nadler (2000) found that female faculty reported higher levels of perceived value of OCC with students than did male faculty.

In order to more fully understand why female instructors are perceived by students as more immediate than are male instructors, it would be helpful to know more about the content of these interactions to determine whether informal contact has different functions for female and male faculty. It would also be valuable to know who initiates these informal interactions.

Perhaps female faculty, who appear to value OCC more than male faculty, take the initiative to engage in these informal interactions, or perhaps students are approaching them because the students perceive them to be approachable. Interestingly, differences for female and male students were less prominent than differences for female and male instructors. Student sex was only statistically significant in two of the two-way interactions.

With respect to interactions between student sex and instructor sex, male students rated female instructors as more nonverbally immediate than they rated male instructors with regard to length of office visits, whereas female students rated male instructors as more nonverbally immediate than they rated female instructors.

Male students who reported spending longer periods of time interacting with faculty in their offices perceived female instructors to be more nonverbally immediate, whereas female students who reported spending longer periods of time interacting in the faculty member's office perceived male instructors to be more nonverbally immediate. It appears that for these office visits, students who interacted for longer periods of time perceived the opposite sex instructor to be more immediate.

A two-way interaction was also significant for nonverbal immediacy regarding student sex and the discussion of personal problems during informal contact. Male students who reported spending a greater proportion of informal contact discussing personal problems rated their instructors, regardless of sex, as more immediate than did male students who spent less time informally discussing personal problems with instructors.

Conversely, female students who spent a greater amount of time informally discussing personal problems with faculty rated their instructors lower in nonverbal immediacy than female students who spent less time in these discussions. This finding indicates that male students who reported spending more time informally discussing personal problems did so with instructors they perceived to be more immediate.

Perhaps male students seek out immediate instructors when they have personal problems. But female students appear to see their instructors as less immediate when they discuss personal problems with them. Once again, knowing the content of the interactions and who initiates the interactions, instructor or student, would be helpful in explaining these results.

Although these findings are difficult to explain at this

time, they do highlight the complexity of relationships between female and male students and faculty. The results of this study point to the importance of studying communication variables in relationship to OCC. For example, students who perceived their instructors to be higher in verbal and nonverbal immediacy were more satisfied with OCC than were students who perceived their instructors to be lower in verbal and nonverbal immediacy.

This result is based on a study with several limitations, however. The first is that these are student perceptions of instructor immediacy behaviors rather than the ratings of actual behaviour. Student perceptions are valuable, nevertheless, because these perceptions may be the basis for student behaviour. A comparison of perceptions of immediacy to actual immediacy behaviors would be helpful, however. It would also contribute to an understanding of causation that is not discernible from the current study.

Although faculty in-class behaviors appear to provide cues to accessibility for out-of-class discussions, it cannot be assumed from this study that instructor immediacy in the classroom is the cause of the increased OCC. Students who choose to engage in OCC with faculty members may, as a result of this personal contact, perceive their instructors to be more immediate in the classroom.

Because this study has indicated a relationship does exist between student perceptions of instructor immediacy and OCC, research investigating the causal relationship is warranted. Finally, because so few students actually engage in OCC, it is difficult to analyse the ranges of contact for those who actually do have OCC as compared with the large number of students who do not interact with faculty outside of class. Again, studies of the content of OCC may help by focusing on the students who are actually engaging in this contact.

This study is one of very few studies on OCC and sex of students and instructors. More studies are necessary to analyse the full range of faculty in-class behaviors and student behaviors as they are related to OCC. More information is also needed to determine whether gender-role expectations influence student-faculty OCC.

Furthermore, future research should continue to distinguish the context of OCC for research on sex differences since OCC appears to function differently in the contexts of the office versus informally on campus. OCC is complex for students and faculty, and sex of student and sex of instructor appear to contribute to this complexity. Continued research on this topic is important to understanding this complexity, especially as OCC is beneficial for students' educational outcomes, for faculty evaluations, and for student retention at the university level.

Chapter 7

Communication and Burnout Toward Social Problems

The term "compassion fatigue" first appeared in studies of job burnout in the helping professions to describe a decline in compassionate feelings toward patients or clients in need. In recent years, however, the term has been used outside the occupational context, in the popular press and in philanthropic and fund-raising circles, to describe a larger societal phenomenon - a numbing of public concern toward social problems.

Frequently, these anecdotal reports suggest that the mass media are a primary contributor to the creation of burnout toward social problems. They portray a public grown weary of unrelenting media coverage of human tragedy and ubiquitous fund-raising appeals. This mass-mediated brand of compassion fatigue is characterized as a negative societal phenomenon, with ominous implications for the way that Americans perceive and respond to social problems.

As one account laments, "Mere exposure through the media to human suffering no longer necessarily raises public consciousness of that suffering, because overexposure to the violent and the desperate dulls the senses, building its own wall of indifference."

This conceptualization of compassion fatigue is a direct contradiction to the press agentry models of public relations and fund raising, whose practitioners have based their communication strategy on the philosophy of "the more media coverage, the better" in terms of generating public support. Kelly has noted that this is the predominant model of fund raising practiced today.

While media observers since Lazarsfeld and Merton have speculated that the mass media may lead to desensitization toward social issues, a review of the mass communication, psychology, and sociology literature during the past thirty years found no previous investigations which examine the relationship between communication about social problems and emotional fatigue toward those issues.

COMPASSION AND SOCIAL PROBLEMS

The empathy/altruism literature reflects several conceptualizations of compassion. It is frequently defined as an emotional response that results from empathy and is synonymous with "sympathy." Researchers, however, have found it difficult to empirically isolate compassion from empathy and the terms are often used synonymously. Empathy is a vicarious response to viewing others in distress, and is an inborn, involuntary response.

It is treated as a dispositional trait that varies in strength from individual to individual but that can be elicited at differential levels according to situational factors. There is substantial empirical evidence that seeing someone else suffer leads to negative affect, such as feeling upset distressed or morally outraged.

The literature reflects agreement that empathy arouses emotional distress, which the empathizing person finds aversive and is motivated to reduce through strategies of avoidance or altruism. Of particular import for the present study, Hoffman suggests that there may be a range of optimal empathic arousal in which individuals are most likely to alleviate their empathic distress through helping rather than avoidance behaviors.

Beneath this optimal threshold is a state of empathic underarousal, in which empathic distress may be insufficient in intensity to break through self-preoccupation, and thus results in neither helping nor avoidance behaviors. Conversely, arousal of empathy beyond the optimal range may create empathic distress so aversive that it motivates avoidance behaviors.

This overarousal hypothesis has been supported by studies of nurses whose work with terminally-ill patients created so much empathic distress that they avoided the patient's rooms as much as was possible. Whether Hoffman's continuum of empathic arousal also exists in relation to social problems encountered through the media has not received examination.

The best parallel to compassion fatigue as it is conceptualized here is found in the literature related to emotional burnout in the helping professions, in which subjects become increasingly desensitized to those they are supposed to help.

This burnout is characterized as a pattern of emotional overload and subsequent emotional exhaustion. Its antecedents include dealing extensively with others who are troubled or needy, an overload of information and demands, and a lack of personal efficacy: "Burnout is a greater risk whenever people feel powerless They have the sense that they are at the mercy of the situation and that there is nothing they can do about it.

"It's hopeless; you can't change things; it's bigger than all of us, so why bother trying?"

In the workplace setting, burnout tends to be manifested in one of two ways: emotional exhaustion, characterized by the feeling that one is no longer able to give of himself to others; or through an "armor" of detachment and depersonalization, characterized by "a cold indifference to others' needs and a callous disregard for their feelings."

While the empathy/altruism literature provides strong evidence of compassion fatigue in the interpersonal realm, it does not address the possibility of emotional fatigue with social problems triggered vicariously through the mass media. The present study examines whether the antecedents and manifestations described by Maslach - in particular the outcomes of densensitization and hypersensitization - might also be associated with a mass-mediated compassion fatigue.

MASS MEDIA AND SOCIAL PROBLEMS

Mass media content, including news coverage, entertainment programming, and advertising, carries an abundance of information about social problems. Media are considered to be a primary source of the public's information about social problems and thus are influential in the public's perception and definition of social problems and the formation of attitudes about them.

Agenda-setting studies have found correlations between news coverage of social problems and those regarded as critical issues by the public. In addition, third-person-effect studies have shown that people rely on media coverage, rather than their own experience, to assess the gravity of social problems.

Beginning with Lazarsfeld and Merton's predictions of a mass mediainduced "narcotizing dysfunction," a number of media observers have speculated that pervasive media coverage of social problems may lead to desensitization. Notes Downs, "the piteous sight of an oil-soaked seagull or a dead soldier pales after it has been viewed even a dozen times."

Issue lifecycle studies, while focusing on the rise and fall of public interest in an issue rather than on fluctuations in emotional responses toward victims, provide support for the idea that there is a limit to the effectiveness of message repetition about social problems.

Public attention eventually reaches a threshhold point, beyond which increases in communication about the issue fail to elicit increased interest in the issue. This decline in interest is attributed to message saturation, the flooding of multiple communication channels with redundant messages.

While most issue lifecycle theorists recognize the competition between issues for public attention, Hilgartner and Bosk suggest that social problems also compete for the "surplus compassion" they can muster for causes beyond people's immediate concerns, although they do not empirically investigate levels of compassion in the issue lifecycle. The saturation phenomenon found in these studies raises the issue of marginality, an economic model which suggests a threshhold point beyond which additional messages would have no effect. By contrast, the concept of compassion fatigue posed by the present study suggests a threshhold point at which saturation has negative, rather than neutral, effects.

Thus, when messages about a social problem reach the point of saturation, rather than simply having no impact on an audience, they may have a negative impact on the audience, which might be measured in subjects' affective, attitudinal, and behavioral responses to the issue.

The literature points to a parallel phenomenon associated with repetitive messages in advertising. Ray et al. suggest that an ad which initially arouses positive affect may actually create negative affect after many repeated viewings. Atkin notes that there is also a clutter of "similar-looking PSA's [which] may be creating a 'PSA glaze' wearout problem."

Characteristics of the mass media which would be expected to contribute to compassion fatigue include its ubiquity in everyday life and journalistic news values which influence portrayals of social problems.

PERVASIVENESS

Pervasiveness is considered tobe a defining characteristic of the American mass media and one of the reasons for its power.

The media's ubiquity is magnified by a proliferation of media channels and the "sameness" of content between media channels, particularly in news content.

Maloney and Schonfeld describe a media "bandwagon effect" in which media follow each other's leads for programme content "to the point that it becomes impossible to turn on the news or open a paper without reading another account of the same bad news."

This pervasiveness may lead to a normalization of social problems, described in a newspaper editorial about violent crime: "Such events have come to seem normal to us, just another part of living in America" and are no longer able to shock.

NEWS VALUES AND PRACTICES

Communication research suggests that contemporary news values and practices have relevance for compassion fatigue. Four factors, in particular, emerge from the literature: an emphasis on the sensational, a preponderance of "bad news," failure to provide context for social problems, and the presentation of problems but not solutions.

The desire to attract media consumers has fueled a preference for conflict, violence, and crises over chronic - but perhaps more profound problems, and for social problems which are visually dramatic and consequential for a large number of people. Thus, the media tend to sensationalize social problems as crises of large and overwhelming proportions.

At the same time, opinion polls have consistently shown a public perception that there is too much bad news. People report more concern with the volume of bad news, rather than the bad news itself, which was found to simultaneously attract and repel.

The bad news syndrome is exacerbated by the tendency of the media to present problems but not their solutions, contributing to feelings of inefficacy among media consumers. News reports often fail to provide "mobilizing information" - suggestions for action and details such as phone numbers or addresses which are necessary for action, In addition, antiinstitutional themes - what Robinson terms "journalistic Naderism" - often present established institutions as inept or incapable of solving social problems.

The result of this failure to provide solutions is that the media overwhelm people by showing "an unending procession of events to which they are expected to react, but which they cannot themselves affect." Feelings of inefficacy may constrain information seeking and interpersonal communications. Americans' feelings of inefficacy were blamed by aid organizations for poor public giving in the aftermath of the 1994 Rwandan massacres.

Finally, the media often fail to provide context or in-depth coverage of social problems, presenting social problems through the coverage of events and not necessarily their meanings. The fact that most news media have no social issue beats and that social issues may not fit into conventional press beats often means that news content about social problems reflects preparation by journalists with a superficial knowledge of the problem.

Thus, the communication literature points to a number of potential antecedent variables which explain how the mass media might foster desensitization to social problems. There is a paucity of research, however, to explicate the relationship between mass media and affective responses to social problems.

The study reported here investigates the existence of a compassion fatigue phenomenon and its relationship to mass media. For the issues of AIDS, homelessness, violent crime, and child abuse, three key research questions are explored:

- RQ1: Does a mass-mediated compassion fatigue exist?
- RQ2: If it exists, what variables are predictors of compassion fatigue?
- RQ3: If it exists, what are its manifestations?

Issue Selection. Issues considered for inclusion in the study were those that (1) met the criteria for definition as social problems, and (2) had high top-of-mind awareness among a general population. First, preliminary research was conducted with two groups of undergraduate students (n=50), who were asked the open-ended question, "What would you say are the current issues of the day?" and a number of follow-up questions.

This technique elicited seventeen distinct issues which could be considered social problems. Next, these issues were compared to issues identified by Gallup Poll data which asked American's to name the "nation's most important problem." Six items which emerged from the pretests and the Gallup poll were intially considered, including the war in Bosnia and the environment, as well as AIDS, homelessness, child abuse, and violent crime.

Several iterations of survey instruments, incorporating

from one to six issues, were developed and pre-tested via telephone, including one in which issues were self-generated by respondents and another which included a control issue with no readily identifiable group of victims to serve as objects of compassion.

These pretests indicated that four issues were optimal: more than four issues became too long for respondents; less than four did not allow for sufficient comparison between issues. The self-generated issues version was found to be unwieldy to administer. The issue of Bosnia was eliminated because it stood out as the only nondomestic issue.

The environment was eliminated because it was overly broad and the only issue in which the most obvious "victim" was not a human being. The final version of the survey, focusing on the four issues of AIDS, homelessness, violent crime, and child abuse, was selected as most feasible because it allowed for comparison of compassion levels between several highly recgonizable social problems, while keeping the time required for interviewing to approximately fifteen minutes.

The literature review and preliminary research with subjects suggested a number of variables that are likely to be associated with compassion fatigue. Survey items assessed each of these variables for each of the four issues studied. These variables included: interest in the issue, emotional arousal toward the issue, information seeking (or avoidance) of the issue, interpersonal communication about the problem, emotional and physical reactions to media reports about the problem, efficacy feelings associated with the problem, attitudes associated with the problem, and media consumption patterns.

The survey consisted of thirty-five five-point Likerttype scales and a series of six open-ended questions related to key manifestations of compassion fatigue. Scaled items included ten questions employing the customary "strongly agree" to "strongly disagree" format, as well as thirteen questions employing response alternatives based on other variables which were scaled on a 1 to 5 continuum, such as "hopeful" to "hopeless," "definitely would watch" to "definitely would not watch" and so on.

Two different versions of the survey, varying the ordering of questions, were used to avoid an order bias. Interview times ranged from eleven to twenty-two minutes, averaging approximately fifteen minutes. Quantitative data analysis procedures employing SPSS(x) were used to assess the research questions.

To determine the extent to which a general population may experience compassion fatigue, a telephone survey of randomly-selected residents of greater-metropolitan Atlanta, encompassing urban, suburban, and semirural locales, was conducted. A random digit generating software programme was used to ensure random selection of telephone numbers. Seven call attempts were made to each number at various times of the day and week. A message requesting participation in the survey was left on answering machines. Call attempts to 550 eligible, residential numbers resulted in 316 completed interviews, for a response rate of 57.4%.

Does Compassion Fatigue Exist? Based on the survey item43 which most directly assessed self-reports of emotional arousal, a substantial proportion of respondents reported feelings of burnout for each of the issues studied. Forty per cent of respondents rated themselves as either burned out or approaching burnout (a response of 1 or 2 on a scale of 1 to 5) on the issue of violent crime.

Thirtyfive per cent reported feeling burned out on AIDS, and 33% on homelessness. Even for the issue of child abuse, which consistently elicited the most compassionate responses, nearly 15% of respondents said they were burned out or approaching burnout.

A reliability check of this survey item with two other items assessing emotional sensitivity yielded Cronbach's alpha scores ranging from.56 for the crime issue to.78 for the homeless issue, indicating that this is a satisfactory measure of emotional arousal. Responses to the open-ended questions (reported below under "manifestations") provide further evidence to support the existence of a compassion fatigue phenomenon, reflecting affective and behavioral responses consistent with desensitization and hyper-sensitization.

Who Is Burned Out? A comparison of means for this item indicates a pattern in which whites, males, and college graduates express greater fatigue with the social problems studied than others. For all four issues, white respondents reported more intense feelings of burnout than black respondents, with t-tests showing the difference to be significant for every issue.

Males reported significantly more intense feelings of burnout than females for the issues of child abuse, homelessness, and AIDS. College graduates reported significantly higher levels of burnout than those with a high school diploma or less for all issues but homelessness. Respondents with household incomes of $50,000 or more reported feeling the greatest burnout for every issue, although income was significant at a=.05 only for the issue of violent crime.

Age was not a significant factor in burnout differences. Media consumption was a significant variable in burnout only for the issue of violent crime. Here, heavy media users (24.7% of respondents) those who reported watching television news five or more times in the past week and reading the newspaper five or more times in the past week - were found to report less burnout than light media users, who watched TV news and read the newspaper less than twice a week (7% of respondents).

No significant differences in levels of burnout were found between those who were highly TV-dependent and those who were highly print-dependent.

PREDICTORS OF COMPASSION FATIGUE

A discriminant function analysis was performed for each issue to predict membership in "burned-out" or "not-burned-out" groups. The burned-out group was defined as those respondents who rated themselves as a 1 or a 2 on a scale of emotional sensitivity ranging from 1= burned out to 5=highly sensitive. The not-burned-out group was composed of those who responded with a 3, 4, or 5. This division of respondents was selected because of the desire to focus on differences between those who clearly identified themselves as burned out or approaching burnout, and everyone else. A split sample approach was used to check for sample bias. Canonical loadings of all variables found to be significant discriminators at a=.05 were examined to determine which variables have the greatest predictive power.

Results suggest a pattern in which four variables are of primary importance in predicting who will be burned out. In particular, likelihood of watching a programme about the issue was the most powerful discriminating variable for three of the four issues: violent crime, child abuse, and AIDS. For these issues, selective avoidance of media content about the issue is a strong predictor of burnout.

For homelessness, emotional arousal to news reports about the issue was the most powerful predictor of burnout; this variable was also a significant predictor for each of the other three issues. Other predictor variables which were significant in predicting membership in burned out groups for all four issues were: feelings that what one has seen in the media has decreased compassion feelings and low interest in the issue.

These findings indicate that mass media are strongly associated with the phenomenon of compassion fatigue. Although the media's role in the development of burnout requires further explication, the link between media and burnout is evident in the manifestations of burnout - with those who report feelings of burnout toward an issue likely to selectively avoid media content about that issue.

Interpersonal communication about the issue was a significant factor only in predicting burnout toward child abuse and AIDS, with those in the burned-out groups far less likely to discuss these issues with others. It is noteworthy that level of media consumption was a predictor of burnout only for violent crime, with the burned-out group watching one fewer day of local TV news per week than those who were not burned out.

In addition, the fact that heavy media users reported less burnout than light users suggests that the development of compassion fatigue is influenced more by individual tolerances to media coverage of "bad news" than level of media consumption. In other words, no one level of exposure is uniformly associated with emotional burnout in every individual.

Finally, the discriminant function analysis does not suggest a clear pattern of association between efficacy and compassion fatigue. Efficacy was a significant predictor of burnout only for the issues of violent crime and homelessness. Contrary to what might be expected, however, those burned out on violent crime reported feeling less overwhelmed by needy causes than those who were not burned out on violent crime.

With the homeless issue, those who reported burnout were significantly more hopeless that the problem could be solved than those who were not burned out on this issue. However, they also perceived that the media provides mobilizing information "about what you could do to address the problem" more frequently than those in the not-burned-out group.

To determine whether compassion fatigue is a situational or "state" phenomenon rather than a personality trait which would be present regardless of issue, a repeated measures MANOVA procedure was performed.

This procedure tests for significance of the main factor effects (burnout on each issue x interest, emotional arousal, and information-seeking subscales) and the interaction effects of the variables.

Significant differences were found for the overall analysis. The variables contributing to the effect were then identified using paired t-tests.

Significant differences, reflecting variation in burnout as a function of issue, were found in 38 of the 48 t-tests. Had burnout been a trait characteristic, the findings would have reflected insignificant results for each of the 48 pairs.

These results suggest that compassion fatigue is a state,

occuring for some issues but not for others, rather than a personality trait.

MANIFESTATIONS OF COMPASSION FATIGUE

Compassion fatigue was conceptualized as resulting in manifestations of desensitization or hypersensitization, with either outcome expected to impact three primary areas: interest in the issue, emotional arousal toward the issue, and information-seeking about the issue. Since the survey included multiple items to assess each of these variables, subscales for interest, emotional arousal, and information-seeking could be created by combining each respondents' scores for the survey items assessing these areas.

Then, the group means of subscale scores for respondents classifying themselves as burned out and not-burned-out were compared. T-tests found significant differences at the.05 level for each variable between those who were burned out and those who were not, with burned-out groups having significantly lower subscale scores for interest, emotional arousal, and information seeking.

To further explicate the strength of the relationship between burnout and the factors of interest, emotional arousal, and information-seeking, the correlations between self-reported burnout scores and subscales for the three variables were calculated. Correlation coefficients indicate a positive relationship between compassionate feelings and interest, emotional arousal, and information-seeking.

Responses to open-ended questions about emotional, physical, and media use reactions confirmed and enriched our understanding of the nature of compassion fatigue and how it is manifested. For purposes of comparison, respondents were asked to describe their reactions to the issue (of the four) they felt most sensitive to, and the issue they felt least sensitive to. Response categories to these questions were coded and analysed.

AFFECTIVE MANIFESTATIONS

When respondents described emotional reactions to

issues they felt least sensitive to, more than half (51.5%) of their responses reflected feelings of desensitization or lack of compassion. Many couched their responses in rationales for their lack of compassion, including:

- Perceptions that conditions were self-inflicted and therefore, deserved
- They were "saturated," "numb," or tired of hearing about the issue
- The issue had received unwarranted attention from the media, at the expense of other issues

The problem was hopeless and there was nothing they could do about it. These rationales are similar to those identified by Hunt as explanations for lack of compassion, and reflect the link between empathy and efficacy and the "just world orientation," or the belief that people "get what they deserve."

By contrast, when respondents described their emotional reactions to the issue they were most sensitive to, 41.4% of responses reflected compassion, through terms such as "sympathetic," "sad," and "upset." The second most common affective response was anger about the issue (36.3%), followed by being shocked or appalled (7.6%).

PHYSICAL MANIFESTATIONS

In open-ended questions, 35% of respondents reported media content about the social problems studied so disturbing that they experienced physical reactions, such as sleeplessness, crying, and loss of appetite. Consistent with the conceptualization of hypersensitization, physical reactions were most likely to occur as a reaction to issues to which respondents were most sensitive.

Other physical reactions mentioned in open-ended responses included nausea, stomach ache, perceptions of increasing high blood pressure and racing heart, feelings of anxiety and depression, nightmares, and headaches. These reactions are similar to somatic manifestations of anxiety found in other studies.

The relatively large percentage of respondents reporting

physical reactions suggests that many people may occasionally experience somatic reactions in response to coverage of disturbing issues, but that these may not necessarily lead them to classify themselves as "burned out" on the issue, or to trigger media avoidance strategies.

It was clear from respondent comments, however, that for a small cohort of the population, physical reactions in response to a particular issue were experienced intensely and consistently, and served as strong motivators for avoidance of the topic in the media.

CHANGES IN MEDIA USE

In open-ended questions, more than half of the respondents indicated that their use of the media had changed as a result of their reactions to the issue to which they felt most sensitive. Only 32% of respondents said their media use had changed as a result of their reactions to the issue they felt least sensitive to.

Overwhelmingly, changes in media use reflected decreased information-seeking. Selective avoidance of the topic was the most common change in media behaviour reported. Specific avoidance behaviors mentioned included avoiding local newscasts, channel switching, turning off the TV or radio or putting the newspaper down, mentally tuning out the story, skimming print articles, turning the volume down, being more selective in choosing programming, decreasing overall media use, and monitoring children's viewing.

Forty-eight per cent of respondents reported using such strategies to avoid the issue they were most sensitive to. Slightly more than 30% of respondents reported avoidance behaviors for the issue they were least sensitive to.

Even when respondents were asked about the issue they were most sensitive to, only 7% of their responses reflected increased information-seeking.

These responses are consistent with the study's close-ended survey item which found that 40% of respondents agreed strongly that they felt "overwhelmed" by the number of needy causes they heard about. Many of those whose open-ended responses were indicative of hypersensitivity described regular and quite intentional efforts to avoid the topic - either in all media or specific media channels. In particular, avoiding local television news coverage of the issue was mentioned by more respondents than any other avoidance strategy.

This finding is consistent with the survey's close-ended question which found that respondents reported feeling more emotionally exhausted after watching local TV news than after reading the newspaper or watching the national TV news.

The affective impact of television news reports was clearly a key to their aversive nature. Respondents mentioned preferring print sources or public broadcasting as less graphic alternatives to network television; choosing programming for mood control (in particular, avoiding the topic when depressed or tired); preferring sitcoms or other upbeat programming to television news; and avoiding the news, regardless of topic, at dinnertime and before bed.

The findings suggest that an issue which is strongly emotionally arousing for an individual is more likely to be associated with avoidance behaviors, ostensibly as a form of self-protection from content which elicits emotional distress. In this situation, the need for emotional self-protection may override the need to know about an issue that concerns us.

Conversely, when an issue holds low emotional arousal for an individual, it appears to be less likely to motivate selective avoidance. Desensitization or lack of concern about a social problem appears to be less aversive than emotional distress, and individuals may "sit through" media coverage on the topic rather than commit the energy required to avoid it. In its most extreme form, compassion fatigue was manifested in total media avoidance, with respondents reporting that their reactions to the issues in the media had caused them to totally boycott television news and drop newspaper subscriptions.

While these respondents were few in number, their reactions reveal the depth of ire directed toward the media, and a tendency to "kill the messenger" when the messenger is perceived to have acted irresponsibly. In sum, the selective avoidance strategies cited by respondents support the predictions of media observers who warned that unrelenting media coverage of bad news would alienate the public and cause them to tune out social issues.

DISCUSSION

The study finds (1) evidence for the existence of a compassion fatigue phenomenon among a general public, and (2) a relationship between compassion fatigue toward four social problems and media coverage of those problems. A compassion fatigue phenomenon associated with lowered interest, emotional arousal, and information-seeking toward these social problems was found in all statistical assessments employed, and confirmed in responses to open-ended questions.

Several defining patterns emerge to give shape to the compassion fatigue concept: Compassion fatigue is issue-dependent. The nature of a particular social problem appears to be a key factor in the development of compassion fatigue. In this study, there were clear differences in the levels of emotional sensitivity to the four issues. AIDS and homelessness did not arouse respondents' concern to nearly the same degree as violent crime and child abuse.

Factors fueling feelings of burnout toward violent crime appeared to be the pervasiveness of crime coverage and the heinous nature of the crime itself. Compassion fatigue also appears to be a particular risk for issues like homelessness and AIDS, which are perceived by many to have low personal salience, and reflect perceptions that victims are to blame for their situations.

Evidence that those who are most burned out on the issues are also the furthest removed from those issues in terms of life circumstances suggests that social cause organizations must do more to promote perceptions of similarity between viewers and victims.

The study also indicates that levels of burnout vary within individuals by issue. Statistical analysis showed no evidence for a "burned out" personality that exhibited compassion fatigue toward all social problems.Compassion fatigue is an individual, multi-dimensional phenomenon.

The findings support the conceptualization of compassion fatigue as being manifested in either desensitization or hypersensitivity toward an issue, with these outcomes producing a range of of affective, physical, and behavioral responses to media coverage about the issue.

It should not be surprising that not all respondents exhibited feelings of compassion fatigue. Consistent with the limited effects school only some of those exposed to pervasive media coverage of social problems would be expected to exhibit symptoms of compassion fatigue. Situational factors such as individual tolerances for bad news and personal salience appear to be intervening variables.

Results of the study suggest that for those who are initially disinterested or biased against victims of a social problem, pervasive media coverage likely serves to entrench negative feelings toward victims and foster desensitization.

However, for those who initially are sympathetic toward the issue, a more diverse range of outcomes is possible: Pervasive media coverage may foster disinterest based on boredom, or feelings that "I know all I need to know" about the issue; it may foster frustration and emotional desensitization when it appears that nothing can be done, or that the victims' own behaviour is to blame for their situations.

For others, it may increase emotional sensitivity toward the issue in an optimal way that encourages empathy with victims. And for a final group of those who are initially sensitive to the issue, pervasive media coverage of some social problems may contribute to empathic distress at a level sufficient to motivate avoidance of topics which are emotionally draining.

Each of these outcomes is identifiable in the openended responses of survey participants. It is plausible that desensitization may be the final outcome for those who experience hypersensitization, as it would serve as a defence against emotional distress. The mass media play a primary role in the development of compassion fatigue. The media contribute to compassion fatigue toward social problems in two primary ways: by providing content that serves as aversive stimuli, prompting avoidance strategies; and by fostering desensitization to social problems through redundant and predominately negative messages which reach the point of saturation.

Respondents blamed their desensitization and avoidance strategies on the nature and content of television news reports, and local news in particular. These findings underscore perceptions of media negativity that were found to be a primary cause of hostility toward the media. Level of media consumption and print versus broadcast dependence do not appear to be as influential in the development of compassion fatigue as individual tolerances for exposure to disturbing media content and perceptions of the victims' "deservingness" of compassion.

Interpersonal communication appears to mediate compassion fatigue toward AIDS and child abuse, suggesting that interpersonal communication may be one key to preventing or reducing desensitization toward issues which deal with societal taboos.

PRACTICAL AND THEORETICAL IMPLICATIONS

The compassion fatigue concept offers an alternative model to the press agentry approach to communication about social problems. It expands our knowledge of the influence of message repetition to the arena of communication about social problems.

Most important, it suggests that burnout need not be the result of direct personal contact with those in need, but that it may also be a vicarious response, associated with exposure to human problems through the window of the mass media.

Over the years, social cause organizations have factored their audience's limited time and financial resources into their fund-raising strategies. However, the public's capacity for emotional arousal has often been treated as an infinite, undepletable commodity. This study suggests that social cause organizations in fact are competing for three limited resources: the public's time, money, and capacity to care. Communication strategists must be increasingly sensitive to the prospect of an informationally-overloaded and emotionally-overwhelmed public.

While news coverage of social problems may initially serve a facilitating role in attracting attention and resources to problem amelioration, pervasive coverage which emphasizes problems without solutions may actually backfire and create a numbing of concern toward social problems and their victims.

The nature of contemporary mass media is integral to the compassion fatigue problem. Acknowledging compassion fatigue as part of the potential fallout from current news values and practices is an important first step for media gatekeepers who are interested in playing a helpful rather than hindering role in addressing social problems.

Chapter 8

Exploring the Impact of Affirmative Action

Anti-discrimination laws and affirmative action procedures theoretically have leveled the playing field in employment. Race, gender, and ethnicity are supposed to no longer have a role in hiring, and, as a consequence, employment rates for the powerful and less powerful groups in society should be indistinguishable.

Because of the supposition that race, gender, and ethnicity no longer play a significant role in hiring, affirmative action-though not antidiscrimination legislation-has come under severe attack in recent years. Affirmative action is often termed a form of reverse discrimination that ought to be outlawed by the anti-discrimination legislation and policy that preceded-and in many ways-spawned it.

Debates within the communication industries have mirrored those in society at large. Media industries are considering the need for continued affirmative action in a period of high employment overall and supposed equality of access to jobs in the economy.

Does discrimination continue to exist in the journalism and mass communication labour force? Is there evidence that anti-discrimination legislation and affirmative action policies on the part of media and related communication employment sectors have eliminated race, ethnicity, and gender as criteria in hiring? This chapter examines that question in detail by documenting, first, the rate of employment of those seeking entry-level jobs in the field of journalism and mass communication and then attempting to explain why discovered gaps in employment rates exist.

Until the U.S. Congress passed the Civil Rights Act in 1964, it was legal to make hiring decisions based on race, ethnicity, and sex. At that time, it was common to use these characteristics in selecting employees and in assigning them to work tasks once they were hired. Such decisions might have made short-term economic sense, given past practices and existing prejudices in the society. They certainly were accepted practice in U.S. industries, including those in the communication sector.

Title VII of the 1964 Civil Rights Act made race- and sex-based segregation in the workplace illegal. Affirmative action resulted from the recognition that outlawing discrimination in hiring would not, of itself, result in equal access for women and members of racial or ethnic minorities to all segments of the labour force. Affirmative action requires employers to do more than refrain from making decisions based on race and ethnicity.

It requires pro-active activities to promote equal employment opportunities to groups traditionally discriminated against in employment. Hiring is one of the important pro-active activities.

Reskin, in her review of the effects of affirmative action on employment, says that the 1964 Federal law banning discrimination in employment curtailed the most blatant forms of discrimination but had little effect on the discrimination that stemmed from the ways that organizations went about recruiting, screening, and evaluating workers.

She continues: "Custom, habit, self-interest and people's aversion to the risks that change entails all favour the status quo. In pursuing ostensibly neutral recruitment, hiring and promotion procedures that were customary before the passage of anti-discrimination regulations, establishments continued to exclude groups of workers from many lines of work."

Reskin said that eliminating forms of habitual discrimination requires employers to actively modify their personnel practices. These modifications, designed to ensure race- and gender-neutral employment practices, are a fundamental part of affirmative action.

According to Reskin, four different types of affirmative action exist. The first type results from presidential and gubernatorial executive orders requiring action by government contractors and subcontractors and actually affects only a very small number of employers and employees. The second type is the consequence of regulations on government itself in its capacity as employer.

The third type is based on court decisions in anti-discrimination cases. The final type stems from voluntary human resource policies of employers. There is no doubt a link between the third and fourth types of affirmative action. The 1972 Equal Employment Opportunity Act amended Title VII of the 1964 Civil Rights Act to allow federal courts to include affirmative action among the remedies they can require of firms found guilty of discrimination and use affirmative-action plans as part of a consent decree in settlement of such cases.

Employers might well have initiated affirmativeaction programs voluntarily with the knowledge of the power of the courts to mandate such programs should a legal complaint be adjudicated. Voluntary affirmative-action programs have been found to have common characteristics. They promote the integration of jobs in organizations and racial and gender neutrality in decision making.

Advertisements that say the organization is an equal-opportunity employer are a common component. Some organizations train and reward managers for their affirmativeaction performance. Estimates of the percentage of firms implementing voluntary affirmative-action policies vary.

Edelman found that 71 per cent of the organizations surveyed nationally had affirmative-action plans, almost one in five had an Equal Employment Opportunity or affirmative-action office, and most had created structures and rules to foster affirmative action. Holzer and Neumark, however, found that fewer than half of the employers in Los Angeles,

Atlanta, Boston, and Detroit said they took into account either equal employment opportunities or affirmative action in hiring workers.

Miller found that only four in ten of the large firms in the New York-New Jersey-Connecticut metropolitan area surveyed reported some form of affirmative action to recruit minorities, fewer than three in ten did so to recruit women, about three in ten employed affirmative action in promoting minorities, and one in four did so in promoting women. Fewer than half of workers have been found to believe their employer practices affirmative action.

The American Society of Newspaper Editors, the National Association of Broadcasters, the Newspaper Association of America, the Radio-Television News Directors Association, and other professional mass communication groups have been outspoken in promoting affirmative action among their members.

The Associated Press in the early 1980s settled a complaint by the Federal Equal Employment Opportunity and seven female, former AP employees requiring the news service to, among other things, develop an affirmative-action policy for the organization. The Federal Communication Commission historically has required stations applying for license renewal to present an affirmative-action plan for hiring and promotion of women and minorities.

Despite these efforts at affirmative action and the existence of antidiscrimination laws, evidence of discrimination continues to exist in the United States. This conclusion is based on evidence of differential employment outcomes, on reports of employers to researchers describing how race and sex affect their hiring decisions, and on the prevalence of organizational practices that have been shown to have discriminatory consequences.

All show evidence that discrimination continues to be a prevalent part of American employment. This is true despite mounting evidence of potential effectiveness of affirmative-action procedures. Reskin, in her review of a research on this topic, found that affirmative-action programs required by presidential executive orders have reduced discrimination against minority and female workers, as have court-ordered affirmative-action and even some voluntary affirmative-action plans.

Bowen and Bok's study of the performance of minority students admitted to selective colleges through racesensitive admission programs similarly documents the positive consequences of that decison. Weaver and Wilhoit have found little evidence that American newsrooms have become much more diverse across time.

Women made up 20 per cent of the journalistic workforce in 1971, 34 per cent in 1982-83, and 34 per cent in 1992. Minorities increased from about 5 per cent of the journalistic workforce in 1971 to about 8 per cent in 1992.

The American Society of Newspaper Editors has found that minorities make up less than 12 per cent of the newsrooms of daily newspapers in the United States-roughly the same percentage as a year earlier and up from 8 per cent in 1990 and 4 per cent in 1978.

Women made up 37 per cent of the daily newsrooms in 1998, the first year that figure was tracked by the organization. In 1997, 27 per cent of the U.S. population was minority; the figure is projected to increase a percentage point by 2000. The recent literature on employment helps to explain why discrimination continues, despite legal prohibition of it. Much of this literature is a departure from the classic economic perspective on hiring, in which it is assumed that individuals looking for jobs, or managers looking for employees, are rational actors and follow the dictates of labour market theory.

Within labour market theory, employers are the buyers of labour, and employees are the sellers. Supply and demand operate to regulate wages and establish equilibrium, and within a strict interpretation of this view, unemployment should not exist." It is also assumed that individuals can possess complete information about the "market." Granovetter, however, has resituated the concept of job search from the rational actor approach of economics to the realm of sociology. Job-finding behaviour, he says, "is heavily embedded in other social processes that closely constrain and determine its course and results."

Granovetter begins with the idea that information is imperfectly distributed in the job-search process. Many top-level jobs are filled by those privy to special information, and he found that 57 per cent of jobs are filled through informal contacts and nonrational avenues. In similar studies other researchers have found percentages ranging from the 30s to the 50s.

According to Granovetter, individuals are most likely to receive new job information from those with whom they have "weak ties."Z' They are less likely to receive new information from those with whom they have strong ties (family and close friends) because they are likely to already have this information. Common examples of weak ties include friends and family of former co-workers and schoolmates, and contacts made from networking at professional conferences.

Weak ties are often occupational rather than social, and those who have fewer ties tend to have more trouble in the job market. Historically, blacks have been at a disadvantage because they have been underrepresented in the occupational structure itself and therefore have been less privy to informal channels of opportunity.

Formality of search is also a major dimension in the literature on hiring theory. According to Marsden and Campbell, informal recruitment (e.g., employees recruiting acquaintances) facilitates the hiring of persons who are already well informed about a workplace. For this reason, informal recruitment can lower turnover, but it may also lead to a lack of diversity in the applicant pool, because those associated with the firm are likely to convey information to socially similar persons.

Coverdill and Finlay, in a study of headhunters and white-collar recruitment, found that the assessment of a job candidate's likely social fit is a highly important factor in the hiring of whitecollar employees. In short, "like hires like."

According to Marsden, formal channels of recruitment-including advertising in the mass media, visiting campuses, and using placement agencies-are more suitable for reaching geographically dispersed and more demographically diverse candidates. Also, larger organizations are more likely to use formal channels of recruitment because they have more resources for formal searches and their needs may exceed the skill resources of the local community.

Barron and Bishop found that economic conditions may also have an effect on the level of formality and on how intensive the search is. When faced with a smaller applicant pool, employers tend to screen potential hires less carefully.

Pfeffer and Cohen found the existence of internal labour markets in organizations to be an indicator of formalized recruitment methods.Zb At organizations with internal labour markets, i.e., formal promotion ladders with few ports of entry at the bottom, employees are expected to stay with the organization for a lifetime and management therefore has a higher stake in their quality.

Similarly, Barron and Bishop found that organizations use more intensive formal methods of recruiting when it is necessary for the organization to invest more training in the position. Little systematic work has been done focusing on hiring and its effects of the journalism and mass communication labour market.

Becker, Fruit, and Caudill did study how media organizations make hiring decisions, but they did not examine how those decisions were affected by gender and race or ethnicity. Becker, Kosicki, Engleman, and Viswanath examined the individual predictors of success in the journalism and mass communication labour market, though the analysis dealt only tangentially with gender and race. Neither variable predicted success of the applicants in finding a job in the field.

Claussen, Lowrey, Anderson, and Becker found evidence that newspapers, at least, do not have elaborate internal labour markets-that is, policy that leads to clear paths of internal advancement-and rely heavily on external markets of the type most likely to be influenced by informal hiring methods.

Research in the sociology of organizations has found that a strong external or "craft" labour market is an indicator of more informal recruitment channels. In a craft market, skills are transferable among organizations, and job openings are often communicated informally among occupational members. News organizations have been viewed as existing in an external "craft" labour market.

Two different types of literature have been reviewed to this point. The first is macro-level, looking at social policy and its outcome in producing a labour force that is not differentiated by race or sex. The second is organizational, looking at factors that come into place as employers make decisions on whom to hire and whom to promote.

The social policy can dictate organizational behaviour, and only if the organizational behaviour is consistent with social policy will the outcome of employment undifferentiated by race and gender be possible. At least that is the assumption of the social policy.

Unknown in the field of journalism and mass communication is the extent to which social policy of equal opportunity and anti-discrimination has led to employment patterns that are not differentiated by race and gender. The evidence at hand has focused only on segments of the industry and only on the cumulative effects of hiring, not on the immediate hiring decisions themselves.

If the social policy of affirmative action and the laws of anti-discrimination have been effective, there should be no difference in employment rates for women and men, or for minorities and those not labeled as minorities.

If the policy has failed in the field of journalism and mass communication-as seems likely given the evidence of its failure in the labour force generallywomen and men should show differential employment rates, as should minorities and nonminorities. We hypothesize this second outcome.

H1: Across time, differential employment rates of women and men and of minorities and nonminorities in the field of journalism and mass communication will continue to exist.

We are not expecting blatant discrimination to continue

to play a significant role. The law has made it difficult for employers to refuse to hire qualified applicants or to openly follow policies that make it impossible for women or minorities to gain jobs. Gender, race, and ethnicity, however, are often linked to other characteristics that play a role in the hiring decision.

Minorities are less likely to have had the same educational experiences, the same opportunities, and the same guidance as their colleagues. The same can be said for women in comparison with men. The result should be that much of the evidence of discrimination should be attributable to the legacy of inequality. What isn't attributable to these should result from what we have termed the informal hiring practices of media organizations-the practices that can be addressed by renewed efforts at affirmative action.

As noted above, the informal hiring procedures often used make it likely that people will hire people like themselves-and those making hiring decisions are not often female or nonwhite. We hypothesize that not all of the variance in employment rates will be explainable by the legacy of inequality of experience. We speculate that such a finding will provide evidence of the effects of informal hiring practices.

H2: Even after controlling for the inequality of experiences of women and men and of minorities and nonminorities, women will be less likely to be hired than men, and minorities will be less likely to be hired than nonminorities.

METHODS

Data gathered as part of the Annual Survey of Journalism & Mass Communication Graduates are appropriate for a test of these hypotheses. The Annual Survey of Journalism & Mass Communication Graduates is designed to monitor the employment rates of graduates of journalism and mass communication programs in the United States, including Puerto Rico. In addition, the survey tracks the curricular activities of those graduates while in college. The survey has employed a comparable methodology since 1987. During that time, more than 24,200 graduates of journalism and mass communication programs around the country participated in the survey.

At present, the Annual Survey of Journalism & Mass Communication Graduates is conducted at the Henry W. Grady College of Journalism and Mass Communication at the University of Georgia. From 1987-1996, the survey was conducted at The Ohio State University.

As a first step in the survey, a sample of schools is drawn from those listed in the Journalism and Mass Communication Directory, published annually by the Association for Education in Journalism and Mass Communication, and The Journalist's Road to Success: A Career and Scholarship Guide, published each year by the Dow Jones Newspaper Fund, Inc. The sample of schools is modified each year to reflect changes in these two directories.

Sample selection is probabilistic, so that schools selected represent the population of schools listed in the two directories. In 1997, as an example, 92 schools were drawn from the 451 unique entries of four-year programs in the United States (including Puerto Rico) in the two directories.

Administrators at the selected schools are asked to provide the names and addresses of their spring bachelor's and master's degree recipients. As the second step in the survey, a questionnaire is mailed in November or December to all spring graduates receiving either a bachelor's or a master's degree from the selected programs. A second questionnaire is sent to nonrespondents in January or February.

The questionnaire asks about the respondent's experiences both while as a student and in the months since graduation. Included are questions about university experiences, job-seeking and employment, and salary and benefits.

Employment rates for each of the survey years are based on responses to a question on employment at the time of completion of the interview. Respondents could indicate if they were employed full time, part time, enrolled in school, or unemployed. Respondents enrolled in school were eliminated from computation of employment rates.

Respondents classified themselves according to sex and race/ethnicity, allowing for computation of employment rates by these social strata. Additionally, respondents indicated if they had sought jobs in the field of journalism and mass communication and if they had received job offers in the field. For those who sought such a job, receiving an offer is an indicant of job-seeking success, whether or not the job was actually taken.

Respondents indicate the type of specialization within journalism and mass communication they completed, the number of internships they completed, in which campus media they participated, and their grade point average.

Respondents were classified as having attended an accredited journalism programme or not and, based on the percentage of students applying to their college and university who were admitted, as having attended a selective university or not.

Return rate for the 1997 survey, computed as the number returned divided by the number mailed minus the bad addresses, was 54.5%. Of the usable questionnaires, 2,169 were from bachelor's degree recipients and 145 were from those who received a master's degree. Earlier surveys produced similar return rate statistics.

Most graduates of journalism and mass communication programs receive an undergraduate, rather than graduate degree, and the graduate survey reflects this fact. The design of the survey was changed in 1989 only to incorporate master's degree recipients.

The analyses that follow are based only on the responses of bachelor's degree recipients from 1987-1997, twothirds of whom were female and 15 per cent of whom were classified as minorities - that is, African American, Hispanic, Native American, Asian American, Pacific Islander American, or Other, In general, there are only small differences between women and men in terms of level of full-time employment six to eight months after graduation from a journalism and mass communication programme.

The figures were nearly identical in 1987, and they vary only slightly in the years that follow. Across all years, the difference in full-time employment rates is 2.7%-a difference that is statistically significant. The difference is in favour of women. Women have a slightly better chance of being employed full time six to eight months after graduation than do men, who are slightly more likely to end up in part-time positions.

The discrepancies between minorities and nonminorities, however, is more striking. In every year except one since 1987, minorities report lower levels of full-time employment six to eight months after graduation than do nonminorities. The exception is 1988, when the number of minorities surveyed was quite small, and, as a consequence, the power of the estimation low.

To be sure, in two years, 1991 and 1992, the differences in level of fulltime employment were slight. Across all years, however, the gap in level of full-time employment six to eight months after graduation was 5.2 percentage points, with minorities significantly less likely to report full-time employment than were nonminorities.

Hl predicted discrepancies in the labour market-as reflected in employment rates-for women versus men and for minorities versus nonminorities, despite the existence of affirmative-action initiatives. Evidence of discrepancies for women are slight and suggest that women have fared just slightly better than men.

The discrepancies are more striking when minority graduates are compared with nonminority graduates. This discrepancy actually increased over time and supports the hypothesis of continued inequalities, based on race and ethnicity, in the labour market.

The employment rates are macro-level indicators of potential discrimination in the labour market. A better indicator of bias in hiring, however, comes from an analysis of any discrepancy between job seeking and the receipt of a job offer. The graduate survey asked respondents to indicate from which types of mass communication employers they sought jobs and from which ones they received offers. These survey questions test hiring discrimination at the individual level and are therefore appropriate for use in a test of H2.

Only those graduates who actually sought work with a communication employer are included 32 The dependent variable is scored as dichotomous, with receipt of an offer coded as 1 and no receipt coded as 0.

Independent variables used in the analysis were minority status (minority scored high), reported college grade point average, accreditation status of the programme at which the graduate studied, selectivity of that programme, sequence specialization (with dummy variables for journalism, RTV, and advertising), number of internships worked by student applicants, number of college media for which the student worked, and gender (female scored high).

In each year, the variables entered into the equation explained a small but significant amount of variance in the receipt of at least one job offer. The R square ranges from a low of.031 to a high of.080. Consistent with findings from analysis of employment rates, gender contributes little to an understanding of the dependent variable, receiving a job offer. Only in 1996 does gender explain a significant amount of variance. In each year, the standardized logistic regression coefficient is positive.

Race/ethnicity, however, is a different matter. Being a member of a minority is negatively associated with receipt of a job offer in four of the eight years analysed, and in each of these four years the standardized regression coefficient is statistically significant.

What is striking is that these are the four most recent years. Minority status appears to be becoming increasingly important in understanding hiring and increasingly negative in its contribution to the hiring outcome.

Other variables that explain a significant amount of variance are grade point average, accreditation status, number of internships received and number of campus media in which the student participated. Having a newspaper major and having an advertising major are also significant predictors.

None of these are consistent across all years. What is consistent is that gender matters little. Selectivity of the university also matters little, controlling for other factors. In a separate analysis (not shown), race/ethnicity was scored as a dummy variable, with African-American, Hispanic and Asian-American status entered into the equation.

The analysis showed that being Black in every year was negatively associated with getting a job offer in the field of journalism and mass communication-among those who sought such a job. In recent years, being Hispanic also produced negative outcomes. Being an Asian American is not associated with receipt of a job offer.

The effects of race/ethnicity on hiring were further examined by using a more refined model in which, across each year from 1990 to 1997, the dependent variable was receipt of a job in a specific communication employment sector for those who sought work in that sector. The predictors, in addition to race/ethnicity and gender, were grade point average, accreditation status of the graduate's journalism programme, and the selectivity of the graduate's university.

In addition, the graduate was scored for having specialized in the area of the job sought, having completed an internship in that employment sector, and having worked for a campus medium linked to that employment sector. In the equation shown for each sector, year is entered as one of the predictor variables, although this final equation was computed only after the separate year-by-year analysis were examined.

Notable first are the increases in predictive power of the models. Only for weekly newspapers and cable television do the R square figures remain particularly small. Also notable is the strong and consistent predictive power of an internship. Clearly completing an internship in the employment sector of the job sought is a very important predictor of success in actually finding work in that sector.

For daily newspaper jobs, for television jobs, and for jobs in advertising, having specialized in college in those areas of study also is extremely important, controlling for other influences. In the cases of public relations and advertising, women are more likely to get a job offer than are men, other things being equal, but otherwise there is no effect of gender.

Only where weekly newspaper and advertising jobs are concerned is race/ethnicity a significant-and negative-predictor of job market success. Even here the effects are small. In general, there is considerable consistency for the equations across the 1990 to 1997 period. For race/ethnicity, for example, the standardized regression coefficient with receiving a job offer is.00 each year.

Neither table offers support for the hypothesis that gender remains a predictor of job market success after controlling for formal qualifications of the applicants. The analyses reported here were intended to serve two purposes. The first is an assessment of social policy-or of the effects of social policy. The second was the development of social and organizational theory.

This chapter's origins lie in the recent debate about the need for the continuation of affirmative-action policy in the United States as a means of addressing social inequalities in the labour market. It has attempted to inform that debate through an understanding of the labour market and of how organizations actually make decisions that have impact on that labour market.

A case might be made for discontinuing affirmative-action policies in hiring in the field of journalism and mass communication if there were no evidence of continued inequalities in the labour market attributable to the social classifications of gender and race/ethnicity. The data presented here suggest the situation is complex, and such action might be premature. While women have fared well in recent years, allowing them to make at least slight gains that will help offset-but clearly not overcome-biases from the past, minorities have not done well.

Being a minority is associated with lower levels of

employment, and the situation became worse in the most recent years studied. This evidence argues that policies that are designed to offset biases in the labour market have not yet been completely effective.

Yet a closer examination of the situation shows that-at least in the specific market sectors analysed-race is not a predictor of job searching success if the applicants have prepared themselves with employer specific internship training, campus media experience, and curricular specialization.

The conclusion is limited to the specific labour market segments for which adequate data for analysis exist. And it does not negate the general findings that summing across labour market segments and using nonmarket specific measures of internships and campus media experience, race/ ethnicity is a slight, negative predictor of job market success.

We speculate that these remaining biases in the labour market are attributable to what we have termed informal hiring methods, that is, methods not based on strict rules but rather stemming from social contacts and interaction.

The contrasting predictive power of the equations where general measures of formal characteristics were used and where specific measures of formal characteristics were employed argue that formal characteristics are important. To the extent informal methods remain in play, affirmative action seems to be called for.

Employers in media organizations should be aware that, if informal hiring procedures lead to a less diverse staff, this may in turn lead to less diversity in the content generated and processed by this staff. While news content may be constrained by organizational routines, the organization's culture and the individuals in the organizations play a role as well.

The policy implications of the paper seem clear enough. Increased attention to the development of hiring procedures that are designed to provide fair access to the labour market is needed. In addition, minorities need to be adequately advised of the importance of specializing in their education so that they posses the formal qualifications that are so essential for success in the job market.

The theoretical implications also seem clear. This study suggests that informal hiring procedures may play an important role in the journalism and mass communication labour market. A more formal test of this relationship in which direct measures of informal hiring procedures are employed is now needed.

Chapter 9

The Main Elements of Management in the Communication

Research into practitioner role enactment is recognized as one of the main areas of theory development within public relations. Traditionally, roles research has focused around one of two dominant investigative frameworks or role typologies: (1) Broom's four role typology, and (2) the manager-technician role dichotomy advanced by Dozier and Broom and Dozier.

Public relations roles' scholars such as Dozier, Broom, Lauzen, and L. Grunig and J. Grunig have based their research around these typologies, investigating role enactment in a variety of contexts, as well as the relationship between roles and variables such as gender and salary, involvement in strategic decision making and issues management, and the status and power of public relations departments.

Despite their widespread use within roles research, these traditional typologies and the associated role inventories used to measure and classify practitioner role behaviour have come under criticism on ideological and methodological grounds.

In the former case, a broad critique of roles research has been advanced by feminist scholars, including Choi and Hon, Creedon, and Toth and Grunig, as well as Toth, Serini, Wright, and Emig, and have highlighted the failure of roles research to recognize how the gender of researchers and practitioners being studied may influence the type of research questions posed and the assumptions made.

The feminist critique also maintains that the manager-technician typology tends to trivialize the technical dimension of the practitioner's role that is performed more frequently by female practitioners.

While acknowledging these feminist arguments, it is the methodological criticisms of roles research that are of interest in the present research, which focuses on examining the managerial dimension of practitioner role enactment. Previous research by this study's authors in the United Kingdom highlighted the limitations of the traditional manager role inventory scale.

Similar criticisms have been advanced by scholars such as Leichty and Springston who noted the manager role scale "lacks a coherent theoretical justification." In reviewing the body of roles research for the first volume of what is generally known as the Excellence Study, Dozier acknowledged that because roles are abstractions of the activities that practitioners perform, conceptualizing and measuring roles is inherently problematic.

Reflecting on the body of roles research and the criticism of the traditional approach to role measurement, Grunig, Grunig, and Dozier recognized the need for revision and updating of the role inventory measures used in roles research to reflect the evolution of the profession. This updating, they suggested, might be best achieved through "intensive observation of what communicators do."

This critique might seem to mark a turning point in thinking about roles research because it acknowledges the need for a fundamental reexamination of the basis on which the role inventory measures are formulated, suggesting that such measures should be derived from empirical observation of practitioner behaviour, rather than from synthesis of various literatures.

To date, there is little evidence of any intensive observation study of practitioner behaviour undertaken by roles researchers, nor of any attempt to undertake a fundamental revision of the role inventory measures used by roles researchers. Turning to the criticisms of the manager role inventory, we have highlighted the absence within the roles literature of any reference to the extensive body of management research conducted into managerial work and behaviour.

Reference to this body of research might help inform understanding of how managerial work and behaviour may be best conceptualized in the public relations context, while offering insights into effective methods of measuring managerial work and behaviour that might be applied in the communications context.

The body of general management literature also contains concepts and models useful to public relations managers. Building from Fayol's classical view of management as a rational profession where managers plan, organize, command, and control, Mintzberg created ten categories of managerial roles, and created a managerial model highlighting the job frame, the manager, and the organizational agenda as key elements of what a manager does and is.

Hales identified the common characteristics of managerial work, and Stewart concentrated on observing managerial behaviour. These management scholars have acknowledged that managerial work can and does vary by function, level, and organizational context, yet the possibility and indeed likelihood of such variability in managerial responsibilities and work activities in the public relations roles context has been largely ignored by roles researchers, who treated the manager's role as a sort of "generic" conceptual typology.

Wright's study is one of the few attempts to distinguish between different levels of practitioner responsibility, using survey, interview, and focus group research to identify a "communication executive" role comprising corporate senior vice presidents who appeared to report directly to CEOs. Further insight into the potential complexity and variation in manager role enactment has been offered by Grunig, Grunig, and Dozier, who distinguished between the knowledge and expertise possessed by the top communicator as an individual, and that residing within the organization's communication/public relations department as a whole.

Second, the authors identified two distinct aspects of managerial expertise they termed administrative manager expertise and strategic manager expertise. The former, they argued, is concerned with the knowledge and expertise needed to deal with the day-to-day operational management of a communications department, while the latter is associated with the expertise required to contribute to the organization's strategic planning process.

While offering a potentially useful insight into managerial role enactment in public relations, questions surround the particular components of expertise labeled as "administrative" rather than "strategic." From a traditional management theory perspective, many of the components of managerial expertise Grunig, Grunig, and Dozier identify as "administrative" (i.e., developing goals and objectives, developing strategies to solve public relations problems) appear to be more appropriately recognized as characteristics of strategic management expertise.

It is not the purpose here to pursue this argument further save to note that such ambiguity continues to characterize the way public relations and management scholars have treated the concepts of management and strategy making. The issue of how managerial roles may vary at different "levels" within functional departments/hierarchies is the basis of the Public Relations Society of America (PRSA) Foundation's Professional Career Guide.

It suggests a hierarchy of skills and responsibilities associated with five levels of job progression embracing the roles of technician, supervisor, manager, director, and executive. It is notable that the differing pattern of responsibilities associated with each of these job descriptors, particularly at the manager, director, and executive levels, is not reflected in the traditional manager role index widely used by roles researchers, nor has there been any explicit attempt to re-examine or reconfigure the way a manager's role in the public relations context is understood and measured to reflect the different responsibilities at these different hierarchical levels.

These limitations in the way the manager's role has traditionally been conceptualized in the public relations context, and the absence of any significant, extensive reference to the body of management literature, are issues we specifically began to address in previous research, first through an intensive qualitative investigation of managerial practitioner work patterns in the United Kingdom and the United States, followed by a nationwide survey of U.K. practitioners that revealed a new five-dimensional model of the work elements performed by public relations managers.

The research reported here is intended to examine whether this five-dimensional model might be applied more widely to describe the core dimensions of managerial-level practitioners' work in other regions and countries, in this case, the United States. These five core areas of practitioner work comprise four areas of what is identified as being essentially managerial responsibility: monitor and evaluator, key policy and strategy advisor, trouble shooter/problem solver, and issue management expert; as well as a further technical dimension labeled communication technician.

This research also used the U.K.-developed survey instrument describing the type of work activities performed by practitioners operating at a managerial level. Specifically, the items were derived from a synthesis of general management studies including Fayol's classical view of management, Mintzberg's managerial categorical roles, Hales' common characteristics of managerial work, Stewart's managerial behaviors observations, and Watson's study of managerial environments.

The work of Broom, Dozier, Grunig and Grunig, and feminist scholars noted earlier also contributed to the eight operational dimensions. Theoretically, the aim was to further test the validity and utility of the five-dimensional model of practitioner role enactment emerging from the U.K. study, thereby extending knowledge of the measurement of role enactment beyond the traditional 24-item role inventory.

As with the U.K. survey, the survey instrument comprised 57 items set in 7-point semantic differential scales, designed to be self-administered, and used to rate a specific variable depending on the relative importance it possesses. Slight alterations were made to reflect U.S. cultural and business terminology, and two separate versions of the survey were created to enable both mailed- or Web-based distribution.

The survey items covered eight operational dimensions of managerial responsibility/work, including (1) counseling and advisory responsibilities; (2) issues management; (3) policy and strategy making; (4) trouble shooting and problem solving; (5) administration; (6) monitoring and evaluation; (7) negotiation; and (8) technical responsibilities. A final segment of the instrument contained the classification and demographic sections. The statements used at the item level were derived from earlier qualitative and survey work, and drew substantially on the analysis of the previous research subjects' accounts of their daily tasks and work activities across the eight dimensions.

Pilot testing of the survey instrument in the U.K. stage significantly improved reliability and eliminated reverse coded items. Closely replicating the U.K. sampling characteristics, the U.S. frame consisted of 1,000 names drawn in a randomized fashion from the Public Relations Society of America (PRSA) directory of eligible practitioners.

Those selected for sampling embodied two important criteria: they held PRSA status, and their job titles suggested practitioner positions at managerial levels. To ensure external consistency, the authors followed the comprehensive sector typology developed during the U.K. work.

The survey of 1,000 mailed questionnaires was dispatched in February 2005 to practitioners in all 50 U.S. states. A return of 248 usable questionnaires achieved a 25.3% return rate, relatively standard for surveys of this type; the U.K. survey achieved a 25% response rate. The sample characteristics helped ensure that the U.S. segment of this work captured a very similar cross-section of respondents to measure the public relations manager's role across a range of U.S. sectors (e.g., government, corporate, not-for-profit).

We replicated the exploratory factor method applied to the U.K. sample and exemplified in other work of this kind. Here the aim was to repeat the factor reduction process with the U.S. data set, and test the relevance and applicability of the five-dimensional model and loaded items. In a classic sense, we wished to uncover the dimensions or constructs and the variables that measure them.

The use of confirmatory factor analysis at this stage would have necessitated detailed knowledge of the variables that load highly on theoretical constructs, and a degree of confidence regarding these loadings. As in previous work, the ultimate objective was to determine the managerial dimension of practitioners' work, and the small number of latent factors that represent relationships among interrelated variables.

Principal Components Factor Analysis on the 40 work activity scales within the survey instrument revealed the presence of ten components, all of which achieved eigenvalues greater than 1.0, and explained 64% of the variance. PCA can overestimate the number of factors and the amount of variance accounted for is also a function of the instrument's scale items/wording.

The analysis was therefore advanced with two further methods and rotation: the computation of total variance explained and a Scree test as verification of this cut-off point. A five-factor model was identified, and the remaining variables were retained for later analysis.

As with the U.K. study, the initial use of orthogonal Varimax rotation identified the factor structure. The five theoretical dimensions emerged, depicting the roles performed by U.S. communication/public relations practitioners operating at the managerial level: monitor and evaluator, key policy and strategy advisor, trouble shooter/ problem solver, issues management expert, and communication technician.

The second stage of the analysis, an Oblimin or oblique rotation procedure, provided the theoretically important underlying dimensions and, because factors were correlated, represented the relatively large number of variables more accurately Basing the judgments on Hair et al. and the U.K. decision criteria, and given the sample size (n=248), a factor loading of.32 and below was considered poor,.40 significant, and loadings of.60 or greater as very significant.

Items with secondary loading lower than.40 were therefore disregarded. Factor loadings on the monitor and evaluator, key policy strategy advisor, trouble shooter/ problem solver, issues management expert, and communication technician dimensions ranged from.40 to.81. Cronbach alpha scores were computed on the items indicating internal consistency and reliability. The first dimension, labeled Key Policy and Strategy Advisor, consisted of ten items, resulting in nine primary loadings (alpha =.87) with two secondary loadings on the Issues Management Expert dimension.

Loadings on the Key Policy and Strategy Advisor dimension can be seen as indicative of the strong relationship public relations practitioners reported that they have with senior management within their organizations, and the active part they seemed to play in the policy-making process.

This latter finding provided an interesting contrast with the previous qualitative investigations, which found that in a significant number of cases U.S. practitioners did not always report playing an active part at the most senior management levels within their organizations, particularly in terms of participation in strategic decision making. Furthermore, the survey of U.K. practitioners also suggested that practitioner involvement in the work of top management teams [dominant coalitions] remains more the exception rather than the rule.

The secondary loadings on the Issues Management Expert and Trouble-Shooting/Problem-Solver dimensions suggested the interrelationship between the Key Policy and Strategy Advisor role and the status of issue expert and trouble-shooter. Items here were perhaps indicative of the type and level of policy advice and contribution that public relations practitioners operating at a managerial level should offer senior management.

The second dimension, labeled the Monitor and Evaluator dimension, consisted of seven items, seven (primary) and one (secondary) loading (alpha =.81). The loading on these items characterizes the task of target and goal setting along with reporting results as elements of working closely with senior management in planning communication strategies.

Analysis also revealed a primary and secondary loading on the Communication Technician dimension, which may be indicative of the continued importance attached to media relations work by U.S. practitioners. Moreover, as both the U.K. qualitative and quantitative stage of the research indicated, differences in department size and resources available may also account for some practitioners retaining a degree of involvement (secondary loading) in media relations even though they may have moved up the organizational hierarchy (Factor 1).

Primary loadings on the second dimension appear to capture the important managerial responsibility for "organizing, controlling, and monitoring" the work of communication/public relations departments internally and externally. The work of setting targets with top management, operating within budget, monitoring performance against targets, and preparing departmental reports are major facets of this management role.

Additionally, the role requires some negotiating for organizational resources and commissioning of external agencies. The third factor, the Issues Management Expert dimension (alpha =.81), consisted of eight items (seven primary and two secondary loadings). These items relate to the public relations practitioner's role in diagnosing and responding to external threats from major or minor issues. In this capacity practitioners create meaning from the information they or others within their departments will have gathered; in this role, practitioners may be recognized as the organization's external "eyes and ears."

Secondary loadings on the items that measure external threats and negotiating with stakeholders may indicate something of the way in which elements of the issues management process may involve other organizational "actors," perhaps working alongside or taking the lead from communication/public relations practitioners.

Factor 4 {Trouble-Shooting/Problem-Solver) represents practitioners' responses to the way they treat internal or external challenges, threats, and/or crises confronting the organization. In this sense, public relations/communication practitioners are generally acknowledged to be the organization's designated "fire-fighters." In this study the dimension encompassed only four items (alpha = null) loading on the Monitor Evaluator, Issues Management Expert, and Communication Technician dimensions. The latter represented the primary loading of the three with the Monitor Evaluator and Issues Management Expert producing secondary loadings.

The very low alpha scores suggest that this factor lacks strength and therefore importance within the context of the public relations management function in this U.S. study. Alternatively, it might also suggest different alignment on the part of U.S. practitioners concerning their understanding of what constitutes "trouble-shooting/problem solving."

In the U.K. study, trouble shooting/problem solving potential threats to the organization was viewed as a separate, but related, dimension of activity. The inclusion and primary loading on one item of the Communication Technician dimension, namely the handling of e-mail, may suggest the increasing importance of e-mail as a source of news within organizations and therefore an early indicator of problem situations.

As in the U.K. study, this research revealed a fifth factor or dimension of the senior practitioner's role, the Communication Technician dimension. Unlike the preceding four dimensions that are defined as managerial elements of practitioner work, this represents the craft and technical side of practitioner activity.

Despite the strong loading on two of the items relating to the handling and/or overseeing of technical work, this dimension produced an unacceptably low alpha score (alpha

=.51) on these two primary items, and as such this dimension has been rejected from the model on the basis that alpha scores below.60 are unacceptable. However, it is worth commenting that the strong loadings on the two technical items represent a similar pattern (albeit to a lesser degree) to that found in the U.K. practitioner survey where practitioners were found to retain some responsibilities for at least overseeing elements of technical communication within organizations.

In this sense, despite what appears to be a strong emphasis on the more strategic managerial elements of their roles, U.S. practitioners still appear to engage in producing or overseeing aspects of technical work-an argument that all practitioners tend to enact elements of both the manager and technician roles.

Finally, the component correlation matrix revealed some interesting relationships that warrant further comment and explanation. In particular, a significant correlation (score 0.38) appeared to exist between component 1 (Key Policy and Strategy Advisor) and component 3 (Issues Management Expert) and also between components 1 (Key Policy and Strategy Advisor) and 2 (Monitor and Evaluator) (score 0.27), suggesting that these three components of the practitioner's role are related.

Lastly, there also appeared to be a correlation (score 0.25) between component 2 (Monitor and Evaluator) and component 5 (Communications Technician). The principal objective of this study was to identify the main dimensions of managerial-level practitioner role enactment in the U.S. context, examining the findings compared to those derived from our earlier analysis of U.K. practitioner behaviour.

Here we were particularly interested in examining whether the five-dimensional model of public relations practitioner role enactment that emerged from the authors' U.K. study would prove an equally valid and effective framework for explicating practitioner roles in U.S. organizations.

In the long term, this international research programme

aims to determine whether it is possible to identify any universal dimensions of practitioner role enactment that might transcend differences in cultural and organizational settings. Although the U.S. study resulted in a number of patterns similar to those found in the U.K. research, there were some significant differences between the two studies in terms of the emphasis and strength of the dimensions that emerged.

Of course, whether similar dimensions would have necessarily emerged had the research been conducted across a more diverse range of cultural settings has yet to be determined. Research by scholars who have focused on the question of cultural and national differences in public relations practice would seem to suggest a rather mixed picture emerges of the similarities and differences in communication/public relations practices across different cultures.

Nonetheless, we believe the model of practitioner role enactment identified through this programme of research represents a more effective positive and normative model of manager role enactment in communication/public relations departments than is offered by the traditional conceptualization of manager role in the public relations context (e.g. Broom, Broom and Smith, Dozier and Broom).

However, looking at more recent roles literature, we acknowledge that our managerial-level practitioner management model does, in fact, reflect a number of the elements of the top communicator/departmental "expertise" associated with the manager role enactment identified by Grunig, Gruning, and Dozier in the final volume of the Excellence Study.

In short, we believe that the multi-dimensional model of managerial practitioner role enactment emerging from this research offers a contemporarily relevant and robust basis for explicating the managerial dimension of practitioner work roles in organizations of various complexions.

While this chapter does not set out to conduct a detailed comparison of the findings from our research into practitioner role enactment in the United Kingdom and among U.S.

practitioners (the subject of a future analysis), some initial broad comparisons are nevertheless inevitable in interpreting the findings of this U.S. research.

Perhaps the most obvious and notable distinction observed between the U.K. and U.S. practitioner research findings lies in the different emphasis and profile of activities identified by respondents as constituting important elements of their job-roles. As outlined earlier, our 2005 U.K. study revealed a fivedimensional model of practitioner role enactment comprising a technical dimension and a four-dimensional managerial component, the latter consisting of activities concerned with monitoring and evaluation, key policy advice and strategic counsel, issues management, and trouble-shooting.

In contrast, the U.S. study revealed a very strong three-dimensional managerial model, emphasizing key policy advice and strategic counsel, monitoring and evaluation, and issue management, but with little explicit recognition of the trouble-shooter dimension. The U.S. study also revealed a technical dimension to practitioner roles, but with a far weaker dimension than the U.K. study.

Looking again at the loadings on items shown in the factor pattern matrix reveals a strong emphasis on carrying out activities concerned with what can be defined as determining the organization's strategic direction; setting out strategies and policies; determining benchmarks and targets and monitoring their achievement; and identifying, tracking, and determining responses to issues that might threaten the organization and the achievement of its goals.

In short, the picture that emerges is one of practitioners who appear to be operating very much as members of the management team in their organizations, contributing not only to the formation and implementation of communication strategies and the management of the communication/public relations function, but also playing an active role in contributing to broader corporate strategy-making and policy.

This argument about practitioners demonstrating a strong managerial orientation in their roles, emphasizing their involvement in areas such as policy advice and strategy, monitoring and evaluation, and issues management can be seen to echo themes found within previous roles research in terms of factors related to manager role enactment.

Thus, what we believe this strong three-dimensional loading found in the U.S. study may imply is that U.S. practitioners (or at least those who responded to the study) generally seem to be displaying a strong managerial orientation; they may, in this sense, be operating in a type of "public relations executive" role similar to what Wright identified.

The picture emerging from this U.S. study is one of a mature, relatively sophisticated profession in which managerial-level practitioners are encouraged to focus on what can be seen as more strategically oriented dimensions of their roles. This picture of a more strategically oriented practitioner role mirrors the findings from the 2005 U.K. study, where such a strategic orientation, particularly in terms of key policy advice and interaction with top management, was also found to figure strongly in the practitioner's role profile.

Notwithstanding this apparent strong managerial orientation found within the U.S. practitioner sample, further examination of the U.S. data revealed interesting correlation evidence relating to the relationship between the manager role dimensions and the relationship to the manager-technician debate.

As suggested earlier, the correlation matrix suggested significant relationships between the key policy and strategy advisor dimension and issues management expert dimension, as well as between the key policy and strategy advisor and the monitor and evaluator dimension. This suggests that, operationally, these three dimensions represent related elements of the practitioner's managerial role-a role that is conceptually and operationally distinct from the communication technician role.

In this sense, while this study suggests a distinctively different set of "managerial dimensions" for the communication/public relations manager's role compared to those originally identified by Broom, Dozier, and Broom and Dozier, as defining manager role enactment, it does broadly support the idea of a multi-dimensional structure to the public relations manager's role, distinct from the largely technical role performed by practitioners enacting or choosing to enact a largely technician role.

However, unlike the original roles studies where there was no correlation between the dimensions of the manager and technician roles, our study did uncover some correlation between one of the manager dimensions, the monitor evaluator role and the communication technician role.

We believe that one possible explanation for this relationship lies in the increasing emphasis and importance attached to measurement and evaluation of all aspects of public relations work, particularly the measurement of all public relations outputs.

Further, this apparently technical element of work performed by at least some senior practitioners may perhaps reflect the specialist nature of communication/public relations function as was suggested in the authors' 2005 U.K. study.

This U.S. study suggests that the retention of some technical work responsibilities by U.S. practitioners might reflect that some sensitive, higher-level communication, such as news releases about corporate earnings or mergers, is too important to be left to inexperienced communicators; and/or that as a result of significant corporate downsizing during the 1990s, some U.S. communication/public relations departments may be still operating with a skeleton staff, where one or two practitioners are responsible for, as well as actually doing, all the work.

Of course, given the relatively small scale of the current survey some caution is needed in suggesting any general principles that might characterize the work of U.S. communication/public relations practitioners, even those operating at more senior levels.

Clearly, in such a large and diverse country and across the relatively vast U.S. corporate and public sectors, it is perhaps inevitable that there is likely to be considerable scope for quite wide-ranging differences in the status and working practices of communication/public relations professionals. Nevertheless, we believe that the findings from this study provide a sound basis for moving forward toward a reconfiguring of the understanding of the managerial role in a communication/public relations context.

We are in the process of gathering survey data from practitioners from other countries, including South Africa, Ireland, Sweden, Singapore, India, and Australia. Drawing on those data, we hope to further refine our understanding of the work of communication/public relations practitioners, particularly in terms of their managerial roles.

Chapter 10

Feminist Reflections on Gender

This is a cautionary tale about a feminist who gendered her work collecting oral histories for a water district's public education project. First, after the district envisioned the project as a history of its "founding fathers." I uncritically adopted a definition of history that privileged "great men." making it difficult to identify the women narrators I was determined to include.

Then I established a less formal, more intimate rapport with women narrators, which produced transcript differences between the women and men. Finally, I unwittingly divided narratives into "private" and "public," which invoked a gendered division of labour.

In addition to demonstrating the value of reflexivity, this chapter explores some ways it is possible to gender interviews, an idea undeveloped in but relevant to communication studies, feminist theory, qualitative fieldwork, interviewing methods, and oval history.

By gendering the interview I mean reinforcing stereotypical expectations regarding women and men during interview research, instead of revealing the processes by which we coproduce gender. I begin with the premise that gender is performed hut argue that researchers by definition have greater power to enable and constrain such performances.

In the present case, I gendered the interviews by approaching and interpreting the project, the women and men who became my subjects, and their stories via gendered categories, which, in turn, informed my interaction with narrators and invited them to respond accordingly. Preferring to call the people with whom we conduct our research "reciprocators," Steier stresses research co-construction and self-reflexivity. It is not simply a matter of letting subjects, respondents, or narrators speak during interviews; nor, as they do so, is it possible for researchers simply to stand aside. Always together we co-produce the linguistic product called research. Nevertheless, because researchers not only act in their own research but also direct and produce it, they ultimately are responsible for the final production.

For researchers, reflexivity means taking on the final role of critic to scrutinize our own performances. Understanding our roles as researchers and their consequences requires both "reflection"-showing ourselves to ourselves-and "reflexivity"-being conscious of ourselves as we see ourselves.

Critical-interpretive qualitative methods and feminist methods converge in the premise that co-construction and reflexivity should be organic to conducting research, although some feminist thought suggests reflexivity might begin with accounting for one's standpoint. "A responsible, reflexive text announces its politics and ceaselessly interrogates the realities it invokes," Denzin writes.

"Such texts make readers work while resisting the temptation to think in terms of simplistic dichotomies". In this reflexive analysis, I examine my "blunders," the ways I deployed simplistic dichotomies that tended to invite particular gender performances that gendered an oral history project. Briggs described "blunders" as "interesting situations" in interviews when participants realise something is awry.

Taking liberty with Briggs' definition, Chase and Bell define interview "blunders" as "awkward moments" when women subjects may seem to contradict themselves to the confusion of the interviewer. In my case, "blunder" refers to my failure to notice how my approach was already awry. The word "blunder" here is a good fit not just because it implies a foolishly heavy-handed error.

"Blunder," as Chase and Bell use it, also addresses the

tensions of probing for gender issues in an interactive oral history interview, the pitfalls of having preconceptions about women's narratives, and the necessity of reflexivity to recognize both.

Below I mine the gender issues I encountered in my interview research. I first introduce the project under analysis. Then I outline gender as performative before examining the literature to theorize ways we may gender interviews. Next I return to the project to explicate my blunders. Last I consider the implications of my blunders before concluding with some comments about the promise of approaching gender as performance in studying the communication of gender.

PROJECT DESCRIPTION

In 1997, the Southwest Florida Water Management District initiated an oral history project in anticipation of its 40th anniversary. The SWFWMD, or "Swiftmud" as locals and news media call it has a complex and controversial history beginning with its creation in the wake of Hurricane Donna's devastating 1960 floods.

Today, the district covers 16 counties, and much of its mission is public education about Florida's fragile and dwindling hydrological systems. Swiftmud's public communication personnel initiated the oral history project hoping to give people a story about the district's charge.

The project's immediacy stemmed from the district's desire to locate its elderly "founding fathers." Intrigued by the environmental and public communication objectives, I conducted the first eight interviews involving nine narrators, which are the subject of this chapter.

I did have concerns, however. First, as a feminist, I had to reconcile myself to a client with an agenda I was obligated to support. Fortunately, while the district did wish to locate the elderly men who founded the district, I had carte blanche to organize the project, and my contacts were not against including women.

Second, choosing narrators was distressing. As the list of names snowballed and my time on the project dwindled, an obvious list of aging high-profile figures, some in declining health, superseded what I considered a more representative pool of voices.

I began chronologically with the district's known "founders." all white men. I also included women, again all white, whom informants identified as key in the district's early history but whose roles, not surprisingly, were organizationally more internat. I interviewed live men and four women, aged 48 to 92.

Third, I fretted over narrative issues. Much as I hoped to allow Swiftmud's history to emerge. I knew I would shape the story: by my personal perspective as a while, able-bodied, heterosexual, middle-class, middle-aged academic feminist trained as a journalist; by my particular knowledge of the district; and by the decisions I made throughout the project given the district's desire to give its mission a human face and to collect compelling water stories for the general public.

Last, I found myself dealing with a series of gender troubles, beginning with the fact that there were no women of comparable status to the "founding fathers." Other issues included the women's hesitation to participate in the project and differences between the women's and men's interviews and narratives. My unease has less to do with gender differences per se than with my realization that I may be responsible for them.

"Gender relations are an important dynamic shaping the interview process which can significantly influence the sorts of data obtained," argues Herod. He theorizes three kinds of gender "influences":

1. How the gender of the interviewer or interviewee may shape the interview process;
2. How gender relations are implicated in the structure of particular research methodologies; and
3. How gendered assumptions can affect how information generated in an interview is interpreted.

Instead of thinking about "gender relations" as independent "influences" impinging "data," I wish to explore how researchers may participate in defining and performing gender. I argue researchers' assumptions about and interpretations of the research, research participants, context, and subjects' narratives all may gender interviews.

Additionally, the symbolic order and language also may lead us to gender our work, and, finally, women's history, like women's research, is always already gendered simply by marking the feminine. Before addressing ways we may gender interviews, however, it will be necessary to clarify "gender" and the paradox of gender for women.

OPERATIONALIZING GENDER

Researchers tend to treat both sex and gender as unproblematic, and clear definitions of sex and/or gender in research are rare. Sometimes studies use sex and gender synonymously without operationalizing either. Historically, scientific studies rather unscientifically have presumed gender differences based in sex before proceeding to explain these differences in unsubstantiated causal links between sexed biology and gendered behaviour.

Because gendered behaviors are mostly performed, they also are historically and culturally contingent. Nationality, race, ethnicity, age, sexual orientation, dis/ability, religion, and economic and social status, among other factors, also confound attempts to make claims about sex- or gender-based differences.

Feminist theorists who adopt performativity as their foundation for gender observe that sex-the biological body-cannot precede gender because sex is already a gendered concept-in discourses, social practices, and historical formations. Gender is not reducible either to physical biology or to cultural text inscribed upon the body.

These theorists view gender as a performance-embodied and enacted. That is, the material body performs gender, usually languaged as "feminine" or "masculine." Furthermore, contemporary gender theory understands that the binary logic that limits, naturalizes, and enforces two genders (as either feminine or masculine) also consolidates the logic that limits, naturalizes, and enforces heteronormativity (as compulsory heterosexuality), and vice versa. Presuppositions about binary gender tend to be used to coerce heteronormativity, and presuppositions about heteronormativity tend to be used to coerce either feminine or masculine performances. Regarding gender as performative allows us to sidestep this closed circuit defining "natural" and to account for multiple forms of gender and sexuality, embodied and enacted by material bodies, without resorting to discourses of biological pathology or social/cultural deviance.

Performing gender is "a practice of improvisation within a scene of constraint. Moreover, one does not 'do' one's gender alone. One is always 'doing' with or for another, even if the other is only imaginary". The material effects of these performances, however-as scenes of constraint due to social conventions, sanctions, and taboos-are quite real. In sum, gender "is the mechanism by which notions of masculine and feminine are produced". The present analysis follows this critical work, even while using the word "gender."

THE PARADOX OF GENDER FOR WOMEN

How to denote women without signifying gender remains an antinomy for feminist thought. Without iterating women or the feminine, gender remains transparent, and women too often remain invisible or absent in a gender system where man/masculine remains the universal, normative, and transcendent category.

Specifying women, however, requires participation in the very symbolic order that constructs women as subordinate or the negative. While symbolic meanings of feminine and masculine are interdependent, the relationship between feminine and masculine is asymmetrical and hierarchical. Sarap summarizes the theoretical point: "The feminine always finds itself defined as deficiency, imitation, or lack".

In symbolic terms, the feminine is always once removed from the masculine in a gender hierarchy. In linguistic terms, all language applied to women and the feminine not only is always "marked" linguistically as "not male" bul also suffers from "semantic derogation," the process by which "any symbol which is associated with the female must assume negative connotations".

Marking the feminine, then, specifies gender, thus genders. If "founding fathers" privileges a masculine point of view, "founders" still fails to account for the specifics of women's experiences. "Founding women" or "founding mothers," while indicative of women's perspectives, necessarily genders by denoting the feminine and further connotes the feminine as a "special case" in ways that "founding fathers" does not.

"Research," "researcher," and "research subject" remain implicitly masculine unless otherwise noted. So "adding women" not only genders but also represents women as an afterthought This explains the paradox of adding the always marked and secondary feminine, whether as women's research, woman researcher, woman research subject, women's communication, or women's histories.

INTERVIEWING, GENDERED PARTICIPANTS, AND THE CO-CONSTRUCTION OF GENDER

Williams and Heikes note the scarcity of research on gender interacting with qualitative depth interviews. They argue that "even when gender is a 'constant,' it is still 'constantly there'". Common wisdom suggests same-gender interviewing is preferable based on the assumption of improved rapport by "natural" affinity, but supporting evidence is mixed or anecdotal.

Some wonder if women make better interviewers because feminine communication styles supposedly make women better listeners. Others argue that a woman's authority as the researcher affords her "honorary male status". Phoenix writes that race and gender certainly impact interviewing, but not in any predictable, generalizable way.

I suggest that when researchers have thought to examine the implications of gender, it mostly has meant "adding" some specific study of women or the feminine. Hence, much like the "addition" of women in the Swiftmud project, what we know about gender in interviewing mostly comes from specifying women researchers or research subjects, women's research topics, or gender transgression because otherwise gender remains transparent, thus moot.

For example, growing numbers of women researchers have produced more thought about situations women face in the field. Spitzack noted her interviews with men were longer and that these men did not hesitate to make "hold" assessments of her appearance, which she interprets as the men's sense of powerlessness in an interview with a woman interviewer.

Yet, in other ways, a woman interviewing a man sets up a stereotypically asymmetrical gender relationship in which the woman finds herself having to listen without being able to challenge. Yow advises oral historians that a "male narrator may tend to talk down to a female interviewer." something "we women may just have to tolerate".

Lee likens cross-gender interviewing to a blind date with its attendant emotional and, for women, physical dangers. Safety issues such as choice of interview sites remain a concern for women as subjects and researchers. Writing for a feminist audience and calling for reflexivity, Sparke admits he misread his women respondents' laughter during interviews as rapport when the laughter actually signaled nervousness toward Sparke as a man and a stranger.

Harding and DeVault point out that being a man does not preclude working with feminist or women's issues. But "doing so successfully requires learning enough to see and understand the consequences of varying social locations, including one's own".

In comparing their interviews with men nurses, a case of gender transgressiun. Williams and Heikes discovered their respondents formed their answers based on expectations that Heikes, a man, would empathize with "masculine" physicians and that Williams, a woman, would identify with "feminine" nurses.

Padfield and Proctor, woman and man respectively, also compared their interviews, this time with young women recounting abortion histories; Padfield and Proctor were surprised in find that their respondents' answers depended not only on respondents' definitions of gender but also on the interviewers' genders and the interviewers' definitions of gender.

Jorgenson calls this process of respondents "fashioning an identity for the interviewer" co-construction, where "the person to whom a research subject speaks is not the person an interviewer thinks herself to be". This, in turn, constrains the interviewer's definition of self, context, and relationship with subject.

Researchers need to be alert for and reflexive about their own and their subjects' definitions, as well as definitions that emerge as part of the co-communicative process. Nevertheless, despite the generation of inter-subjective understanding during interviews, I argue that researchers do have greater influence to define the research, and, because they generally initiate contact with interviewees, they also have greater responsibility for constructions of gender, which we can think of as co-performative.

Gendered Communication, Women as Research Subjects, and Male Register Communication styles performed during interview research will depend on participants' interpretations of one another, their relationship, and the communication context. But if the researcher has greater responsibility for co-constructed gender performances, then the researcher also has some influence on resulting gendered communication.

The literature on gendered communication suggests that while it is possible to identify typically feminine and masculine communication patterns, most individuals can call on a range of feminine and masculine-styles.

Others note a persistence in using gendered criteria to assess women's and men's communication differently, which results in evaluating women's communication as deviant, inferior, or incompetent relative in a transparently gendered masculine standard.

Furthermore, most claims about women's communication implicitly focus on white middle-class women without considering variation, for example, across race, ethnicity, class, or age or generation. Gendered communication performances also depend on participants' status and power, and U.S. women historically have had less status and power socially, institutionally, and in cross-gender relationships.

Moreover, feminist theory persuasively argues that women as research subjects do merit some consideration. Women have been described as a "mute group" because men have controlled the production of language, weighted it with their meanings, and used it for their purposes, including the control of women.

When women use language, they, in essence, are forced to translate or "tell it slant". Women's outsider relationship to language has implications for women us research subjects it they are attempting, to express subjectivities generated from living as women for which there may be no vocabulary or to translate their experiences into masculine codes and modes of expression.

Researchers also may emphasize events and actions without probing for emotions and human relationships, and they may overlook mela-communicalion about how women subjects want to be understood. Yet I suggest there is a difference between understanding the possibility of observing these phenomena among women as research subjects and ascribing or assigning them a priori to women as research subjects.

Also germane is the concept of "male register," referring to men privileging discourses of the public sphere while prohibiting women from participating in those discourses. In the West, the symbolic gendering of "public" as masculine and "private" or "domestic" as feminine is the result of what is often called the sexual division of labour into separate spheres of influence.

In discursive terms, male register "is both the meaning and the form in which that meaning is expressed (in public discourse) that has been encoded by men and is controlled by men". Historically, male register has enforced gendered communication practices that censure women's public speech. Wholly absent from conceptions of "public," women and the feminine mostly have been excluded from and silent in public discourses and contexts, and when women, however competent, have been present, they have been evaluated negatively as women.

Thus, Spender writes of a "hesitancy" that comes from "the contradiction of being muted and a speaker". Male register may explain, in part, the women's initial reluctance to participate in Swiftmud's "public" oral history project. As I will argue, however, whether or not a context is public or private is not always fixed or clear.

The same site may become public or private, masculine or feminine, depending on the participants' co-constructed interpretations, which, in turn, lead participants to perform what they perceive as appropriate communication. At the same time, women as speakers as well as feminized contexts will suffer from semantic derogation. I believe that I initiated gendered interpretations of interviews with men as public speech contexts and interviews wiih women as private speech contexts.

In terms of interview topics, I additionally unreflectively urged the men to speak as officials to official events-male register-while I probed the women for unofficial stories about the district as an internal organization. All of this led to differences between the women's and the men's narratives and transcripts.

Because of semantic derogation, the resulting women's history of the district may be interpreted as less important than the men's.

"Macho Methods," Gendered Histories, and Histories of Gender Feminist critiques of what Herod calls "macho" research methods, including interviewing, are well developed. Likewise, oral history has been the subject of feminist critique, although oral history is a valued feminist method because it privileges women's voices.

Nonetheless, feminist methods urge a cautious approach to oral history and interviewing women, given: the asymmetry of power between researcher and subject; the difficulties of mute groups telling it slant; the symbolic order's semantic derogation of women and the feminine; the slipperiness of language, interpretation, and meaning; and the high probability of neglecting, obscuring, misrepresenting, or appropriating alternate and subaltern realities. Not so well developed, however, is discussion about women's history or the paradox of "adding women" to history.

Unmarked (masculine) history is for everyone; women's history is only for women. In history, the absence of women in numbers proportionate to their population has been explained by the overall inferiority of women as a group compared to men, rather than historians' masculinist worldview and women's exclusion from "public" life. "Throughout historical time, women have been largely excluded from making war, wealth, laws, governments, art, and science." wrote Kelly-Gadol.

"Men. functioning in their capacity as historians, considered exactly those activities constitutive of civilization". Where we do find women's history, it generally follows two patterns: either exceptional women, judged to he as great as men in (the) history (of men), or histories of women, "another subgroup of historical thought to place alongside the list of diplomatic history, economic history, and so forth", Additionally, histories of women often are judged to he "of less political, economic or social consequence" because women's activities have been limited to domestic family life apart from public life controlled by men or within the invisible low-status strata of public society.

Reclaiming great women and women's histories does not change the fact that both versions arc gendered. "Great" women remain rare in an otherwise masculine definition of history that privileges male register. Celebrating otherwise lost women's histories marks the subject matter as feminine. In other words, rather than gendered histories, we need histories of gender that make the communication and institutionalization of gender-such as definitions of history that privilege men's experience-apparent instead of transparent.

This, by my reading of the late feminist historian Joan

Kelly-Gadol, requires the introduction of "sex as a social category" to reveal relations between the genders. Historical analysis focusing on gender is necessary because traditional social categories such as class, race, caste, minority, etc. fail to explain women's universal experiences of "Other" and inferior status within all such categories, even if the experiences of women as a group differ by degrees across such categories.

The disparate histories of women as women do not result from a fact of (heir biology, but rather from man-made rules governing (the performance of) gender. Revisiting history through a gender lens radically revises theories of human progress and social change, argued Kelly-Gadol: "there was no 'renaissance' for women-at least not during the Renaissance". If we account for man-made gender segregation and specialization as well as relations between women and men during historical "periods of so-called progressive change," we discover those very eras exhibit "a fairly regular pattern of relative loss of status for women".

Additionally. Kelly-Gadol observes, when social divisions between private/domestic and public have increased in Western history, from Athenian culture to the U.S. industrial revolution, women's status and relative prosperity have decreased. Thus, like race analysis, systematic gender analysis forces us to rethink what we have considered "great" periods for "mankind" by asking great for whom and at whose expense.

Gender analysis explains gender as the apparatus that produces the social, political, and economic status of women us women and men as men. This is an altogether different kind of history from "adding" a few "great women" defined by androcentric criteria or from appending segregated women's histories viewed as interesting historical footnotes but with little contribution to progress deli tied by men.

Gendered histories naturalize gender differences while obscuring the relational patterns that generate such differences. But histories of gender demystify gender differences by locating the relations that produce them, "Sex as a social category" would seem to reinforce the dualisms of binary gender, but this is not a "blundering" gendering resulting from unexamined foundational assumptions. This is a self-conscious enterprise alert for the stakes and strategies that tend to disadvantage women as a group, despite differences among women.

Regarding the Swiflmud project, while it was important to include women, the result was not a history of gender that unpacked definitions of history that presume "founding fathers," Instead it became a gendered history: marked women narrators who did not qualify as "great," who were added secondarily and encouraged to speak on topics outside the "public" sphere, all of which may seem trivial compared to unmarked (masculine) histories of great men.

GENDERING THE INTERVIEW

If gender is performed during interview research, then researchers should be reflexive about: assumptions about women and men as gendered participants; co-performed definitions of gender and gendered communication styles that emerge during interviewing; and gendered interpretations of material, social, and symbolic contexts such as private or public.

Researchers also should he cognizant that the symbolic order and language-including concepts, metaphors, themes, motifs, frames, and narrative formulae-may lead researchers to deploy gender, such as women as a marked category, the semantic derogation of the feminine, and myths that naturalize gendered spheres of influence. Additionally, research models and methods may gender, such as definitions of history that privilege men. Studying these processes shifts the focus of our analysis from gendered communication to the communication of gender

In the following analysis, I did begin with a definition of history that privileged great men operating in the public sphere, which left me to search for great women. Because no great women appeared in the historical record. I specifically "added" women narrators by different criteria, which marked, thus gendered, the women and their roles as different from the men's.

Then, because the men were "great" and me women were not, I directed gendered communication performances from the women and men respectively; I interpreted the men's interview contexts as public, directed public speaking performances from the men, and urged them to speak to topics featuring official public events that occurred externally to the district as an organization.

Conversely, I interpreted the women's interview contexts as private, directed private conversational speaking performances from the women, and urged them to speak to unofficial topics about the internal "domestic" culture of the district as an organization. Once I invoked gendered spheres of influence, I consigned the women and their narratives to an interesting historical addendum to the great men's public oral history of the district's public mission.

Analysis: Historic, Additional, Classic, and Divisive Blunders To illustrate the ways I gendered my interviews, the following analysis organizes my blunders into four areas: (1) "A historic blunder" refers to the masculine definition of history that shaped the project. (2) "An additional blunder" covers "adding women" to a history of founding fathers. (3) "Classic" blunders reinterpret textbook examples of gendered communication patterns in terms of the researcher's responsibility for co-performativity. (4) "Divisive" blunders expose the artifice of gendered dichotomies such as "private" and "public."

A HISTORIC BLUNDER

When the district expressed interest in locating its "founding fathers," I assumed that meant high-status figures vested wilh official power At the same lime, in an effort to get a handle on lour decades of nearly unintelligible political and scientific gobbledygook, I began my background research looking for a timeline of significant "public" moments.

So my first blunder was to frame the project with a masculine definition of history: "great men" influencing larger-than-life events affecting the general "public." My background research included "public" records promoting the district's people and work, including external news accounts and internal documents in the district's extensive library.

The resulting chronology highlighted natural disasters, such as Hurricane Donna; "public" controversies, such as a proposal to turn Tampa Bay into a freshwater lake; engineered "public" works, such as dam and canal construction; and water policies affecting business and industry. Those same records also presented the "great men" who became my priority narrators.

Four of the five men narrators I interviewed were august "public" figures with reputations preceding them. Through newspaper articles, their own writing, and district publications, I learned a great deal about these men before I met them. For example, the politically connected 89-year-old who literally founded the district also traced his family's political influence continuously from Florida's homesteading days.

The 92-year-old, known as Florida's "dean of hydrology," had discovered and named Florida's major aquifers during World War II. Two of the three younger men had equally impressive vitae. Three were still active in politics. Indeed, these men were "legendary." As I collected their biographies in preparation for interviewing, I intimidated myself, even though once we met they turned out to be rather ordinary, even frail, individuals.

Defining traditional history turns out to he rather tautological: History means historical significance. The criteria for historical significance, however, become more recognizable in a related area, one of my "public" sources: news media. In terms of narrative news values, a good story requires drama: conflict and heroes.

In terms of news measurements, a big story requires some combination of "prominence" of actors' status, "magnitude" of event, and "consequence" to numbers of people. Hence, history and news share similar approaches to recording the historic; a good story on a grand scale increases the likelihood of significance. Women's media historian Elizabeth Burt writes that "we typically view the world through a set of male-defined values that give preference to male characteristics such as competition, novelty, and physical ability," as well as to the public activities of "politics, war, crime, and natural disasters."

Such a worldview precludes: women; feminized values "such as community, cooperation, and support"; women's work in the "private" sphere; the feminized "private" sphere itself, including "social issues and the life of the family"; and women's labour and careers in the "public" sphere-all considered "inconsequential".

In sum, I gendered the interviews from the outset by adopting a detinition of history that privileged men visible in the "public" sphere. This would complicate the inclusion of women's oral histories in the project because, as Burt observes, "if we measure women against male-defined values, they often fail."

AN ADDITIONAL BLUNDER

Unlike the men, who were eager to become narrators, the women initially were skeptical that they could add anything of value. Burt explains. "Women have often internalized this institutionalized lack of acknowledgement, which has led to their own failure to recognize the importance of their efforts". Because there were no "great" district women by the project's definition of history, I had to expand the criteria for choosing narrators if I were in include women.

My next blunder was to make those "additional" criteria women-specific and to limit "additional" narrators to women. Thus I unwittingly constructed a second-tier of marked women-only narrators. By definition, symbolic order, and ordinal rank, the women's interviews were feminine and subordinate to the men's.

Although I was determined to include women in the project from the beginning, identifying which women to include posed a problem. The "public" record did not present any high-profile women comparable to the men. So I resorted to the district's internal records, such as newsletters. I queried informants for the names of women who had been with the district early enough and long enough to offer interesting stories about the district's formation. Once I idenlified a list of potential women narrators, it was difficult to learn much about them prior to interviewing since they did not have "public" reputations or biographies.

Looking back, me criteria for choosing women narrators were feminine "firsts" and longevity with the district. One narrator was the first woman hired. Another spent 30 years at the district to become the highest-ranking district woman. The third woman narrator, with 25 years of district service, had been the first "public" communication employee. I chose the fourth woman because of her longevity-the first employee to retire with 30 years of service. It turns out that feminized "firsts," as a substitution for "prominence," sometimes meant "oddity," one of the least prestigious news values. Furthermore, "oddity" tended to mean gender transgression, such as the communication specialist who leaned out of Cessna planes to take aerial photography. In fact, she described herself as "eccentric."

Interestingly, the women offered me stories of other women hascd on their oddity, such as the story about the district's first woman engineer, described as "gutsy" and "a real characler." Other women were feminine exemplars. For example, informants described the human resources director as "everyone's grandmother" and the "mother you don't want to cross." So the men, notable for their professional accomplishments, became leading actors, while the women, notable for their personal idiosyncrasies, became supporting or character actors.

In order to avoid gendering the women and their interviews, I would have had to make the criteria for including second-tier narrators applicable to both women and men and to enlist men as well as women as second-tier narrators. That might have avoided marking the women and their interviews as feminine.

But since the project's definition of history remained

transparently masculine, it would not have produced a history of gender that makes the institutionalization of gender opaque. Instead of marking the women as "additional" narrators who deviated from the "original" men narrators, using "gender-neutral" criteria would have been a clear case of "add women and stir" to a masculine enterprise that has always excluded women and de-valued the feminine.

Finally, although I had little information about ihe women prior to interviewing. I apparently did have preconceptions about them, which guided our interactions.

CLASSIC BLUNDERS

Minister describes her women narrators' hesitance to participate in oral history because they understand it as a masculine "public performance" in which "they are expected to 'take the floor.'" Beyond oral history's staging with recording equipment standing in as an imagined "ghostly" audience. Minister acknowledges that interviewer and narrator together co-construct the oral history production.

When the participants are women. Minister (1991) observes, the talk is likely to be driven by women's communication conventions, such as turn-taking, cooperative overlapping, joking, and inclusive pronouns, among others. Mostly barred from "public" speaking, women developed these conventions for "private" conversations with women. Minister urges oral historians to try to "feel the dilemma posed by oral history method for women who do not use male communication strategies."

Again, however, I suggest that naming the phenomena of women's communication after the fact, or even anticipating them, is not the same as stage-directing them. Furthermore, because the interview's performance is largely co-constructed, whether or not the interview plays out as a public or private performance also is largely co-constructed-and the researcher, as producer and director, has greater responsibility for the performance, regardless of whether or not narrators are asked to improvise.

After conceiving of the Swiftmud project as a traditional

masculine history and casting women narrators in supporting roles, my next blunder was to direct different kinds of performances from the women nnd men.

So I further gendered the Swiftmud interviews because I, as a woman, deferred to the men's status, and, by my manner, invited them to make speeches for it "ghostly" "public" audience.

Perhaps because the woman did not intimidate me, I initiated a more intimate, informal, "private" kind of conversation with them, something Oakley (1981) finds particularly onerous when interviewing women since the charade of rapport is likely to be abandoned once the research is complete.

Hence, the Swiftmud transcripts exhibit classic patterns of gendered communication, not as "natural" phenomena, but as performances I directed.

Shortly after I began transcribing the interviews, I recognized Tannen's "rapport-talk" and "report-talk," Tannen characterizes rapport-talk, associated with "private" speaking situations, as a communication style adopted for establishing egalitarian relationships through turn-taking, supportive interruptions, and matching stories.

Tannen's work indicates white women often feel more comfortable in this mode. In contrast, Tannen's "report talk," associated with "public" speech contexts, is a typically masculine communication style adopted for establishing independence and status. Tannen describes report-talk as "I'll explain it to you," an interaction where one lectures as another listens.

Closer examination validates my suspicion that my performance invited the men to do report-talk, while I tried to establish cooperative rapport with the women. Transcripts show the men tended to speak in long blocks of text, often going on for more than a single-spaced page. I rarely interrupted except to clarify or urge them to continue; "So you talk about anything you want to talk about.

I'm just taking it in," "What a great story. Keep going." and "Can you give me an example?" These excerpts from the men's transcripts illustrate how I communicated my role as audience ("I'm just taking it in"), encouraged the men to hold forth ("Keep going"), and probed without editorializing ("give me an example").

The women as narrators, on the other hand, tended to speak in much shorter blocks of talk, measured in lines rather than pages, which frequently were "matched" by my own lines of talk.

The conversation about aerial photography provides an example:

Narrator: It never occurred to me that I could be hurt, and we had a great time.

Interviewer: It sounds like fun, but I'm just thinking, now, I lake pictures, but that's a lot different.

Narrator: You don't lean out of the door of a doorless airplane to do it?

Interviewer: (laughs)

Narrator: It's a lot more fun (laughs)

The women and I also did more joking and laughing, another characteristic of women's conversational patterns. Unlike the men's transcripts, the women's transcripts also show patterns of feminine cooperative overlapping, as in me following example:

Narrator: But the conservation issues are coming into their own

Interviewer: I know But in a real sense there is sort of that idea that the '60s were for flood control

Narrator: because we had Hurricane Donna that started the whole movement

Interviewer: which formed the district

However, there is evidence that I was offering the matching stories ("I take pictures") and often initiating the interruptions and overlaps ("I know"), something I rarely attempted with the men. and never successfully because we had established a relationship in which I was an audience, not a conversational partner.

Also, by using "we" and "us" in conversation with the women, I communicated that I framed the interviews as conversational partnerships, as in the following transcript excerpt in which I say, "The story goes that before we bought the property (district headquarters), we were leasing it for $1 a year."

Additionally, when it came to probing the women, I did not retrain from gelling personal or editorializing. For example, I asked one woman, "Was that a tough transition tor you?

This is off subject, hut I'm just curious." Indeed, with the women, I did not hesitate to go off topic into areas that interested me, even if it meant asking personal questions. Two of the narrators talked about sitting through long-winded "public" meetings from which they had to transcribe minutes for the "public" record.

In both cases. I probed for their experiences of typing these long documents without the benelit of computers: "And that's when you'd do a draft on typewriters?" "This was before word processors?" and "Highly undervalued job, I would say."

While I did not construct the women as "great," I did value them and their siories as important contributions to an otherwise invisible wonu'n's history. I now recognize my stage direction toward rapport talk as conspiratorial, an attempt to subvert the project a little hit with alternative narratives.

The blunder was to make only the women responsible for those alternative points of view. Had I directed all the narrators toward the same kind of communication performances, I may have avoided the problem. Nevertheless, the question of choosing which kind of communication performance to direct would remain.

Indeed, only the "addition" of women as narrators raises the dilemma. Minister's description of oral history as a "public" speaking platform and Tannen's distinctions between "private" rapport talk and "public" report talk beg a question: Is an interactive oral history interview a public or private speaking context? The answer, of course, is a matter of interpretation.

DIVISIVE BLUNDERS

If an oral history interview is a performance, then Goffman provides dramaturgical insight on scenes, scripts, and roles. First, regarding scenes, Goffman notes that a setting may function as either formal front stage or informal backstage: "By invoking a backstage style, individuals can transform any region into a backstage" second, regarding scripts, Goffman describes a friendly, familiar honesty present in backstage social interaction where participants may share gossip and secrets.

Third, while the ceremonial roles of "visible leadership" are front stage performances, there are less visible "discrepant" roles, such as the "servant" who roves between front stage and backstage regions. Ignored as "someone who isn't there", the servant is still essential for pulling off front stage performances. A history of gender would explore the ways discrepant roles enable the ceremonial ones.

To answer my own question, interviews with men became formal front stage contexts, and interviews with women became informal backstage contexts, regardless of whether the interview took place in a home or office. Even more illuminating, I generally aligned the men with visible front stage ceremonial scripts and roles, directing their narratives toward topics in which they and the district interacted with the "public."

I aligned the women with backstage scripts and roles, directing their narratives mostly toward "privjie" topics internal to the district. Put simply, I blundered by directing scene, script, and role on the basis of" gender. I gendered the interviews by dividing the women and men into separate spheres of influence, which produced gendered narratives and contributed to gendered histories.

The men's oral histories are full of "external" front stage events, such as making "public" presentations to teach citrus growers about the dangers of well draw-down; "public" policy, such as regulating local water utilities; and "public" works, such as designating "public" wetlands. Compared to stories of the men taking leading roles as officiates in "public" performances, the women's stories focused on organizational culture. The women's oral histories are full of "internal" behind-the-scenes events, such as burying time capsules to celebrate district anniversaries; embarrassing secrets, such as a Hood in the district headquarters building; unofficial district culture, such as maintaining a voluntary employee fund to aid coworkers in need; and interpersonal relationships, such as who mentored whom.

Even when the women described front stage events external to the district headquarters building, they did so from the backstage perspective of an invisible servant, such as detailing catering menus and guest lists for dam dedications.

In truth, I relished the women's backstage perspectives, which I now understand were offered mostly as a result of my interests. I was asking the women for those kinds of stories.

In hindsight the men's "public" and "professional" narratives are both typical of masculine history as well as the result of our report talk style and my stage direction toward official ceremonial narratives.

The women's "private" and "relational" narratives are atypical of masculine history as well as the result of our rapport talk and my stage direction toward unofficial backstage narratives.

Granted, the men undeniably were "public" figures, and the women were not. But those facts did not preclude the women from speaking to "public" policy issues; nor were the men precluded from sharing backstage organizational stories.

Furthermore, while the women may not have heen media figures, a consistent number of informants did name them as "historically signiticant," which meant they had heen both visible and respected enough to have garnered strong reputations.

But. as I unwillingly relied on gendered categories such as public and private to label external and internal respectively.

I never reflected on the ways those divisions guided me toward gendered spheres of influence. In this instance, in order to produce a history of gender, I should have avoided assigning gendered topics to women and men respectively and, instead, probed for the ways the district assigned gendered scenes, scripts, and roles, as well as how that particular dramaturgy wrote a reciprocal relationship between the district's external mission and its internal culture.

Feminist oral history seeks overlooked, unsaid, and invisible women's voices and perspectives. But it is important to retlecl upon what we classify as women's and men's, feminine and masculine, and then to be reflexive about the ways we assign gender to backstage and front stage, unofficial and official, private and public-as well as what we feature or sidebar in the collective memory.

Clearly, an androcentric definition of history privileges public communication, public history, general public, public record, public events, public figures, public works, public land, and public policy.

However, as Ribbens and Edwards argue, divisions between private and public are not stable. During the "niity-gritty" of fieldwork, theories of fixed boundaries shift to a series of conscious and unconscious, arbitrary and negotiated labeling decisions, such as treating some interviews as public and others as private contexts, or aligning the district's "external" affairs with "public" and men, and its "internal" affairs with "privaite" and women.

Caring relational work such as employee assistance funds and mentoring, for example, is inherently neither private nor public.

Still, caring work usually is delegated to women and mostly remains as undervalued as the women who do it. Just as "private" homemaking enables "public" institutions, "internal" organizational relationships, labour, and technologies-be it word processor. Cessna, or backhoe-are integral to any organization's "external" business.

I did not err in collecting internal backstage narratives. My blunders were to gender them feminine, assign them to women, and then to foreground masculine external and front stage narratives. Instead of imposing a template of gender relations onto the Swiftmud project, a history of gender would have explored ways the district's organization and culture evolved to communicate gendered roles and relations.

Understanding gender as performed and co-constructed-co-performative-affords us the opportunity to witness-and witness to-gender as a communicative process with material consequences.

Bell and Blaeuer write: gender is a complex matrix of normative boundaries-constituted in discourse, materially embodied and performed, and mobilized through culture to secure political and social ends.

Nor is gender a singular constitution, but gender is always articulated in, on, and through sexuality, race, ethnicity, class, age, and abilities.

If we locate gender in performance, perhaps we may move with greater facility from sighting/citing material effects after the fact to intervention in process. But with this understanding comes greater responsibilities for researchers to be reflexive about their own roles in enabling and constraining gender performances.

My blundering performances in the Swiltmud oral history project gendered my own interviews, an especially rueful insight for a feminist.

I directed, acted in, and produced a gendered history. I began with a masculine definition of history that cast high-status white men in leading roles. Using feminized criteria, I added while women as marked, secondary narrators. I then directed gendered communication performances from the women and men and I divided their narratives into gendered spheres of influence.

The result is a "public" history that so thoroughly reinforces stereotypical gender expectations that I doubt anyone will notice. Indeed, I produced two gendered histories: a (masculine) regional water history of "great men" influencing "public" works and a women's history of the organization itself.

Maybe an explicit history of gender was beyond the district's objective, but there were opportunities to reveal ways relations between women and men constructed the district's unique history.

For example, although the district's 40-year regional existence does nut qualify as a great historical period of "so-called progressive change," there are localized parallels. My background research revealed public "periods" within the district's history, from flood control and engineering construction, to wetlands acquisition and environmental conservation, to water shortages and utility wars, which I adopted, and the key actors in these "public" periods tended to he men.

Rather than accepting a definition of history that privileged male register, the "public" sphere, and the men who starred in its "public" events, a history of gender would have explored the social and institutional relationships between men and women that supported such an arrangement.

Additionally, there were other less obvious "periods" that had profound effects upon the district's mission, such as changing technologies.

The district's adoption of computers, for example, evolved into highly gender-segregated internal functions: masculine scientific data analysis versus feminine word processing administrative support.

Both internal functions, however, enabled the district's external mission, even as women's administrative roles also supported the internal work of science. Exploring otherwise invisible periods for their gender relations, and those relations' impact on the district's history, would not have been outside the project's objective but would have offered something closer to a history of gender.

Furthermore, the district's mission to preserve limited water resources represents a kind of "progress" to which every narrator, woman and man alike, was deeply committed, a fact I took for granted and did not explore.

All the narrators" commitments to water preservation may have been a way to cast the women and men narrators initially into more equitable roles as historical voices, which in turn may have revealed more organic gender differences within the district instead of those that I imposed.

I share my blunders not just for feminists, historians, interpersonal experts, or researchers dependent on fieldwork and interviewing methodologies.

Even scholars immersed in text and consultants working off campus enact a gendered presence in their work and participate in scripting gender.

Understanding gender as a co-performative process and practicing reflexivity to observe our own roles in the production of gender performances become the lessons here for everyone studying communication.

Additionally, just as the literatures of both history and interviewing methods fail to notice gender until the addition of women, communication research also traditionally has assumed gender is moot unless the presence of women forces the issue.

So how do we include women in communication research without resorting either to exceptional women within masculine frameworks or to marginalizing women's research?

And how do we avoid making the search for an answer to that question women's work and avoid feminizing the work of analyzing gender? Instead of studying gendered communication, we ought to be studying the communication of gender. Recognizing gender as performed encourages us to consider the myriad ways we enact, invite, react to, and write gender.

Bell and Blaeuer challenge communication research to "risk" theorizing gender differently: "to depart from the sex/gender system as foundation for claims about communication, to return the body to research questions, methods, and findings as materially performed, and to account for power structures that produce the subject named in discourse."

We can begin with a consciousness of the ways we participate in gendering not only bodies (such as women researchers and narrators) but also practices (such as women's research), social contexts (such as women's interviews), and abstract ideas (such as women's history) in a symbolic order that marks and derogates women and the feminine. Facilitating communication by fulfilling gender expectations notwithstanding, deploying gender does have its uses: to unsettle assumptions, as in gender bending; to appropriate and rehabilitate the feminine, as in feminist strategic essentialism; or to make the gender system apparent, as in histories of gender or the communication of gender.

If we approach gender as performative then we may avoid the blundering, unreflective gendering that results from and in "simplistic dichotomies."

We also afford ourselves opportunities to play with rather than recite our roles, to subvert rather than re-inscribe the semantic derogation of women and the feminine, and to expose rather than sheath the ways we edify gender.

Chapter 11

Communicative Rationality

German critical theorist and philosopher Jürgen Habermas has become a challenging source of ideas for many communication scholars, particularly those concerned with community communication ecology, cultural studies, discourse ethics, participatory communication, and public journalism. Habermas's critical-theoretical project has evoked a great deal of interest among scholars in the social sciences and the humanities. Dryzek asserts that Habermas's critical theory stands out in its ability to engage social science in fruitful dialogue. Capra says that by integrating numerous philosophical strands, Habermas has become a leading intellectual force and a major influence on philosophy and social theory. Scholars have paid particular attention to his analysis of the transformation of the public sphere and the formal pragmatics he used to develop his theory of communicative action.

However, a number of scholars have criticized these two aspects of Habermasian social theory because of their implicit Eurocentric bias and their "universalizing" tendencies that promote domination through globalization. For instance, Giddens asserts that Eurocentrism raises its head when Habermas treats "oral cultures as inferior to civilizations, and particularly to the modernized West".

Kaufman argues that "Habermas's theory of communicative rationality relies strongly on notions of common sense and, more seriously, cannot stand without the notion of Western superiority on which it is founded". Huang argues that the binary opposition between state and society in Habermas's theory of public sphere "is an ideal abstracted from early modern and modern Western experience that is inappropriate for China".

On the other hand, Tong contends that Habermas's theory of modernity associated with his theory of communicative action "provides an ideal basis for a new and rewarding interpretation of the Chinese discourse on modernization and the idea of 'socialist modernization with Chinese characteristics'".

The relationship between the theory of the public sphere and the theory of communicative action, which I shall elaborate in greater detail in the next section, needs a brief explanation here. Habermas began his early scholarship by analyzing the emergence and spread of an enlightened, politicized "public sphere" of open rational debate in the 18th century and its gradual emasculation under advanced capitalism.

He described the public sphere as the realm that enabled a "discursive will formation" or free uncoerced debate among equals. The bourgeoisie, which emerged with the rise of capitalism, sought to limit the authority of the state and affirm the principle of public accountability.

Eventually, Habermas developed the notion of communicative rationality based on an in-depth reading of what he originally termed "universal" pragmatics and implanted the public sphere in the lifeworld realm, as opposed to the system realm, of society built into his communicative action theory.

He divided the lifeworld into private and public sectors-the former revolving primarily around the intimacy and solitude of the nuclear family, and the latter concerned with the networks that shape public opinion and social identity through rational social dialogue. The system realm, divided into the economy and the state (public administration), uncoupled itself from the lifeworld with the rise of the welfare state-the economy from the lifeworld's private sphere and the state from the public sphere.

This uncoupling gave rise to the pathologies of

modernity, or "colonization of the lifeworld," because the system realm, associated with the media of money and power, used cognitive instrumental rationality to impose purposive-rational action upon the lifeworld. The latter, on the other hand, used communicative rationality for action related to cultural and societal reproduction.

Habermas's critical theory is an attempt to emancipate the lifeworld from system "colonization" through the revival of an uncoerced and unrestricted public sphere operating on the "universal" pragmatics of communicative rationality. Its modus operandi helped participants reach agreement through argumentation based on the validity claims of truth, moral rightness, and sincerity.

Max Pensky says that Habermas has been an influential advocate "for an unashamed universalism in political and moral questions" as reflected in Habermas's insistence that "we find a universal, if modest, basis for the great political innovations of popular sovereignty, legally enforceable human rights, democratic procedures, and the inconspicuous but vital solidarity that binds humans together".

Pensky goes on to say that globalization "has also globalized the political public spheres of citizens, and has thus globalized the focus of public intellectuals operating within these public spheres as well".

In the light of the attempts to globalize the public sphere in this putative age of globalization, which is more or less a euphemism for Westernization, it is pertinent to re-evaluate the Habermasian metatheory of society, particularly with regard to the aspect of the public sphere, which Habermas developed for his post-doctoral Habilitationschrift, and the aspect of communicative action, which he consummated two decades later.

His Legitimation Crisis served as a crucial transitional work separating his public sphere concerns and his work on communicative action. His Gauss lectures and essays of the early 1970s, which provide a good introduction to the theory of communicative action, also formed a bridge between his work of the 1960s and that of the 1980s.

The purpose of this monograph is to examine the thesis that Habermas's theory of the public sphere, as well as the more elaborate theory of communicative action, requires revision in order to remove the "universalizing" tendencies that promote domination through globalization. Universalism at the level of theory-whether it is the theory of the public sphere or the theory of communicative action-has its counterpart at the level of practice through lending support, perhaps uncritical support, to dominant versions of globalization.

The themes of universalism tend to be associated with the negative expressions of globalization (viz., Eurocentric hegemony). Habermasian theory is clearly a product of Eurocentric verticality, for it sees no positives in the historical development of non-Western societies or non-Western epistemology.

"Verticality," therefore, refers to the tendency to interpret world developments through the narrow confines of a particular region or civilization.] Habermas's depth hermeneutics or critical theory, a dialectical synthesis of the empirical-analytic and the historical-hermeneutical disciplines, relies heavily on evolutionary theory to claim the "universalism" of rationality in communicative action. The move to "universalize" the Enlightenment concept of rationality in this manner through a global public sphere, associated with putative globalization, is tantamount to a revival of the "developmentalism" notion of the Parsonsian structural-functionalist modernization paradigm.

Although Pensky credits Habermas as an advocate of an "unashamed universalism," Habermas himself had decided to abandon the term "universal" and related forms as early as the 1970s, when, for example, he selected the term "formal pragmatics" in place of the term "universal pragmatics" for his theory of communicative action, a point he seems consistently bound to repeat against several critics. In a footnote to the 1979 English translation of his 1976 essay on "universal pragmatics," Habermas expresses his dissatisfaction with the label "universal" and his preference for the term "formal pragmatics." The footnote states Hitherto the term "pragmatics" has referred to the analysis of particular contexts of language use and not to the reconstruction of universal features of using language (or of employing sentences in utterances). To mark this contrast, I introduced the distinction between "empirical" and "universal" pragmatics.

I am no longer happy with this terminology; the term "formal pragmatics" - as an extension of "formal semantics" - would serve better. Substituting his preferred terminology, the first sentence of his 1976 essay would read: "The task of formal pragmatics is to identify and reconstruct formal conditions of possible mutual understanding (Verständigung)."

This change in terminology led to an important problematization of the critique of Habermasian "universalism," including by Habermas himself in the book Postmetaphysical Thinking, after which "one is hard-pressed to charge Habermas with the development of something like hegemonic universalism, grand in its ambition though Habermas's project may be." Habermas himself has said that his work is of importance only to Western societies because of its Eurocentrically limited view; and that "modernization" is not synonymous with "Westernization".

Therefore, the questions one must ask is: What remains of the Habermasian universalizing impulse today? Can we not circumvent the dangers of globalizing its Eurocentrism-or rather the lingering traces or remaining strains of Eurocentrism-through what subaltern historians call provincializing "Europe" or what Robertson and others call "glocalization"?

PROVINCIALIZING AND GLOCALIZATION

Provincializing "Europe," Chakrabarty explains, is not a project of shunning European thought, but rather a project of "globalizing" such thought by exploring how it may be renewed both for and from the margins-"how we create conjoined and disjunctive genealogies for European categories of political modernity as we contemplate the necessarily fragmentary histories of human belonging that never constitute a one or a whole".

Elaborating further, Chakrabarty says that the project of provincializing Europe "refers to a history that does not yet exist"; and that it does not involve "a simplistic, out-of-hand rejection of modernity, liberal values, universals, science, reason, grand narratives, totalizing explanations, and so on". Thus, "it cannot be a project of cultural relativism," and "it cannot originate from the stance that the reason/science/universals that help define Europe as the modern are simply 'culture-specific' and therefore only belong to European cultures".

Chakrabarty argues that not only Europeans but also Third World nationalisms have been equal partners in equating a certain version of Europe with "modernity." For example, both have been responsible for the universalization of the nation-state as the most desirable form of political community.

Drawing from Marx, Chakrabarty (2000) distinguishes between two types of history: the linear, developmental, and universal type (analytical histories) anchored on rationalism, objectivity, and the driving force of capital (History 1); and the nontotalizing, heterogenizing, and pluralizing type (affective narratives) that examines the lifeworlds of postcolonial people (History 2).

The project of provincializing "Europe" entails the production of History 2 "charged with the function of constantly interrupting the totalizing thrusts of History 1"-the instrument of Western hegemony, repression, and violence on the modern, the contemporary, and the historical.

The subaltern project of provincializing "Europe" is not the same as what Robertson defines as globalization-"a process involving the increasing domination of one societal or regional culture over all others".

Robertson identifies "glocalization" (roughly meaning "global localization") as the heterogenizing aspects of globalization. Robertson maintains that "globalization-in the broadest sense, the compression of the world-has involved and increasingly involves the creation and the incorporation of locality, a process which itself largely shapes, in turn, the compression of the world as a whole".

More recent studies have refined the concept of glocalization. For example, Helvacioglu (2000) used Robertson's notion of glocalization, Castells' notion of polarization, Sassen's notion of global city, and Appadurai's conception of imaginary worlds to elucidate, both in theory and in practice, a series of contradictions, ambiguities, and irregularities that result from particular articulations of global and local developments.

Using Turkey as a case study, Helvacioglu analysed the practical implications of globalization(s) at both the national and local levels and at the level of neighborhoods. Ritzer (2003), on the other hand, sees globalization as the sum of two conflicting sub-processes: glocalization and grobalization [sic], which form a continuum.

Glocalization is "the interpenetration of the global and the local resulting in unique outcomes in different geographic areas" whereas grobalization focuses on "the imperialistic ambitions of nations, corporations, organizations, and the like, and their desire and the need to impose themselves on various geographic areas". Ritzer argues Supporting the glocal as an alternative to the grobal may be a more successful strategy, recognizing the fact that the glocal is an increasingly important source not only of cultural diversity, but also of cultural innovation.

Subaltern scholars may argue that Robertson's "spin" on globalization via glocalization has some serious flaws from the point of view of non-Western contexts, whereas Chakrabarty's poststructuralist position seeks to open up a conceptual space to understand contemporary postcolonial realties.

Because of this monograph uses the framework of the theory of living systems (incorporating the theories of autopoiesis, cognition, and dissipative structures) to detect the scientific fallibility of Habermasian theory, it adheres to the same framework to derive the relevance of the concepts of provincializing "Europe" and globalization/glocalization.

The theory of living systems presumes that the world-system is a far-from-equilibrium dissipative structure wherein nation-states function as autopoietic cells that recursively reproduce themselves. Each nation-state is operationally closed but cognitively and structurally open to its environment-the other nation-states, organizations, and the world-system at large, all of which are structurally coupled through cognition, the process of living.

Autopoiesis is what enables nation-states to preserve their distinctive cultures. Nation-states differ from one another in their receptivity toward globalization/glocalization or toward provincializing "Europe." Thus, the two concepts, irrespective of how they are defined, can relate to different nation-states in different ways.

I use the concept of provincializing "Europe" in the sense of translating "modern" universale (associated with Eurocentric historicism and discourse) into the History 2s of non-"Europe" and the concept of glocalization in the sense of adapting "Europe"-imposed globalization trends to suit the socio-cultural contexts of "non-Europe."

It would have been much more appropriate had Chakrabarty avoided the term "globalizing," which implies the deleterious domination of all aspects of Westernization as well, to argue the case for embracing the universals of "modernity." In the subaltern sense, the history of non-Europe has much to do with these universals although they bear the European imprint, and digging that history is part of the project of provincializing "Europe."

Elsewhere, Chakrabarty clarifies that thinking about political modernity is impossible without engaging some universels of "European thought." However, he points out, the problem with these universals is that they come packaged as though they have transcended the particular histories in which they were born.

Chakrabarty says, "When we translate them-practically, theoretically-into our languages and practice, we make them speak to other histories of belonging, and that is how difference and heterogeneity enter these words". Thus, Chakrabarty elucidates that the project of provincializing "Europe" also involves "the translational processes through which concepts and practices are made one's own". Chakrabarty continues that being attentive to the translational processes makes people aware of horizons of human existence that speak of histories other than those encoded into European political thought.

Now it is up to us to build an archive or repository of these other horizons so that we can use them creatively to fabricate our lives as we live them. It means further that while one can acknowledge, without seeking revenge, what one owes to Europe, one can at the same time also investigate the histories that provided the grounds on which European thought was situated and translated in our pasts. At present, most of us studying modern Indian history do not do this digging.

This statement makes it quite clear that subaltern scholars are keen to dig the local links to "modern" universals associated with Eurocentric discourse. Thus, differences between provincializing "Europe" and glocalization is a matter of how one perceives the phenomenon of globalization.

In what follows, I shall first describe the Habermasian theory in some detail (relegating those criticisms that do not strictly concern the focus of this monograph to two appendices for the benefit of the broad spectrum of readers). Second, I shall examine the relevant concepts of Habermasian theory-civil society/public sphere, communicative rationality, and liberal democracy-in terms of Eastern philosophy and history, as well as modern subaltern historiography.

Thereby I hope to uncover the Eurocentric strands of Habermas's project that have received inadequate attention in the ardor for globalizing his theory of modernity based on communicative rationality and formal ("universal") pragmatics.

This attempt also complies with Dhareshwar's call to "interrogate the western theories to construct a metatheory which specifies the intelligibility conditions of the claims and problems of those theories"-a call based on Balagangadhara's theory of religion that unravels Orientalism.

Third, I shall examine Habermas's critical theory through the lens of the emerging theory of living systems-incorporating the theories of autopoiesis, cognition, and dissipative structures-to show that operationally closed but structurally and cognitively open subsystems comprising a dissipative structure like the world-system form a formidable barrier against the emergence of a global public sphere. Fourth, I shall briefly present my conclusions.

HABERMASIAN THEORY

Habermas was not the originator of the notion of "civil society" or the idea of the "public" (or the "public sphere") that are central to Habermasian theory. Rather he reconstructed some of the essential philosophical and sociological discussions since the Age of Enlightenment culminating in Hegel and Marx. The concept of civil society as a realm distinct from the state emerged in the 17th-century works of Hobbes and Locke and of the later thinkers of the French and Scottish enlightenments.

The distinction between the private and the public spheres also arose in the 17th century when almost all Enlightenment theorists followed the lead of Locke's famous Letter on Toleration in demanding freedom of religion. They argued for the removal of religion from public life and public authority, so it would fall into the private sphere of individual preference and individual practice.

Kant linked the concept of public space with the right to publicity that provided the moral legitimacy of democracy. Negt and Kluge say that Kant ascribed to the public sphere the status of a transcendental principle, that of the mediation between politics and ethics. The public sphere is, according to Kant, a principle of the legal framework of society and simultaneously a method of enlightenment; it is the only medium within which the politics of the revolutionary bourgeoisie can articulate itself.

Some identify Habermas as the last rationalist, for he borrowed the concept from the Enlightenment rationalists via Weber and gave it a new twist. Rationality, science, liberalism, and individualism, all of which emerged as interlinked concepts in the late 17th-century Europe, reached a high point during the Enlightenment.

As Wallerstein points out, the presumed rationality of the social world, just like the presumed rationality of the physical world, implied the ability to formulate lawlike propositions that held true across space-time. Because Habermas thought it essential to mix the empirical-analytical approach with the historical-hermeneutical to develop his version of critical theory, he too implicitly subscribed to linear thinking associated with Newtonian mechanics.

One may interpret Western rationality as the pragmatic formulation of the ontological concept of "rationalism," a philosophical view that goes back to Pythagoras, Plato, and Aristotle in ancient Greece, and was later adopted by Descartes, Spinoza, Leibniz, Kant, and Hegel. Rationalism, which has long been the rival of empiricism, has come under severe challenge by the 20th-century logical positivists.

Habermas believed that philosophy in its postmetaphysical, post-Hegelian currents was "converging toward the point of a theory of rationality". He used Weber's theory of rationalization-perhaps a subtle attack on historical materialism, which explains capitalism as a mode of systematizing consciousness rather than of class exploitation-as the groundwork to derive the concept of communicative rationality.

Habermas attempted to establish a cooperative relationship between rationality and empiricism by introducing a theory of communicative action that clarifies the normative foundations of a critical theory of society. Thus, Habermas emerges as a different kind of "pragmatist" than Mead, whose pragmatism is highly tilted toward instrumental manipulation of man and nature-not the rules of communicative understanding and democratic will formation.

Habermas conceptualized the bourgeois public sphere as

"the sphere of private people come together as a public". They "soon claimed the public sphere regulated from above against the public authorities themselves, to engage them in debate over the general rules governing relations in the basically privatized but publicly relevant sphere of commodity exchange and social labour".

The public use of reason was "peculiar and without historical precedent". The apolitical literary precursor of the public sphere, which was not "autochthonously bourgeois", provided them the training ground for critical-rational public debate. Economically, culturally and politically, the "town"-with its coffee houses, the salons, and the table societies (Tischgesellschaften)-served as the life centre of civil society. The line between state and society divided the public sphere from the private realm.

The public sphere in the political realm evolved from the public sphere in the world of letters, and "through the vehicle of public opinion put the state in touch with the needs of society". Thus, Habermas argued for the existence of two kinds of public spheres: the political public sphere concerned with rational discourse leading to agreement on public policy, and the literary public sphere concerned with matters of taste and general social behaviour.

Some version of the public sphere has always existed as an appendage to democratic theory. Benhabib identifies three different versions of public space that correspond to three main currents of Western political thought: the agonistic, the legalistic, and the discursive. The agonistic view, associated with Hannah Arendt, belongs to the "republican virtue" or "civic virtue" tradition.

The legalistic view, exemplified by Bruce Ackerman's conception of "public dialogue," belongs to the liberal tradition of Kant that emphasizes a just and stable political order. The discursive view, associated with Habermas, envisages a democratic socialist accommodation within late capitalist society in hopes of reforming it. Benhabib says that because questions of democratic legitimacy are central to Habermas's public sphere, it has strengths that the other two lack. Villa, who compares the public realm theory of Arendt with that of Habermas, says that both attempted to theorize the minimal conditions necessary for a discursive realm free of structural coercion or manipulation. Both saw the public sphere as a specifically political space-distinct from the state and the economy-for citizen debate, deliberation, agreement, and action.

Antipolitical forces unleashed by modernity, however, overwhelmed the public sphere. Arendt argued that "household" concerns had "devoured" the public sphere while Habermas argued that the universalization of instrumental rationality had enabled technical-administrative imperatives to "colonize" the public sphere.

As developed by Habermas, the concept of the bourgeois public sphere should be understood as an analytic category. It emerged along with the development of capitalism as a dynamic nexus that linked "a variety of actors, factors and contexts together in a cohesive theoretic framework". It was this configurational quality, with its emphasis on institutional and discursive contingencies that gave the concept its analytical power.

The ascending bourgeois classes generated this new social space between the private sphere (consisting of the economy and family) and the sphere of the public authorities (formed by the state and the judiciary), especially during the 18th century. Early to mid-19th century saw the highpoint of the bourgeois public sphere, which disintegrated in the modern industrialized welfare states of advanced capitalism.

The bourgeois public sphere was a forum accessible to as many people as possible to express and exchange a large variety of social experiences. Individuals used this forum for rational discussion to confront various arguments and views. Its primary task was to check on government policies systematically and critically. The public sphere functioned on the basis of rational critical argument. The Frankfurt School's attempt to ground a vision of social transformation and human emancipation on the proletariat had foundered.

The public sphere, which provided a mode of social

integration by ignoring the Marxian concept of class, was an attempt to reground the project of critical theory. Public discourse (or communicative action) enabled the coordination of human life with state power and market economies. Britain, France, and Germany served as the models to trace the development of the public sphere.

A refeudalization of society occurred as private organizations began increasingly to assume public power while the state penetrated the private realm. Thus, the public sphere became more an arena for advertising than a setting for rational-critical debate. The public sphere designates a theater in modern societies in which the medium of talk enacts political participation. Fraser sees it as an institutionalized arena of discursive interaction conceptually distinct from the state, as well as from the official economy.

Ambrozas argues that Habermas salvaged "the emancipatory promise of the bourgeois public sphere," where any and all individuals came together (in principle), around issues of general interest, without concern for social status, to achieve rational consensus by means of critical discussion. Here, Ambrozas presents the consensus theory à la Parsons: All actors more or less possess the same values, which necessarily must cut across all classes and cultural strata. They created public opinion.

The public sphere first emerged in 17th-century England in dialectical opposition to the nuclear family and the modern state. Ambrozas says, "The family was a necessary precondition for the public sphere as the realm where private persons were individuated. Factors promoting individuation in the family were humane interpersonal relations as well as solitary reading, especially of the new domestic novels that depicted bourgeois family life".

COMMUNICATIVE ACTION THEORY

Habermas's theory of communicative action represents the outcome of his efforts to develop a new critical theory of modern society by "synthesizing a tremendous range of approaches and elucidating their implications and interconnectedness". His social theory of rationality appropriated the major currents of 20th-century Western philosophy and social theory-speech-act theory and analytic philosophy, classical social theory, hermeneutics, phenomenology, developmental psychology, and systems theory.

Venturelli says that Habermas's theory of communicative action, which redefines the problem of reason and rationalization, "recentres the principle of communication into the emancipatory project of modernity". Habermas says his theory intertwines three topic complexes: a concept of rationality that is free from the subjectivistic and individualistic premises of contemporary Western philosophy and social theory, a two-level concept of society that connects the lifeworld and system paradigms, and a theory of modernity that explains the social pathologies and paradoxes of modernity.

By exhaustively assessing and recasting the ideas of classical social theorists and critical theorists to meet his own immediate needs, he formulated a new theoretical approach that combined the methods and problematics of both philosophy and empirical social science.

On the first topic complex, Habermas tried to compensate for the weaknesses inherent in the older subject-object paradigm by formulating a paradigm of intersubjectivity. Whereas the former emphasized purposive rational action (based on cognitive-instrumental rationality), the latter emphasized the pragmatics of communicative action (based on communicative rationality).

His aim was to derive a universalistic (and, therefore, nonrelativistic) theory of rationality, which he grounded socially rather than transcendentally. Arens clarifies this point: Because Habermas's discourse ethics stood in the neo-Kantian tradition, it attempted to be not only universalistic, but also deontological, cognitivistic, and formalistic. Habermas used Weber's treatment of world religions to derive a broader theory of cultural rationalization (of worldviews).

He did so by drawing upon Mead's communication-theoretic approach ("social behaviorism") and from Durkheim's theory of the origins of religions and ritual. Applying the speech-act theory, Habermas claims that reaching understanding (rather than action oriented to instrumental success) is the essential aspect of language. Thus, he "roots communicative rationality in the very nature of language-mediated communication, and thereby implicitly claims that it has universal significance".

On the second topic complex, Habermas argues that modern society reflects both lifeworld (a concept derived from phenomenology and hermeneutics) and system (as conceptualized by Parsons and carried further by Luhmann) dimensions as differentiated aspects of social life. Forms of action and reason differentiate these two dimensions. Habermas relates each of the two dimensions to a determinate form of action and rationality-communicative versus cognitive-instrumental.

Outlining a theory of social evolution, Habermas grounds the lifeworld in an evolutionary development of societal learning whose superstructural location vitiates the analytic truth claims of Marxist materialism. (This method makes him axiologically neutral on issues of moral judgments and assertions.) System evolution, on the other hand, reflects a linear increase in a society's steering capacity-engendered by the steering media of money and power-that encodes purposive-rational action and instrumental reason.

This dialectical interaction between the two dimensions results in an uncoupling of system integration from social integration entailing the differentiation of state and economy. From a methodological point of view, social integration presents itself as part of the lifeworld's symbolic reproduction while functional integration becomes the standard for system maintenance at the level of organizing the political and economic spheres.

Both paradigms, life-world and system, are important From the life-world perspective, we thematize the normative structures (values and institutions) of a society. We analyse events and states from the point of view of their dependency on functions of social integration (in Parsons's vocabulary, integration and pattern maintenance), while the non-normative components of the system serve as limiting conditions.

From the system perspective, we thematize a society's steering mechanisms and the extension of the scope of contingency. We analyse events and states from the point of view of their dependency on functions of system integration (in Parsons's vocabulary, adaptation and goal-attainment), while the goal values serve as data.

The public and the private spheres served as the environments of the system. Habermas says the imperatives of capitalism and democracy clash in the political public sphere, "where the autonomy of the lifeworld has to prove itself in the face of the administrative system". What emerges as public opinion there takes a different meaning from the action-theoretic lifeworld perspective than it does from the system-theoretic systemic perspective of the state apparatus.

From the lifeworld perspective, social consensus is identified "as the first link in the chain of political will formation and as the basis of legitimation," whereas from the systemic perspective, "the same consensus counts as the result of engineering legitimation".

On the third topic complex, Habermas reformulates the notion of the loss of meaning and loss of freedom in terms of his thesis on the colonization of the lifeworld by the system world, which advances his analysis of postliberal capitalism.

Habermas says that neither the secularization of worldviews nor the structural differentiation of society is the cause of the pathologies and paradoxes of modernity. He attributes these effects to "the penetration of forms of economic and administrative rationality into areas of action that resist being converted over to the media of money and power because they are specialized in cultural transmission, social integration, and child rearing, and remain dependent on mutual understanding as a mechanism for coordinating action".

Habermas's system perspective, like Parsons's, excludes

any meaningful consideration of class, mode of production, and the thermodynamics of nature. Nevertheless, Habermas introduces the dynamic of capitalist market imperatives into his model of interaction between system and lifeworld-an essential characteristic of his critical theory.

Drawing from Weber, Habermas argues that the enduring features of modernity are the three institutionally differentiated cultural value spheres of science and technology, law and morality, and art. As a specification of these three value spheres, Habermas's theory of communicative action takes the following form:

The modern differentiation of the lifeworld into three structured components (culture, society, and personality) is the opening up to experience of three 'worlds' (objective, social, and subjective), along with basic attitudes that can be adopted to those worlds (objectivating, norm-conformative, and expressive), their corresponding rationalities (cognitive-instrumental, moral-practical, and aesthetic-practical), and the three validity claims (truth, rightness, and truthfulness) thematized respectively in three uses of language (constative, interactive, and expressive).

In this description, each of the three structural components of the lifeworld is assigned its own validity claim, and each is conceived of as having a unique 'inner logic" that expresses itself in a specific type of rationalization. According to this model of three autonomous spheres, the validity claim of truth is lodged in the cultural space of science and institutionalized in the 'scientific enterprise," whereas the rightness validity claim is attached to post-conventional law and morality and the institutions of the liberal democratic state.

As for the cultural and institutional space of the truthfulness validity claim, Habermas refers to an 'artistic enterprise".

Billings and Scott (1994) provide a thumbnail sketch of Habermasian theory for contextualizing national religious conflicts over legitimation. They say that for Habermas world mastery meant instrumental rationality, social interaction meant communicative rationality, and rationalization of the lifeworld meant "linguistification of the sacred". Heath (2001) argues that "despite being pitched as a critique of instrumental rationality, Habermas's work is informed by only a somewhat vague grasp of the details of the instrumental views".

Therefore, Heath has brought Habermas's theory into dialogue with Bayesian decision and game theory, "the most sophisticated articulation of the instrumental conception of practical rationality".

LINGERING TRACES OF EUROCENTRISM

I shall now examine the relevant concepts of Habermasian theory in terms of Eastern philosophy and history, as well as modern subaltern historiography, to uncover the Eurocentric strands of Habermas's project that have received inadequate attention in the ardor for globalizing his critical theory of society and modernity. Habermas's metatheory encompasses two aspects of particular interest to communication scholars-the public sphere and communicative action.

An exploration of these two aspects will help the project of provincializing or glocalizing the emancipatory potential of Habermas's work for the benefit of non-"Europe" while circumventing the "universalizing" tendencies that promote domination through globalization. I begin with some insights from the project of subaltern studies.

Although postcolonial subaltern studies recognize the value of European thought for modernizing non-"Europe," subaltern historian Chakrabarty (2000) points out the negative impact that "Europe"-centered "universalism" (History 1) has had on the lifeworld of the colonial subjects. He says that "Europe" remains the sovereign, theoretical subject of all other histories because "Europe" is reified and celebrated in the phenomenal world of everyday relationships of power as the scene of the birth of the modern.

Philosophers and thinkers, Chakrabarty says, have produced theories that embraced the entirety of humanity in relative, and sometimes absolute, ignorance of the majority of humankind.

He refers to Husserl's identification of Greek-European science as theoria (universal science) while characterizing oriental philosophies as "practical-universal," and hence "mythical-religious." Also, Marx's categories-such as capital and pre-capital-carry a similar epistemological proposition.

Chakrabarty (2000) then goes on to point out that British rule had put in place the practices, institutions, and discourse of bourgeois individualism in the Indian subcontinent, which became the staging ground of many of the public and private rituals of modern individualism. India became a nation-state, a conceptual entity "whose theoretical subject was Europe," and in Gandhi's words India continued with "English rule without the Englishmen". Indians became constitutionally recognized citizens in the classically liberal sense-a modern individual with a private self.

This modern individual ? is also supposed to have an interiorized "private" self that pours out incessantly in diaries, letters, autobiographies, novels, and, of course, in what we say to our analysts. The bourgeois citizen is not born until one discovers the pleasures of privacy. But this is a very special kind of "private self - it is, in fact, a deferred "public" self, for this bourgeois private self, as Jürgen Habermas has reminded us, is "always already oriented to an audience [Publikum]".

Thus, Chakrabarty says, "Indian public life may mimic on paper the bourgeois legal fiction of citizenship" but the fiction of bourgeois private self fails to come through even in Indians' autobiographies. The ambiguity of the public-private distinction may appear to be another example of the "incompleteness" of bourgeois transformation of India. The metaphor of the sanctified and patriarchal extended family in India and elsewhere clearly does not fit the private-public dichotomy so central to Habermasian social theory.

However, Chakrabarty argues, European imperialism and Third World nationalism have combined to universalize the nation-state as the most desirable form of political community. He rejects the "stance that the reason/science/ universals that help define Europe as the modern are simply 'culture-specific' and therefore only belong to the European cultures".

Our task should be to "find a form of social thought that embraces analytical reason in pursuit of social justice but does not allow it to erase the question of heterotemporality from the history of the modern subject". Chakrabarty disagrees with Rorty for crossing cudgels with Habermas and implying that democratic societies had self-contained histories of their own when Habermas stated that modern philosophy had backed the democratic societies' attempts at self-assurance.

Chakrabarty writes, "Rorty ignores the role that the 'colonial theater' (both external and internal)-where the theme of 'freedom' as defined by modern political philosophy was constantly invoked in aid of the ideas of 'civilization,' 'progress,' and latterly 'development'-played in the process of this 'reassurance'". Chakrabarty takes the position that European thought is at once indispensable and inadequate in helping the non-Western nations to think through the experiences of political modernity.

The thesis of this monograph-that Habermas's theory of the public sphere requires provincializing or glocalizing in order to remove its "universalizing" tendencies that promote domination through globalization-does not mean an aversion to Western thought.

Chakrabarty asserts that non-"Europe" needs universals derived through European analytical heritage and hermeneutical heritage to produce critical readings of social injustices. Perhaps, one can construe that Chakrabarty's call for History 2s also justifies the glocalization (in the Ritzer sense rather than Robertson's) of such Eurocentric universals (like those built into Habermas's social theory) to reflect the realities of each country's lifeworld.

If such "glocalization" were possible, an exploration of the Eurocentric verticality of the Habermasian project should help determine its adaptability in the non-Western social environment. In the rest of this section, I do this exploration in terms of Habermas's (a) description of the evolution of the public sphere and civil society; (b) use of formal pragmatics in hopes of "universalizing" communicative rationality; (c) treatment of non-Western philosophy and history; and (d) idealization of liberal democracy associated with a discursive public sphere.

My intention is to show the consequences of attempts to push Habermasian theories in the direction of universalism, which promote a Eurocentric discourse of Western universalism that makes non-Western theories relatively invisible in the global academy. Because much of Habermas's work is rooted in modern Europe, I shall examine the usefulness of his concepts in the context of not only classical Eastern philosophy but also of modern subaltern perspective of Chakrabarty.

PUBLIC SPHERE AND CIVIL SOCIETY

The Habermasian blueprint of the public sphere represents an evolutionary phase of European history, although Sparks (2000) rejects the existence of a "bourgeois public sphere" in the 18th century. This blueprint asserts that a political public sphere (preceded by a literary public sphere) evolved between the realm of public authority (viz., state and judiciary) and the private realm (viz., family and civil society, including the economy).

The bourgeoisie used the public sphere for rational debate on matters of public concern that often challenged the realm of public authority. The question arises whether this model conducive to promoting liberal democracy and emancipation can claim "unashamed" universalism.

Baynes clarifies that the model of the public sphere that Habermas envisioned comprised a vast array of institutions in which a wide variety of practical discourses overlapped. It ranged "from the more or less informal movements and associations in civil society where solidarities are formed, through the various institutions of the mass media, to the more formal institutions of parliamentary debate and legal argumentation".

Under European imperialism, the public spheres that emerged in the colonies from the second half of the 19th century onwards contradicted the Habermasian mold. For instance, in British India, the public constituted the European elite, not the native nationalists. Public opinion was the opinion of the "nonofficial" European community.

The imperial government enacted the Vernacular Press Act of 1878 to suppress native public opinion. In colonial society, as Chatterjee points out, the political domain was under the control of aliens, who excluded the colonized from its decisive zones. In colonial society, the public sphere in the political domain, and its literary precursors in the debating societies and learned bodies, did not emerge out of the discursive construction of a social world peopled by "individuals."

Nor was there an "audience-oriented subjectivity," by which the new conjugal family's intimate domain became publicly transparent and thus consistent with and amenable to the discursive control of the public sphere in the political domain.

Clearly, the putative public sphere that arose in colonial India was not associated with civil society of sovereign individuals. It contrasted with the Habermasian public sphere that supposedly functioned in a space outside the supervision of the political authority and thereby marked both the distinction and the unity of state and civil society.

Li points out that the Western division of public sphere and private sphere simply does not exist in Confucianism, the pervasive philosophy in East Asia. De Bary explains that in Chinese philosophy, "private (si) is a familial concept, marked by a cooperative spirit that extends into the community or public sphere (gong) as a single interdependent continuum". This is in general true of Indian philosophy as well.

Therefore, Habermas's public sphere theory, which connects the rise of a market economy with the emergence of civil society in which contractual ties and horizontal integration between economic actors challenge primordial ties to the family and to the state, cannot fit the socio-cultural patterns of much of the non-Western world.

Under alien rule, however, the conflict between the culturally disparate state and its subjects disrupted the cooperative spirit that marked the single interdependent family-community-state continuum-the indigenous "public sphere." Apparently, just like the modernization theorists, Habermas implies that the non-West must eventually go through Europe's "exceptional" historical experience before a bourgeois, rational public sphere can emerge.

This aporetic presumption, in fact, becomes evident in his reliance on the empirically weak evolutionary theories or the "reconstructive sciences" of Piaget and Kohlberg to claim a connection between language and rationality. Calhoun says the notion of civil society is basic to Habermas's account of the public sphere. Habermas asserts that in the 17th and 18th centuries, civil society developed as "the genuine domain of private autonomy [that] stood opposed to the state".

Capitalist market economies formed the basis of this civil society, which "came into existence as the corollary of a depersonalized state authority". Doctrines of laissez-faire and free trade among nations brought the development of "civil society as the private sphere emancipated from the directives of public authority". Civil society served as the precondition for free, rational, informed discourses on the political ends of society.

[However, the links between the public sphere and history are disputatious. Pinter says recent research into the history of the public sphere questioned some interpretation of facts on which Habermas based his early theory.]

Contrary to the presumptions of the bourgeois public sphere, Flower and Leonard point out that the notion of a clear boundary between state and society implicit in the discourse of civil society is problematic in the Chinese context, where the vectors of social interaction involve both horizontal and vertical linkages of exchange and expectation.

If the idea of civil society were to have salience in the Chinese countryside, they argue, it must be reworked to embrace the blurry interpenetration of state and society, and understood in terms of cooptation, negotiation, and historicity at the heart of the interaction. Hann too argues the need for a more inclusive usage of civil society such that it is not defined negatively in opposition to the state, but positively in the context of ideas and practices through which cooperation and trust are established in social life.

He says the narrow, Western liberal-individualist idea of civil society has long been in need of such ethnographic investigation because the term civil society is riddled with contradictions, with its current vogue predicated on a fundamental ethnocentricity. Furthermore, he says that the exploration of civil society requires paying careful attention to a range of informal interpersonal practices that scholars have overlooked.

White adds that the term civil society has become entangled in political currents wherein it has become a litmus test for the democratic potential of non-Western regimes. "The meanings attributed to the term have followed the trajectory of Western philosophical thought, beginning in the seventeenth century when the term took on attributes of reason and rationality in opposition to revelation and the state of nature".

The "classical" sense of civil society is of little or no use in describing most of the non-Western world below the level of government and the activities of a segment of educated Westernized elites. Moon, on the other hand, uses the concept of civil society in the "classical" sense when she blames Korea's Chosön dynasty for choosing neo-Confucianism as the state ideology thereby excluding women from the civil society and the public sphere.

However, Moon concedes that the Korean women do not fit the "liberal model of the self as atomized individual isolated from social relations". Koo clarifies that the public sphere that might have existed in Chosön society "was too limited in scope and nature to comprise what can legitimately be called a civil society" because of the lack of an economic base.

Rabo asks not to create a dichotomy between state and society in which the state is simply a locus of repression. Instead, one should look at the interdependencies between state and civil society. He adds that Western scholars lean heavily on traditional Orientalism to show that the Orient, the Middle East, and the Islamic world are always lacking some basic ingredient for a happy marriage between the rulers and the ruled.

The Eastern perspective of state as part of the public is also evident in the writings of American philosopher Dewey (1927/1954), who defines the state as "the organization of the public effected through officials for the protection of the interests shared by its members". He points out that for long periods of human history, especially in the Orient, the state ruled but did not regulate.

Dewey sees the state as inseparable from the community, which thrives on associated (rather than individualistic) activity thereby bringing into existence a public. The state, Dewey asserts, is "a distinctive and secondary form of association". Implying a Confucian view, Dewey claims that the democratic ideals of fraternity, liberty, and equality are inherent in the "communal experience," and not in individualism. Implicit in Dewey's notion of associational connections is the concept of civil society.

In retrospect, Habermas explains that contemporary discussions of the central question in The Structural Transformation of the Public Sphere nowadays take place under the rubric of the "rediscovery of civil society." He says the current meaning of civil society no longer includes a sphere of an economy regulated via labour, capital, and commodity markets.

The institutional core of civil society is constituted by voluntary unions outside the realm of the state and the economy and ranging from churches, cultural associations, and academies to independent media, sport and leisure clubs, debating societies, groups of concerned citizens, and grassroots petitioning drives all the way to occupational associations, political parties, labour unions, and "alternative institutions". He says that the concept of civil society owes its rise in favour to the criticism leveled against the totalitarian annihilation of the political public sphere. Just as much as Habermas willingly takes "the apologetic role of a Western participant in a cross-cultural discussion of human rights", he appears to say that the non-West must catch up with the modern West by striving to achieve the preconditions necessary for the emergence of a discursive public sphere conducive to the operation of a liberal democracy.

If this interpretation is correct, then the claim for a global public sphere falls apart while strengthening the case for a value-free sphere of the "third realm" (wherein the state and society work in harmony). Such a "third realm," as Huang points out, reflects the reality of the Chinese lifeworld.

Elaborating further, Huang says "the value-laden teleology of Habermas's bourgeois public sphere" does not fit either contemporary China or its conditions under the Qing dynasty and the republic. Huang argues that what's relevant to China is a value-free "third realm" that shows the simultaneous influence of the state and society. In late imperial China, the "third realm" played a major role in the justice system, subcounty administration, and local public services.

Since the reform era began in the late 1970s, China has witnessed a tremendous expansion in the realm of private society and economy, but the private realm pales in comparison with the third realm. Thus: Instead of continuing to insist on equating China and Europe, we need to try to explain the difference between the two. Contrary to the vision of the public sphere/civil society models, actual sociopolitical change in China has really never come from any lasting assertion of societal economy against the state, but rather from the workings out of state-society relations in the third realm.

Chakrabarty's subaltern analysis also points out that even in modern India the private-public dichotomy in the lifeworld remains a fiction, particularly in the context of the extended family system. The rural Bengali institution of adda or majlish-the customary gatherings where people talked informally about all kinds of things affecting their lives-was far from a fledgling public sphere.

The ideals of the adda and those of the modern civil society were mutually antithetical. Conversations in an adda were "by definition opposed to the idea of achieving any definite outcome".

However, because of the imperial imposition of British institutional structure, India is perhaps more ready than China to mimic a glocalized version of the public sphere or more likely two versions-one serving the minority of "Europe"-oriented urban elite, a carryover from the British rule; the other serving the "third-realm" sphere associated with the large majority of the non-Westernized "citizens," who have exercised universal franchise since India's independence from Britain in 1947.

Chatterjee distinguishes between a public sphere appropriated within the narrative of capital, and a community public sphere that belongs to the domain of the natural.

Chatterjee clarifies that in the contemporary Indian context, "the old idea of civil society as bourgeois society" is limited to "a relatively small section of the population whose social locations can be identified with a fair degree of clarity" whereas the large majority belongs to political society because they have a certain political relationship with the state although "this relationship does not always conform to what is envisaged in the constitutional depiction of the relation between the state and members of civil society".

Chatterjee's political society represents the "third realm" that befits Eastern thinking. These two-civil and political-represent the capital/community opposition, "the great unsurpassed contradiction in Western philosophy". Provincializing the Habermasian public sphere in terms of History 2s has its distinct advantages for non"Europe": Whenever the state attempts to move toward authoritarianism, the "citizens" can cry foul, invoking the emancipatory properties of the fictive "public sphere" and the notion of "communicative rationality" associated with it.

Some may argue that the idea of the East implicit in the

term Eastern philosophy posits a major problem because the formation of public spheres and differential rationalities in the Third World societies as a product of the encounters with modernity have left the East in a much more complicated situation. The dominance of History 1 in postcolonial society clearly documents this complexity.

However, as Chakrabarty points out, History 1 does not document the achievement of a bourgeois revolution in non-"Europe." Thus, in the absence of bourgeois revolutions in postcolonial societies, bourgeois public spheres or a global public sphere in the Habermasian mold are unlikely to take hold. The more likely are the capital-detached community public spheres in the domain of the natural-the grist for History 2s.

Chatterjee hypothesizes that "an investigation into the idea of the nation, by uncovering a necessary contradiction between capital and community, is likely to lead us to a fundamental critique of modernity from within itself.". He elucidates that the alien rulers introduced the institutions of civil society, in the form in which they had arisen in Europe, into the colonies precisely to create a public domain for the legitimation of colonial rule.

However, this process was fundamentally limited because the colonial state could confer only subjecthood but not citizenship on the colonized, who refused to become members of this civil society. Instead, they chose to build their national identities within the traditional narrative of community, which differed from the domain of the bourgeois civil-social institutions. Chatterjee points out

The irony is, of course, that this other narrative is again violently interrupted once the postcolonial national state attempts to resume its journey along the trajectory of world-historical development.

This interpretation clearly shows the problems of provincializing the Habermasian public sphere and civil society, as well as the tension between History 1 and History 2s. Rajeev Bhargava concludes that if one were to conduct an empirical-cum-interpretative inquiry into the presence of civil society, political society, public sphere, and the state in Indian society and polity applying the mainstream (Western) understandings of these terms, one may not find these entities in India.

CONCEPT OF RATIONALITY

For Habermas, rationalization is a two-world process-instrumental (or means-end) rationality, as conceptualized by Weber and the earlier critical theorists, associated with the operation of the system world; and communicative rationality associated with the lifeworld, the corner stone of Habermas's contribution to critical theory.

Communicative rationality supersedes instrumental rationality because the latter is a byproduct of the former, whose communicative action created the system world. As already noted, Habermas developed his theory of communicative action on the foundation of formal pragmatics, which claims to have universal characteristics.

Communicative rationality, which refers to "the institutionalization of mechanisms of open criticism and defence", is a distinct feature of Habermas's project. Habermas says that one has to analyse communicative rationality in connection with achieving understanding in language.

This suggests a rationally motivated agreement among participants that one can measure against "criticizable validity claims". Because objectivity in social-theoretical knowledge is essential from both metatheoretical and methodological points of view, the corresponding concepts of communicative action and interpretation, Habermas says, "would have to be shown to be universally valid" and not "interwoven with a particular cultural tradition".

He, therefore, anchors those concepts into an internal structure of processes of reaching understanding in terms of (a) the three-world relations of actors [originally proposed by Popper] and the corresponding concepts of the objective, social, and subjective worlds; (b) the validity claims of propositional truth, normative lightness, and sincerity or authenticity; (c) the concept of rationally motivated agreement, that is, one based on the intersubjective recognition of criticizable validity claims; and (d) the concept of reaching understanding as the cooperative negotiation of common definitions of the situation.

Habermas's main contribution to philosophy has been the development of a theory of rationality. Rationality, in a general sense, means the ability to think logically and analytically. In the Habermasian sense, rationality is a form of communicative action aimed at achieving agreement with others in an "ideal speech situation" where people put forward moral and political claims and defend them based on rationality alone.

However, despite the admirable criteria Habermas applied "to expound the universality of the concept of communicative rationality", his grand theory does not reflect an effort on his part to understand or analyse the non-Western philosophical thinking on action and rationality. This is because he chose to pursue that task by following the path of Occidental sociological approaches to a theory of societal rationalization by using the "conceptual strategies, assumptions, and lines of argument from Weber to Parsons".

Habermas says his concept of rationality is a reconstruction of Weber's theory of rationalization built on "the restricted idea of purposive rationality"-a concept that Marx, Horkheimer, and Adorno also shared. Habermas asserts that Weber "did not regard rationalization process as a phenomenon peculiar to the Occident". Habermas then goes on to work out the logic of the rationalization of worldviews from Weber's studies on the sociology of religion.

Weber had differentiated three rationality complexes derived in formal pragmatic terms from basic attitudes and world-concepts: cognitive-instrumental rationality institutionalized in science and social technologies; aesthetic-practical rationality instituted in eroticism and art; and the moral-practical rationality instituted in law and morality.

In Weber's account, modern life had increasingly become an "iron cage" resulting from the institutionalization of cognitive-instrumental rationality (associated with purposive-rational action) in the economy and the state. Habermas finds conceptual bottlenecks in Weber's theory of action because of Weber's action-theoretic assumption that "processes of societal rationalization could come into view only from the standpoint of purposive rationality". Habermas asserts that from a sociological point of view, it makes more sense to begin with a communication-theoretic line of inquiry. Then he goes on to connect Karl Bühler's theory of language functions-cognitive, expressive, and appellative-with the methods and insights of the analytic theory of meaning to make it "the centerpiece of a theory of communicative action oriented toward reaching understanding".

Habermas takes the view that it is not possible to deal with rationalization adequately within the conceptual framework of the philosophy of consciousness. Therefore, he shifts the paradigm from purposive activity to communicative action by incorporating Mead's communication-theoretic concept of "social behaviorism" and Durkheim's theory of social solidarity connecting social integration to system integration. Habermas says communicative action serves as a reference point for analyzing the contributions of the components of the lifeworld-culture, society, and personality, which, together with organism, make up the four subsystems of every action system in the Parsonsian theory of social evolution. Parsons specified society as an autarchic action system placed in an environment. Habermas delves into general systems theory, as does later Parsons, to give system characteristics to state and economy dimensions of society that intrude into its lifeworld dimension. Predominantly, the lifeworld operates on communicative rationality whereas the two system-dimensions operate on cognitive-instrumental rationality.

The Indian perspective: In contrast, Eastern philosophy in general does not recognize such gradations of rationality. Habermas's treatment of different types of rationality as separate, autonomous validity spheres has come under criticism in the Occident as well because he fails to explain how actors determine the specific standard to apply in a given situation. Fleming has drawn attention to McCarthy's concern that Habermas's schema of three spheres of validity-truth, rightness, and truthfulness-might be Western and idiosyncratic rather than universal features of human interaction. Fleming says that Habermas "seems strangely untroubled by suggestions that his theory might contain Eurocentric prejudices".

Delanty points out that Habermas "fails to grasp that universal morality can be articulated in more than one cultural form and in more than one logic of development". To lessen the residual Eurocentrism still pervading the Habermasian theory, Delanty suggests a shift of its emphasis from a de-contextualized and transcendental critique of communication rooted in Occidental rationalism to a cosmopolitan model of contemporary cultural transformation.

According to Indian philosophy, as Dissanayake points out, "the realization of truth is facilitated neither by language nor by logic and rationality. It is only intuition that will ensure the achievement of this objective". Thus, Habermas's reliance on speech-act theory on the presumption that linguistically mediated interaction would promote understanding (communicative rationality) appears to clash with this interpretation of Indian thought.

However, as White asserts, Habermas relies on the "intuitive knowledge" of participants in imputing the ideal speech situation, a condition necessary for actual discourse when a validity claim is explicitly challenged and justification demanded for it.

Mohanty takes issue with the interpretation that Indian philosophies (darsanas) focus on intuition rather than intellect. He asserts that no Indian philosophy uses a pramäna (or means of true knowledge) that "suffers rendering into the much misused word 'intuition'".

He points out that in the Sanskrit philosophical vocabulary, the words "reason" and "experience," which are so fundamental to Western philosophy, have no exact synonyms. The epistemological question the Indian philosophies asked was whether perception is the only pramäna or whether anumäna (or inference) is also pramäna.

Unlike the Western epistemologists, who also worried about the subjective and the objective, as well as the private and the public, Indian philosophers made "unabashed use of 'mentalistic' discourse and never really [worried] about problems such as psychologism or private language". Moreover, unlike the abstract ontologies of Western philosophy, the Indian prameya (ontologies) dealt with more concrete entities.

According to Indian tradition, science and metaphysics are one continuum. This Indian tradition is in accord with the modern philosophy of monistic idealism, which combines quantum physics with transcendent consciousness to explain how sentient beings collapse coherent superpositions or possibility waves into manifest reality.

Habermas was not concerned with the notion of rationality derived from the Indian darsanas even though Matilal points out that India's dharma tradition-as evident in the discourses in the two great epics, folktales, stories, and fables told at different times-exhibits the rudiments of a theory of rationality.

Matilal argues that neither Hinduism nor Jainism or Buddhism is incompatible with the search for a rational basis of dharma because none of them cites God as the authority on dharma. He claims that the dharma tradition, which does not have a definitive form, developed through an attempt of rational criticism of itself.

Stories in the epics and the puranas mention Cärväka's use of tarka or hetusastra, the science of reasoning, to ask questions and challenge the validity of Vedic rituals. Matilal concedes that probably the karma doctrine "was intended to provide a 'rational' basis for the apparently irrational practice of caste-hierarchy or social inequality".

Sankara, the Indian philosopher who flourished about C.E. 800, expounded thoughts that had the closest parallel to Occidental rationalism. Sankara held that the Absolute is the unattainable goal toward which the finite intellect strives. In the Buddhist sphere, Nägärjuna, the third-century founder of the Mädhyamika school of Mahayana philosophy, used logic to show that nothing in the phenomenal world had full being, and all was ultimately unreal.

Therefore, every rational theory about the world would be a theory about something unreal evolved by an unreal thinker with unreal thoughts. Such ontological nihilism, practiced by the Präsangika sub-school of logic that produced works of great subtlety, reduced all rational argument to absurdity.

However, Siderits asserts that to understand the force of the Mädhyamika claim that the ultimate truth is that there is no ultimate truth, one must begin with the traditional Buddhist distinction between conventional truth (based on warranted assertiblity or community standards) and ultimate truth (based on philosophical rationality).

The point of Nägärjuna's dialectic is not that reality transcends conceptualization, but that truth must conform to human practice, that philosophical rationality is doomed precisely insofar as it seeks a truth free of all taint of human needs and interests.

Bitbol (2003), who points out some similarities between the philosophy of Kant and that of the Mädhyamika, asserts that both involve an analysis of the dialectic of reason, and that Kant's distinction between phenomenon and noumenon is similar to the Mädhyamika distinction between conventional (samvrti) and ultimate/absolute (paramärtha) truth. Wallace argues that "many Buddhist theories are obviously expressions of rational public discourse" and that Buddhism presents rational descriptions of how the mind functions.

Moreover, considering that scholars have very often called Buddha "a rationalist" for various reasons (e.g., for being non-dogmatic, non-mystical, and non-metaphysical, and for implanting his views on the strong ground of reason with emphasis on empiricism), a theory of rationality would be incomplete without delving into Buddhist scholarship.

An examination of Buddhist rationality methodically vis-à-vis Occidental rationalism, outside of Weber's prejudiced analysis of Eastern philosophies, would help the project of provincializing or glocalizing Habermasian theory. Jayatilleke points out that Buddhist rationality is incongruent with the rationalism (i.e., the anti-empirical theory of philosophy wherein the criterion of truth is not sensory but intellectual and deductive) of Descartes, Leibniz, and Spinoza, whose stand was similar to the rational metaphysics associated with tarka or hetusästra in the time of the Buddha.

As evident in Sandaka Sutta, the Buddha rejected theories based on mere reasoning as unsatisfactory because such reasoning may be valid or invalid; and even if valid (i.e., internally consistent), it may or may not correspond with fact. Drawing from Sunakkhatta, a monk who left the Buddhist order dissatisfied, Jayatilleke, in almost dialectical contrast to Weber's view of Buddhism, asserts

Buddha's doctrines were a product of pure reasoning and were not based on extrasensory perception or extraordinary insight ? Nothing in the Nikäyas suggests that any doctrines were taught or were considered to follow from premises which were held to be true in an a priori sense. On the contrary, we always find the Buddha recommending doctrines which are claimed to be true in an empirically or an experientially verifiable sense.

Because subaltern studies see the need for provincializing "Europe" in the context of Indo-European hybridization of postcolonial Indian society, Habermas's theory of communicative action has a degree of relevance to the "Europe"-oriented urban elite.

An essential task of the project of glocalizing Habermasian theory would be to examine India's dharma tradition, including Carvaka's use of the science of reasoning to ask questions and challenge the validity of Vedic rituals, to distinguish between ontological rationalism and empirical rationality.

A provincialized (glocalized) version of the theory of communicative rationality would see the remarkable similarity between the validity claim of prepositional truth (related to the objective world) and the Buddhist focus on empirically verifiable truth, and between the validity claim of moral lightness (related to the social world) and the Mädhyamika concept of conventional truth (based on warranted assertiblity or community standards). The Mädhyamika concept of ultimate truth (based on philosophical rationality) belongs to the realm of rationalism, which Habermas opposed.

A revision of the concept of communicative action on the suggested lines will help diminish the perceived extent of Western universalism that makes non-Western theories relatively invisible in the arena of global academic discourse. It will also help counterbalance Habermas's Eurocentric, evolutionary, or civilizational analysis of what I call non-"Europe" as exemplified by his acceptance of what Levy-Bruhl calls the "savage mind" of the African Azande.

In a remarkable rebuff to Habermas's Eurocentrism, Kim has documented that "(a) scientists are not more able to distinguish what is social from what is objective than the Azande, and (b) scientists are not freer to express dissenting views than the Azande, and therefore their discourse not closer to the ideal speech situation than that of the Azande".

The Chinese perspective: The work of the Chinese sage Zhu-xi shows the nearest parallel to thoroughgoing rationalism in Chinese thought. Zhu-xi believed that a single reason, "the Way," was at work in all human minds that enabled the understanding of the world. However, classical Chinese philosophy does not readily agree with Habermas's distinctions of rationality, or his use of formal pragmatics in the theory of communicative action.

At least three basic principles of Chinese philosophy-embodiment of reason in experience, epistemological-pragmatic unity, and infinite interpretation-appear to conflict with the Occidental concept of rationality. The epistemological separation of reason and experience rooted in the ontological separation of form and substance stands in contrast to the Chinese view of unity of all things.

Shalin points out that in Habermas's communicative

action theory, reason appears primarily as thinking (consciousness, understanding, cognition) with no obvious relation to the human body and the noncognitive processes (emotion, feeling, sentiment).

Shalin says that Habermas shows little appreciation for "nondiscursive communication." Because Habermas elevates the cognitive form of universality above all others, he "inadvertently devalues human experience as merely private and intellectually mute". Shalin implicitly agrees with Chinese philosophy when he asserts that to "divest reason from living experience is to disembody it" and that "knowledge uninformed by feelings and stripped of emotive elements can be rational without being reasonable".

As Kupperman points out, neither Confucius nor Mencius had anything to say about reason if one thinks of reason along the lines of what is operative in mathematics or in formal logic. Although irrationalism had no place in Chinese thought, philosophical Daoism remained anti-rationalist in contrast to orthodox Confucianism, which was often "rational" but not "rationalistic," and Later Mohism, which was "rationalistic".

Furthermore, as Cheng explains, "Reason is not simply logic as such; it is also the respecting of norms and conventions that have been accepted in the community and that have a practical and aesthetic value". Because the concept of rationality in China differs from Habermas's concept, its relevance to the emergence of a political public sphere, where citizens put forth and defend their claims based on communicative rationality alone, becomes a moot point.

Jung says that the Confucian idea of ren (humanity) emphasizes intersubjectivity or sociality. Thus, Habermas comes closer to Chinese philosophy in general when he nearly concedes rationality for communicative action presupposed on the actor's social world and the validity claim of normative rightness.

However, he adds the caveat that "the teleological structure is fundamental to all concepts of action". Responding to his critics, Habermas says, "The critique of reason contends that every tradition, worldview, or culture has inscribed its own-always incommensurable-standards for what is true and false.

But this leveling critique fails to notice the peculiar self-referential character of the discourse of modernity". However, this defence is not adequate to buttress Habermas's view that the public sphere must invariably lie between the state and the economy, and his insistence that it is the space where citizens put forth and defend their claims based on communicative rationality alone.

Glocalizing Habermas's concept of communicative rationality-the three-world paradigm requiring three types of validity claims-in terms of classical Chinese philosophy presents a dilemma. The principle of infinite interpretation states:

Reality can be understood in an indefinite number of ways, and there is absolutely no fixed procedure for generating understanding because the object of understanding has no absolutely fixed nature, and there are no two things which are the same.

Based on the elaboration of this principle by Daoist philosopher Zhuangzi, Cheng provides two conclusions in terms of modern communication theory: first, participants should explore parallel modes of representation, determine a specific point of view, but use many points of view to illuminate what is communicated; second, communication should not be limited to the application of conventional means, such as language. Thus, in relation to the second conclusion, Habermas's formal pragmatics-communicative action in the form of argumentation or discourse-represents a limiting case.

The project of provincializing "Europe" does not call for "a simplistic, out of-hand rejection of modernity, liberal values, science, reason, grand narratives, totalizing explanations, and so on". In this sense, Tong (2000) appears to play the role of subaltern scholar in China, for he sees parallels between Habermas and the modernity advocate Li Dazhao, who tried to blend communism and liberalism into an organic unity. Li sought to find a middle path between communitarianism and liberalism or universalism. Because China is, at present, trying to combine socialism with a capitalist market economy, Tong asserts that "a modern civil society as conceived by Habermas can help to tame not only the subsystem of state administration, but also the subsystem of market economy" by, inter alia, setting normative standards for the economic system.

Tong, as an apologist for Habermas, ignores the fit of the Chinese concept of rationality to that of Habermas, as well as the potentially deleterious effects of "globalization."

DE-EMPHASIS OF NON-WESTERN HISTORY/ PHILOSOPHY

As Chakrabarty mentions, philosophers and thinkers have produced theories that embraced the entirety of humanity in relative, and sometimes absolute, ignorance of the majority of humankind. Habermas ignores non-Western history altogether when he traces the emergence of a literary public sphere to Europe alone.

He fails to acknowledge the existence of a literary sphere (undifferentiated as "public" or "private") in China, where widespread block printing produced a literati several centuries prior to Europe. Tsien writes

In both (East and West) printing promoted culture, widened the scope of subjects that interested scholars, helped shift the bias from religious to classical learning, popularized education, spread literacy, and enriched art and literature; though it did so to a different degree in each.

[In China, printing] facilitated the continuity and niversality of the written language and thus became an important vehicle for sustaining the cultural tradition [as evident] in the printing of the Confucian classics and similar material for the civil service examinations.

Moreover, Tsien says, China had always produced an optimum number of books without pecuniary motivation because of its extensive literary tradition. This suggests the existence of a literary sphere in China at the time when China was also the centre of global trade. Poetry made up the mainstream of Chinese literature. Tam points out that in the ancient Confucian ideal, poetry served "both functions of expressing personal wishes and admonishing the ruling body as well as the people". Daoist philosophers Laozi and Zhuangzi were renowned poets as well. The poetry of Li Bo, Wang Wei, and Du Fu marked the reign of Tang emperor Xuan-zong.

Poet Bo Zhui appeared thereafter with two of the dominant figures in the Confucian revival: Yan Yu and Liu Zong-yuan. Another notable development was the appearance of fiction writers who produced the so-called "tales of marvels." Drama flourished during the Yuan dynasty. Ming China stood out for its voluminous scholarship in many realms.

The short story and the novel developed, e.g., The Romance of the Three Kingdoms, The Water Margin, The Journey to the West, and The Golden Lotus. Tang Xianzu emerged as a leading playwright. The Ming literati were avid bibliophiles, both collectors and publishers. They established public libraries, such as the Dien-i-ko collection of the Fan family at Ming-po.

Scholars put together huge anthologies of esteemed writings of the entire Chinese heritage. An example was the 11,000-volume Yong-luo-da-dian of 1407. Yan Shen, one of the all-around literati of the Ming period, produced poetry and belles lettres in huge quantities.

Weber too refers to China's literary tradition of more than 2000 years. The literati of the feudal period were officially called bo-shi (living libraries). Weber says the literati were "opponents of feudalism from the very beginning"; and "the originally free mental mobility of the literati came to a halt" with the growth of Chinese prebendalism. The literati exhibited "a highly exclusive and bookish literary education".

However, a bourgeois political public sphere did not materialize in China as it did in Europe probably because such a concept was inconsistent with Confucian philosophy. De Bary and Bloom say that in 1017 the Northern Song set up a board of policy criticism (jianyuan), a sort of political sphere identified in the West with "civil society," by which "public opinion" could be brought to bear on the formulation of state policy.

The board, which "was intended to provide oversight, policy options, and even criticism for the emperor himself lasted only 65 years when autocratic rule resumed. Scholar-poet Su Shi lamented the subversion of the board and the Censorate (yushi tai) in his Ten Thousand Word Memorial of 1069.

During the Ming Dynasty, De Bary says, China had "no infrastructure by which popular sentiment could become informed, articulated, or autonomously structured so as to contribute its authentic voice to the decision-making process".

Habermas, despite his original ardor for universalism, failed to analyse why a bourgeois political sphere failed in China despite its long-standing literary tradition. Nevertheless, Habermas has argued that regardless of different cultural traditions, "autarkic isolation against external influences is no longer an option in today's [globalized] world".

The underlying presumption behind this assertion is that modernization requires the absorption of Europe-centered "universals" by the "non-modern" non-"Europe"-a point of view that receives qualified support from subaltern historians.

Despite the absence of printing, a literary sphere of the Brahmans (scholars/priests caste) and the Kshatriyas (warrior caste) emerged in India as well, particularly during the Gupta dynasty (320-550). Epics, lyrics, drama, and fiction flourished under literary giants like Kalidasa and Vishnu Sharman. Other celebrated literary figures followed them in the seventh century: Arnaru, Bana, Bhartrihari, and Dandin, among others.

Of course, India's literary tradition goes far back to the Vedas (dated from about 16th to 10th centuries BCE) and Upanishads (dated from eighth to fifth centuries BCE). India also produced the Buddhist Tripitakas, which it exported to the Far East, and the epics Mahabharata (attributed to Vyasa) and Ramayana (attributed to Valmiki) well before the Gupta period. The Vedas, the Upanishads, and the epics were so much a part of Hinduism that they affected the lifeworld of Vaisyas (merchant caste) and Sudras (laborer caste) as well. It appears that Habermas chose not to compare and contrast these non-Western literary spheres with the "unique" European literary public sphere.

Despite the alleged Eurocentric bias of Weber's Protestant-ethic thesis, Habermas has leaned heavily on Weber's analysis of non-Western religious-metaphysical worldviews to derive the claimed "universalism" for his work. Although Habermas points out the deficiencies of the Weberian analysis, he does not do so with a thorough grounding of non-Western philosophers, philosophy, and history.

However, in the long chapter on Weber's theory of rationalization, he shows a degree of second-hand awareness of non-Western religion and philosophy. He accepts Weber's classification, according to content, of Buddhism and Hinduism as cosmocentric and world rejecting, Confucianism and Daoism as cosmocentric and world affirming, and Judaism and Christianity as theocentric and world rejecting. On attitudes toward the world based on rejection of the world in salvation religions, he again accepts Weber's analysis that Judaism and Christianity exhibit mastery of the world while Hinduism exhibits flight from the world.

On the rationalization potential of worldviews, he places the Orient in the low category: Hinduism low on the ethical dimension, and Confucianism low on the cognitive dimension; and he places the Occident in the high category: Judaism and Christianity high on the ethical dimension, and Greek philosophy high on the cognitive dimension. He comments, "It is remarkable that the two worldviews with the structurally greatest potential for rationalization came together within the same European tradition".

Habermas says that rationalized Western culture seems to be developing in the direction of a morally skeptical, purely purposive-rational type of action although early Buddhism provides evidence of the converse case of rationalization of value orientations while impeding purposive-rational action. Weber had identified early Buddhism as a rationalized ethic "in the sense of constant, alert mastery of all natural instinctive drives," but which at the same time leads its followers away from getting hold of the world in a disciplined way.

As examples of irrationality of action that are technically rationalized, Weber had mentioned "methods of mortificatory or of magical asceticism or contemplation, in their most consistent forms, for instance in yoga or in the manipulation of the prayer machines of later Buddhism". On the other hand Weber, in his book The Religion of India, hailed the linkage between caste and karma as a pure product of rational ethical thought.

Weber wrote: "Karma doctrine transformed the world into a strictly rational, ethically-determined cosmos; it represents the most consistent theodicy ever produced by history"-a point that Habermas fails to record.

Habermas does not deal with Islam because "Weber was not able to carry out his plan to include Christianity and Islam in his comparative studies" of religious-metaphysical worldviews. It's puzzling why Habermas depended predominantly on Weber's rather controversial interpretations of Asian religious philosophies without a serious attempt to seek other, balanced interpretations of both Western and non-Western authorities.

In passing, Habermas (1984) does refer to Joseph Needham's "pioneering investigations," which show that the Chinese "were evidently more successful than the West in developing theoretical knowledge and in using this knowledge for practical purposes" until the 15th century. Therefore, Habermas suggests that the "rationalization potential of these [East Asian] traditions might have been studied first of all from the standpoint of cognitive and not of ethical rationalization" as Weber had done.

Habermas expresses his suspicion that "the Chinese traditions would appear in another light if one considered them primarily from the standpoint of theory rather than of ethics and compared them with the classical Greek traditions". Tong (2000) latches on to this Habermasian concession to Chinese traditions to argue that Habermas's "theory of modernity and modernization based on his theory of communicative action is most relevant to modernization in China and provides the ideal basis for a new rewarding interpretation of the Chinese discourse of modernization and the idea of 'socialist modernization with Chinese characteristics'" even though Habermas "rarely mentioned China, or developing countries in general, in his discussions".

Tong admits that the Japanese case of modernization "poses difficult problems to Habermas's theory of modernity and modernization". Yet, Tong goes on to assert that the Chinese tradition of dialectical logic-the paired concepts of ti (substance) and yong (function)-that contemporary neo-Confucians like Liang Shuming, Mou Zongsan, and Yu Yingshi frequently used in the discourse of modernization can also be looked at in terms of lifeworld (ti) and system (yong) or value rationality (ti) and instrumental rationality (yong). Tong (2000) sees much merit in Habermasian theory in contrast to Huang. Tong disregards the criticisms of Fleming, who says that "Habermas's theory is not universalistic enough because the basic categories of the theory are gender coded".

Tong rejects the criticisms of Habermas's theory of modernity because they relate only to the dynamics of modernization whereas Habermas was mainly concerned with the logic of modernization. Tong goes on to say that the anomalies found in the Japanese case against Habermas's theory "can be seen as anomalies of Japanese society itself according to this theory".

Tong skips Huang's point about the "third realm" in China. Rather than "glocalizing" Habermasian theory, Tong glorifies it to support "the official Chinese programme of modernization", namely, a socialist modernization with Chinese characteristics, with high emphasis on science and democracy.

Provincializing Habermasian theory requires the inclusion of the missing literary spheres in China and India, among other histories, and modifying the emphasis on the distinction between the public and the private spheres. We cannot skip the past to enter the future. As Chakrabarty says, "Pasts are there in taste, in practices of embodiment, in the cultural training the senses have received over generations".

IDEALIZATION OF LIBERAL DEMOCRACY

Even though Fleming has pointed out the flaws in Habermas's expansionist strategy in relation to rationality, Habermas presents communicative rationality (associated with the lifeworld) as the ingredient that lends "universalism" to his critical theory. The problem, however, lies in linking this society-contextualized (self-referential) rationality with his idealization of liberal democracy.

Habermas wanted to make "democracy an integral part of philosophy" because he saw the need to avoid a repetition of the traumas of German history. His idealization of liberal democracy-the liberal constitutional state prior to its transformation into the constitutional social-welfare state-implicit in his theory of communicative action and the concept of public sphere becomes explicit in his later political essays, with statements such as

- "Asiatic societies cannot participate in capitalistic modernization without taking advantage of the achievements of an individualistic legal order."
- "These dictatorships [Singapore, Malaysia, Taiwan, and China] consider themselves authorized by the 'right of social development'-apparently understood as a collective right-to postpone the realization of liberal rights and rights of political participation until their countries have attained a level of economic development that allows them to satisfy the basic material needs of the population equally,".

Li has already documented the incompatibility of Confucianism with liberal democracy. However, Perera says that democracy, in its sense as rule by majority decision, has historically appeared in three forms: direct democracy, representative democracy, and liberal or constitutional, democracy. Sharma says that his analysis of the Vedic texts reveals the existence of at least four forms of "government by discussion" in the early Vedic period from 1500 BCE to 1000 BCE. Buddhist and Jain texts, as well as the works of Pänini and Kautilya, also attest to the existence of a number of republican states from 600 BCE to 480 BCE.

Domes defines (liberal) democracy in terms of three principles: liberty (guaranteed and institutionalized human rights for everyone and guaranteed and institutionalized civil rights for all adult citizens), equality (securing equal life chances for all citizens), and pluralism (guaranteed existence and operation of competing organizations that articulate and aggregate the different political, economic, social, and cultural interests).

His definition also includes three basic rules: people's sovereignty, division of powers, and competitive elections. Schumpeter provides a minimal definition of democracy: "institutional arrangement for arriving at political decisions in which individuals acquire the power to decide by means of a competitive struggle for the people's vote".

Habermas's concept of the public sphere is primarily related to the democratic value of pluralism, which includes the division of powers. However, his concept of rationality fails to appear as an integral characteristic of democracy in most definitions. Of the three strands of Chinese philosophy-Confucianism, Daoism, and Chan Buddhism-Buddhism comes closest to the values of democracy.

The democratic value of liberty is compatible with both Daoism and Buddhism; equality is both a democratic and Buddhist value; and freedom is a characteristic that Daoism (negative freedom), Buddhism (positive freedom), and democracy (negative or positive freedom) all share. Li has argued that because the Chinese can adjust their minds to accommodate three different philosophies, it would not be too difficult for them to accommodate democratic values as well.

Ironically, this shows the greater capacity of the Chinese, as well as others in the so-called Orient, to accommodate pluralistic thinking much more readily than their counterparts in the Occident. Habermas is an advocate of "deliberative democracy," in which a government's laws and institutions would be a reflection of free and open rational discussion in the public sphere.

Habermas claims that the "universalism" of his theory of communicative action comes from communicative rationality, which denotes agreement on propositional truth (in the objective domain of culture and science), moral rightness (in the social domain of society), and sincerity (in the subjective domain of personality).

Thus the cultural and social context of the individual determines what is rational. If that were the case, how that process ipso facto leads to an ideal democracy incorporating liberty, equality, and pluralism needs further elucidation. Would communicative rationality based on the cultural and social context of Confucianism promote the ideals of liberal democracy when they are inconsistent with Confucian values?

Tu Wei-ming says that the dominant ideology in the Western world today is still that of 18th-century Enlightenment marked by "the arrogance of rationality". Tu claims that Habermas's writing holds that the task of Enlightenment is in fact far from completed, and that this state of being unfinished explains all of the social problems that have surfaced in the course of modernization.

Therefore, our historical task is not to find a new model but to reform the old value system by placing greater emphasis on the ideas of liberty and equality, and to reconfigure the democratic system so as to assure greater freedom and a fairer distribution of power and wealth.

Tu's view stands in contrast to that of Tong and the subaltern school. Can liberal democracy dominate the world through globalization? Gunaratne points out that libertarianism cannot exist without its complement authoritarianism. The principles of part-whole interdetermination and the dialectical completion of relative polarities in Chinese philosophy, as well as the revelation of modern physics that every particle has an antiparticle, attest to this. A revision of Habermasian theory requires the dissociation of communicative rationality with libertarian democracy alone, although this should be the most desirable outcome. The public sphere, by Habermas's own admission, has been rendered ineffective by advanced capitalism. Under such circumstances, the prospects for a global public sphere, which would further strengthen Western domination, appear to be unrealistic.

On the other hand, as subaltern scholars would argue, "modernity" demands the propagation of universals enshrined in History 1 (such as democracy, liberalism, rationality, liberty, equality, and pluralism) for which the subjugated colonial people also fought. The continual tension between these universals and the axial-age Eastern philosophies would engender creative solutions reflecting what Chakrabarty calls the "translational processes through which concepts and practices are made one's own"-the grist for narrating History 2s.

HABERMAS AND THEORY OF LIVING SYSTEMS

I shall now examine Habermas's critical theory through the lens of the emerging theory of living systems-incorporating the theories of autopoiesis, cognition, and dissipative structures -to show that operationally closed but structurally and cognitively open subsystems comprising a dissipative structure like the world-system form a formidable barrier against the emergence of a global public sphere.

Although Capra (2002) praises Habermas for "integrating insights from the natural sciences, the social sciences and from cognitive philosophies, while rejecting the limitations of positivism", Capra's assessment is based largely on Baert's review of 20th-century social theory.

Habermas's underestimation of Eastern philosophy stands in stark contrast to Capra's attempt to show the parallels between modern physics and Eastern "mysticism." Moreover, Habermas's quasi-systems theory lacks the three fundamental characteristics that Capra says are essential for a new scientific understanding of living systems: autopoiesis, the pattern of organization of living systems as defined by Maturana and Varela; cognition, the process of life as defined by Maturana and Varela; and dissipative structure, the structure of living systems as defined by Prigogine and Stengers.

Habermas has subjected his critical theory, which he calls deep hermeneutics, to many of the weaknesses inherent in nomothetic social science by merging in it both empirical-analytic and historical-hermeneutic disciplines. Although some may argue that Habermas's theory is "critical-hermeneutical rather than analytical" because his "notion of publicness, particularly in the sense of critical publicity, can only play the role of some kind of comparative standard or of a radical democratic vision on the normative level," Habermas thinks otherwise.

For Habermas says unequivocally "any sociology that claims to be a theory of society has to face the problem of rationality simultaneously on the metatheoretical, methodological, and empirical levels". Moreover, Habermas identifies his work as a "theory of society based on the theory of communicative action", and as a "theory of modernity"-a quasi-systems theory sans non-linear dynamics or autopoiesis.

First, Habermas explicitly distances his quasi-systems theory from Luhmann's "boundary maintaining and autopoietic" systems theory, which says that "actions and interactions can be understood as psychological and social systems that form environments for and reciprocally observe one another". Habermas criticizes Luhmann's systems functionalism for cutting "itself off from the intuitive knowledge of the lifeworld and its members".

Elsewhere, Habermas expresses "fundamental doubts about the usefulness of a systems theoretic concept of social crisis" because of the difficulty of systems theory to clearly determine "the boundaries and persistence of social systems". Thus, by excluding autopoiesis as a feature of society, Habermasian theory fails to meet the first of Capra's criteria for a new scientific understanding of living systems.

The key characteristic of a living network, including any

social system, is that it continually produces itself. This is the pattern of life called autopoiesis. Because all components of an autopoietic network are produced by other components in the network, the entire system is operationally closed even though it is structurally open to its environment (e.g., other social systems) with regard to the flow of energy and matter (e.g., goods, services, and information).

Autopoiesis is the pattern underlying the phenomenon of self-organization. In this sense, autopoiesis of each social system acts as a natural defence against globalization. What is more likely to happen is adaptation, which I call glocalization. Thus, the emergence of a global public sphere is incompatible with the theory of living systems. Habermas adamantly maintains, "I am by no means sure whether a surplus value will accrue to social theory from the most recent developments which systems theory has undergone and which have been labeled autopoiesis".

Second, although Habermas deals extensively with rationality, he does not deal with cognition-the next requirement for a new scientific understanding of living systems-as the process of life. Cognition, the activity involved in the continual embodiment of the system's pattern of organization, is inextricably linked to autopoiesis. Interpreting the Santiago theory, Capra says

Human cognition involves language and abstract thinking, and thus symbols and mental representations, but abstract thought is only a small part of human cognition and generally is not the basis for our everyday decisions and actions. Human decisions are never completely rational but are always colored by emotion, and human thought is always embedded in the bodily sensations and processes that contribute to the full spectrum of cognition.

Eastern philosophy, in general, is consistent with this interpretation of cognition as a continual bringing forth of a world through the process of living. Habermas focuses on rationality as if emotion were less significant in human decision making.

The theory of living systems is at odds with the

Habermasian preoccupation with rationality, a concept that reached a peak during the Age of Enlightenment when science and rationality fit hand in glove. Nonlinear dynamics, however, has made it abundantly clear that a preoccupation with rationality is rather inconsistent with how things occur in reality in a predominantly nonlinear universe.

The phenomenon of nonlocality (or nonseparability that transcends space-time) and the uncertainty principle in quantum physics make a mockery of rationality. Luhmann's self-referential autopoietic systems theory also rejects the Habermasian system's obsession with consensus-oriented communicative action because communication requires dissent to continue its operation. "If universal consensus could ever be reached, it would terminate the system's autopoiesis".

Third, despite Habermas's "integrating insights," he remains within the fold of classical linear thinking. Habermas does not look at society as a far-from-equilibrium dissipative structure-another essential requirement for a new scientific understanding of living systems. Gunaratne sums up the underlying presumptions of classical (social) science as follows:

- That precisely determinable initial conditions determined every element in natural processes. (Heisenberg's uncertainty principle challenges this presumption.)
- That trajectories of most natural phenomena are linear and that such trajectories always tend to return to equilibrium conditions. (Quantum jumps do not follow predictable trajectories. The second law of thermodynamics says equilibrium is virtual "death.")
- That time is not relevant to the understanding of natural processes because all laws are mathematically "reversible" as the fundamental relations of those processes never evolve. (Time may not be relevant to quantum particles, which cannot have a history because they die quickly. But the arrow of time applies to all "matter.")
- That knowledge is universal and can ultimately be

expressed in simple covering laws. (The Aspect experiment's proof of nonlocality-the superluminal interaction of correlated quanta beyond space-time-defies causation.)

Thus, classical (social) science presumed the ability to predict outcomes with the knowledge of the initial conditions and the relevant universal law. Although Habermas calls his theory of communicative action "less a promise than a conjecture", he apparently developed it as an empirically testable "simple covering law," which can both predict and retrodict. It clearly reflects the attributes of determinism, linearity, reversibility, and reductionism.

The concept of the public sphere illustrates this point well. The 16th-century take-off of modern capitalism in Europe resulted in the creation of a potent bourgeois civil society, which initiated a political public sphere (preceded by a literary public sphere) for the rational discussion of issues within a framework of deliberative democracy.

When these initial conditions appear elsewhere, they would reproduce similar linear developments conducive to deliberative democracy irrespective of time. The structural-functionalist modernization paradigm, which presumed that nation-states changed in parallel lines from tradition to modernity, belonged to the same genre of Newtonianism.

On the other hand, nonlinear dynamics asserts that irreversibility (or the arrow of time, which can only move forward) leads to continuing change and increasing complexity in open systems, where even a small input of change could trigger positive feedback that engenders massive, unpredictable structural changes.

Thus, the theoretical approach of nonlinear dynamics precludes the repeatability of the circumstances that produced Europe's bourgeois public sphere or the so-called Protestant ethic within the world system of interdependent states. Van Ginneken demonstrates the importance of positive feedback, which involves amplification and circular reaction, in understanding communicative action-a phenomenon that Habermas ignores.

Whereas Habermas analyses communication solely in terms of rationality, Van Ginneken asserts There is hardly any rational behaviour that is not colored by accompanying emotions, and there is hardly any emotional behaviour that does not also have an underlying ratio.

The theory of communicative action says that social disequilibrium occurs when the imperatives of the system dimensions, engendered by cognitive-purposive rationality, clash with the lifeworld dimension of cultural reproduction, social integration, and socialization. Habermas says that in modernized societies, "stubborn systemic disequilibria"-in the form of crises or pathologies in the lifeworld-appear because of such disturbances.

Prigogine and Stengers have pointed out that far-from-equilibrium conditions are the norm in all dissipative systems, which thrive in open system environments. Had Habermas adopted the dissipative-systems approach of nonlinear dynamics, he could have explained the resulting tension between lifeworld and systemic dimensions as reflecting the usual far-from-equilibrium state associated with all dissipative structures.

Habermas explains that he used the system-environment model of the general systems theory for his two-level concept of society because "it is more suited to application in the social sciences than are the earlier biological equilibrium models".

My thesis of the uncoupling of lifeworld and system only implies that the dynamics of demarcation vis-à-vis a more complex environment infiltrates into society itself... The system model.. submits that subsystems mark themselves off from one another in the course of processes of differentiation and define themselves reciprocally as environments.

He adds that the systems model is appropriate for purely analytical use, as does Parsons, but not for essentialist use, as does Luhmann. Habermasian theory, in its current formulation, presumes that social equilibrium is the norm. Thermodynamically, however, equilibrium means the virtual "death" of a system.

Habermas (2001b) praises Weber for brilliantly conjoining

the rational choice theory on the purposive rationality of individual actors and the systems theory on the functional rationality of large organizations. Parsons used Weber's formulation as a reference system.

Habermas says, "Unlike many systems theorists of a more recent vintage, Parsons was not tempted to forget the constitution of the object domain 'action' or 'society' in the process of applying the systems model to it". This makes it clear that Habermas did not favour the new systems theory or nonlinear dynamics.

He points out that systems theory isolates and overgeneralizes the systemic aspect while action theory does the same for the lifeworld aspect; the theory of structural differentiation, on the other hand, does not sufficiently separate either of these two aspects.

Because the theories of modernity derived from these three approaches remained insensitive to what Marx called "real abstractions," Habermas says he formulated his theory so as to get at such abstractions "through an analysis that at once traces the rationalization of lifeworlds and the growth in complexity of media-steered subsystems".

In other words, he rejected the "systems theorists of more recent vintage," as well as their reliance on nonlinear dynamics, because of the primacy he attached to the Occidental concept of rationality. For him, the arrow of time was not a matter of concern.

Habermas (2001b) goes on to explain, "For systems theory, modern societies collapse into a multiplicity of independently operating, self-referential closed [my emphasis] systems, which constitute environments for one another and can communicate with one another only indirectly, through mutual observation".

However, he omits the distinctive aspects of a living system-the pattern of organization, the process of life, and the structure. It's the pattern that's operationally closed. The dissipative structure itself is always open to its environment. Referring to human rights, Habermas observes, "The autarkic isolation against external influences is no longer an option in today's world". To be sure, it is the fact that a living system is cognitively opens that allows external influences; and it is the fact that it is operationally closed that allows each system to maintain its distinctive culture and choose from among the external influences. Is it not autopoiesis that prevents cultural annihilation through globalization/Westernization?

This monograph has documented that Habermas's emancipatory critical theory of society and modernity is a totalizing Eurocentric product, which contains some significant "universalistic" elements. Habermas carried further the sociological preconditions of universalism that Parsons set through the crucial dimension of rationality.

Piaget allowed Habermas to claim that universalistic critical thought is grounded in the normal development of the human mind. Habermas used formal pragmatics to claim universalism for his theory of communicative action. One may construe the uncritical globalization of such "universalistic" theory as a kind of Eurocentric hegemony as we move from theory to practice.

We can circumvent the potential dangers of Eurocentric hegemony through the process of glocalization (revising Eurocentric theory to fit non-"Europe") or, in the jargon of subaltern studies, through provincializing "Europe." The latter means discarding the chaff and retaining the wheat irrespective of Eurocentrism in theory.

From the postcolonial perspective, the emancipatory elements of Habermasian critical theory provide a useful purpose against non-democratic tendencies in non-"Europe," for the colonies too were participants in upholding liberty, equality, and other rights in the fight against European imperialism.

Habermas's theory of communicative action was an attempt to clarify the normative foundations of a critical theory of society, and to provide an alternative to the philosophy of history on which the earlier critical theory of the Frankfurt School relied. Habermas comments that he "attempted to free historical materialism from its philosophical ballast".

He constructed a theory of rationality to establish a cooperative relationship between social science and philosophy. The task he completed was indeed monumental. Yet, as this monograph has documented, his achievement suffers from vast cultural shortcomings. The project of glocalizing the public sphere and communicative rationality should proceed.

In implementing this project, we should incorporate the history of the literary sphere in China and India that preceded the bourgeois literary sphere in Europe. We should also note that democracy had an early start in pre-Buddhist India with republics such as those of Sakiyas and Vajjians. Because Habermas is involved in the implicit political project of promoting democracy, linking his theory to the history of democracy in the East would be a worthy strategy.

Global public sphere: Although a global public sphere may appear to be on the horizon because of the ongoing process of globalization, a euphemism for Western domination within the context of the highly lopsided telecommunication infrastructure of the world, the very absence of distinct public and private spheres in many societies in non-"Europe," renders such a concept unviable. The pattern of autopoiesis in living systems would engender local public spheres, if any.

A revision of this concept is imperative because of the prevalence of the "third realm," which is neither public nor private, in many societies. Thus, the call by Habermas (2001b) to bring global economic networks-the postnational constellation-under democratic political control is premature. As Hill (2002) observes, Habermas's model of global political participation is devoid of a global, normative standpoint.

Hill points out that a single public sphere may not befit multicultural societies. Moreover, Hill says, principles of popular sovereignty, commonly embedded in national constitutions, are not necessarily applicable at the global level. In addition, "critics have targeted a perceived ethnocentric bias in the universalistic ambitions of the [public sphere] theory".

Sparks (2000) has concluded that there is at present no global public sphere because of regulation and control of satellites, and the small audience for global channels and global newspapers.

He has pointed out that the local public sphere is not an aspect of globalization. Furthermore, Sparks has said that the function of the state-oriented public sphere remains crucial, and that, very far from replacing the state, the new localities need the state to represent them.

Communicative rationality: As documented in this monograph, contrary to Weber's Eurocentric analysis, there is much in Eastern philosophy that pertains to communicative rationality.

Buddhist philosophy encourages the validity claim of propositional truth through empirical observation. Both Buddhist and Chinese philosophy recognize the validity claim of rightness (conventional truth) derived through social consensus.

The provincializing of the theory of communicative action on these lines would make the theory more appealing to non-"Europe" and help bring nonWestern theories back to visibility in the global academy.

The project of provincializing or glocalizing Habermasian theory should also involve looking at the public sphere, communicative rationality, modernity, and related concepts through the lens of the theory of living systems and world-system analysis.

These theories are more consistent with the cosmological philosophy of the so-called Orient, which has unabashed faith in the ability of nature to spontaneously derive order out of chaos ad infinitum. Occidental "science," which slighted the Oriental "myths," used empirical measurements to derive universal "laws" without pausing to think about the unseen Supreme Ultimate (in the Daoist sense) behind such (teleological?) "laws." Thus, "myth" is common to all humanity.

Scholars should reconcile the separate worlds of Western and Eastern philosophy and theory. Balagangadhara (1998), on the one hand, attributes the East-West separation to Orientalism: Social sciences generate Orientalism when the West looks at other cultures.

Looked at in isolation from Orientalism, social sciences are how the West experiences itself. Social sciences teach us about Western culture. Patomäki (2002), on the other hand, asserts, "Globalization as a coming together of humanity requires an open-ended dialogue about philosophical and religious fundamentals".

Chapter 12

Re-telling and Talking about Telling

We begin this discussion of incest disclosure with disclosure of the story that led us to this place. We first met as colleagues when our careers brought us to the same university. We became friends and also, over time, became collaborators on research projects that integrated our interests in community development, intercultural communication, health communication strategies, and women's issues.

In 1998 this relationship acquired a new, if temporary, definition, that of research interviewer/interviewee. When Leigh was working on a study about the communication dialectics experienced by incest survivors, Robbin, a survivor, asked to be interviewed as part of the study. The in-depth interview resulted in a transcript filled with Robbin's narratives within narratives, and the interview process and our subsequent talks about that process became our shared story.

We often spoke of our desire to "do something" with what we learned, to tell others about this lived experience, but how we should do this remained problematic. The last year has been one of change for us; our conversations now unfold via email and telephone, but we have agreed that it is time to try to tell this story.

This chapter then is about the significance of telling the story in all its dimensions for incest survivors. It is also about disclosure and relationships, our friendship relationship, our relationship as research interviewer and interviewee, and our present relationship as co-authors. Influenced by the experimental moment in ethnography, we privilege lived experience, including here the survivor's tale, the listener's story, and the research collaboration.

Further, we use our self-conscious, subjective involvement in the creation of the text. In this text we reflexively examine ourselves as subjects and objects, and through the dialogic form become both authors of our experience and audience to each other.

Finally, we juxtapose this lived experience against the codification of experience as represented in traditional research practices. Through this juxtapositioning we hope that as readers engage the text, understanding emerges "in the spaces between".

DISCLOSING PRIVATE INFORMATION

Accounting for the complexities of disclosing private information in interpersonal relationships has been an important focus of recent disclosure research. Framed by an understanding that personal relationships are challenged by contradictory demands for autonomy and intimacy, an ongoing tension between the desire to keep some matters of the self private and the equally strong desire to reveal aspects of the self characterizes the disclosure process.

Using boundary as an organizing metaphor, this process has been represented in communication boundary management theory. Briefly, in this perspective individuals establish boundaries demarcating the private and the public and seek to control access to private information through the loosening or tightening of these boundaries.

According to Petronio, this public-private dynamic rests on feelings of vulnerability or risk for both the discloser and the recipient. Guided by a set of acquired relational rules, individuals engage in a potentially complex calculus of factors including but not limited to the length of relationship, level of trust, type of information, and relevant contextual factors in order to determine vulnerability and, ultimately, to manage the private-public boundary.

Clearly, not all private information carries the same valence in the assessment of vulnerability. In particular the revelation of stigmatizing information intensifies risk to the discloser and the recipient alike. Stigma refers to a stable characteristic or attribute of an individual that is perceived as damaging to an individual's reputation.

In this definition stigma appears to be owned by the individual, but in truth stigmatization is a relational process controlled and defined as "other" by the dominant group. In Goffman's terms, stigmatized persons fit within two categories: the "discredited" where the stigma is known and apparent to others, and the "discreditable" where the stigma is not immediately known or apparent, such as being HIV positive or being a survivor of sexual abuse. In the latter form, the potential for stigmatization arises through the specific communicative choice to disclose.

For the discreditable stigmatized individual then, managing the disclosure process is critical and complicated. The complexities of this process can be found in the disclosure experiences of adult incest survivors. For them the power to reveal risks the possibility of significant loss (e.g., loss of family relationships, friendships, and romantic partners) and marginalization (e.g., the assertion and/or intensification of social stigmatization).

Further, the discourse practices associated with incest disclosure present survivors with "two intertwined, and paradoxical challenges: reliving the communicative dilemmas of their childhood relations with the perpetrator and other family members and managing the complicated communicative dilemmas of discourse as adults".

Nonetheless, adult survivors have been encouraged to tell their stories as a part of their healing. While researchers and practitioners acknowledge that this disclosure process is neither prescriptive nor linear, specific disclosive acts such as the initial disclosure of the incestuous relationship to another or disclosure to an intimate partner, have been viewed as hallmarks in the recovery process.

It is our desire to examine specific disclosure forms found

in the experience of one survivor. First, we examine telling the secret and then re-telling the survivor story within personal relationships such as with family members and friends. Second, we wish to address the disclosure practice of talking about telling, disclosure in the confidential research interview and the consequent disclosure in the public domain of scholarly research.

In this process we find ourselves, as friends and scholars, engaged in the ongoing struggle with the boundary between private and public.

FEMINIST STANDPOINT THEORY AND THE LAYERED ACCOUNT

It is our belief that feminist standpoint theory offers an important framework from which to understand the experience of incest and the significance of survivors' telling about their experiences. Further, we believe that the layered account provides a method for representing experience that captures the current epistemological tension between commonality and difference in feminist scholarship.

We present our argument in three steps: (1) we describe the historical view of feminist standpoint theory; (2) we briefly sketch the commonality-difference dialectic in feminist theorizing; and (3) we outline the utility of the layered account to accommodating that tension.

Historically, feminist standpoint theory rests on the assumptions that all knowledge is socially situated and that what has usually been taken to be "real" knowledge has been based primarily on the lives of men in dominant races, classes, and cultures. Such knowledge claims function to confine women and other marginalized persons to "Other," or outsider status.

Thus, in the view of feminist standpoint theory, the creation and legitimation of knowledge claims are key to the maintenance of-but also to the alteration of-unjust power systems.

Because dominant knowledge claims are based on men's lives and experiences, feminist standpoint theory advocates the use of women's everyday lives as the foundation for constructing knowledge and, ultimately, for the emancipation of women.

Standpoint feminism encourages women (and other marginalized persons) to discuss their lived experiences. When women speak from and about their reality, unseen aspects of the dominant social structures are revealed, a "consciousness raising" occurs, and acts of resistance emerge. Incest survivors, mostly women, are at the margins, oppressed by patriarchal structures and the institutionalization of the incest stigma.

As a survivor finds her voice or "unlearns not to speak" and tells her story, her individual act of resistance counters the false reality created by the perpetrator and contributes to the delegitimation of the patriarchal power system within which the incest act occurs. In second wave feminist language, the personal becomes political.

Indeed, feminist standpoint theorists have argued that a privileging of the knowledge of the oppressed opens the opportunities for "envisioning more just social practices". However, this emphasis on women's common experience has been challenged by postmodern theorists and by women of colour. In this debate postmodern and third world feminists argue that when feminist scholars focus on similarities, one set of claims is simply replaced with another.

This universalizing of women's experiences minimizes differences and obscures the experiences of more marginalized women, differences rooted in elements of class, race, and sexuality. For example, the research on incest survivorship, while giving voice to individual women through in-depth interviews and the presentation of survivor stories, simultaneously creates a survivor identity that universalizes that identity as almost always White and mainly middle class.

Facing a system of interlocking inequalities and oppressions, defined as a "matrix of domination" by Collins or "multiple jeopardies" by King, poor women and women of colour who are survivors may find little about that identity that fits their experiences of and expressions about incest. It is this sort of tension between the commonality and uniqueness of women's experiences of oppression that is at the centre of current debates in feminism.

Since the mid-1990s feminist standpoint theorists have been grappling with this tension in their research and theorizing efforts. Feminist standpoint researchers encourage and are committed to the value of individual women's voices, women who encounter domination and work at resistance in unique ways.

Simultaneously, standpoint scholars wish to retain the notion of commonality: first, as central to analytical efforts, and second, as a defining feature of feminist political commitments to work for social justice for all women. Hence, current work in feminist standpoint theory attempts to "accommodate difference and to preserve analytical and political force in feminist theory".

To accomplish the accommodation of the commonality-difference tension, current feminist standpoint theorizing begins with the foundational belief that knowledge always arises in social locations and is structured by power relations. As a consequence of being positioned within a patriarchal culture, women share the experience of subordination in relation to men as a group and from this position can critique the patriarchal institutions and ideological systems that support those structures.

In the dominant patriarchal culture women function as "outsiders within" as they occupy positions both inside and outside of the dominant male culture. In other words, women's common experience or standpoint as women is informed by their own knowledge and by knowledge of the dominant culture's worldview.

Simultaneously, according to feminist standpoint theorists, women retain their interpretive agency or their individual ability to interpret their own experiences and to make sense of their own lives. Thus, a standpoint is an "achieved" position.

It emerges through an ongoing struggle with the social, cultural and political powers that dominate the structure of knowledge. Fundamentally, standpoints are developed as individuals meet and become engaged in dialogue and collective interaction. According to O'Brien Hallstein (2000), this process "creates the space for both commonality and difference".

If one goal of feminist standpoint theorizing is to account for this dialectical tension between commonality and difference, our methods must find a way to support the expression of "both-and" worldviews. In general, the strength of feminist standpoint methods is their diversity. For example, Dougherty and Krone (2000) argue that any method can be counted as appropriate to feminist standpoint research if the method accounts for two issues.

First, the method must improve the quality of knowledge. Specifically, the knowledge cannot simply recount women's experiences. Better quality knowledge results when women's experiences are understood in relation to political, social, and material contexts. In addition, the knowledge produced by the selected method in feminist standpoint research should create positive change.

Notions of change and degrees of change may vary. For example, change may involve concrete plans of action for redressing grievances or it may involve the beginnings of consciousness raising in which collective experiences of oppression and pain become sources of individual and collective development of standpoint.

We concur that the methods of feminist standpoint research should be diverse and believe that methodological diversity will enrich knowledge and broaden understanding. From within this position then, we wish to advance the layered account as a method of research and as a means of representation for feminist standpoint theorists and researchers in communication.

As a postmodern method first articulated in sociology, the layered account as form emerges from the dialectical relationship between subjectivist and objectivist moments in human experience. More specifically, as a postmodern ethnographic reporting technique, a layered account integrates a theory of consciousness and a method of reporting. The layered account is purposely structured to resemble the duree, or the stream of consciousness as experienced in everyday life.

It is constructed from many points of view and presents them to the reader as representations of lived experience. It de-centers the science-ing of research as the understanding of the world and places layers of experience in non-hierarchical relationship to each other.

The lived experience of the individual is positioned as equal to but differentially represented from the experience of the aggregate as determined by statistically defined generalizations or phenomonologically derived themes. Such juxtapositioning of representational forms resists the ongoing bifurcation of knowledge claims.

Further, this technique of the layered account offers a means for representing experience that operates in the space between commonality and difference in feminist scholarship. While highlighting women's common social position as women, the layered account also can illuminate, for example, the ways women of colour often face multiple intersections of oppression.

How such intersectionalities operate for different incest survivors from distinctive social standpoints can be revealed as the experience of one survivor is presented against and with the experience of another. Through this method and means of representation we avoid the outmoded and essentialist notions of female experiences such as incest and sexual abuse while preserving the collective experience of oppression by and resistance to the patriarchy within which such abuse occurs.

Additionally and/or alternatively, through the use of the layered account individual standpoints may be contrasted to and emergent from the dominant knowledge representation structures of the discipline. In the layered account, then, Dougherty and Krone's (2000) criteria for feminist standpoint methods are met: (1) the political, social, and material contexts of women's experiences are foregrounded, and (2) positive change can emerge from developing individual and collective standpoints.

Finally, a layered account as a method and a representation form acknowledges the involvement of the Other in the generation of knowledge and understanding. Through the stream of consciousness design, layered accounts rely on the reader's involvement in and interpretation of the text. The reader is understood as "participant with" rather than as "recipient of knowledge and as a participant, the reader engages both rationality and emotionality in this involvement.

Further, the layered account suggests diverse readings as different readers of different standpoints engage the text, and likely alternative interpretations emerge as a reader approaches the text again in a different time and space. Such readings and re-readings encourage self-reflexivity and dialogue with others, including the author of the layered account and other readers.

This participation in dialogue raises the possibility of collective action. In support of our argument, in the following pages, then, we develop a layered account to represent one woman's experience of incest disclosure. As in autoethnography, we turn the ethnographic lens on ourselves, while simultaneously viewing the larger context where that experience unfolds.

Through systematic introspection, we examine ourselves as authors and audience for each other in this tale and we become subjects and objects, reflexively disclosing from various conceptions of self(ves) and relational identities. Robbin foregrounds her survivor experience as a middle-class, educated, bisexual, feminist of Jewish-American heritage.

Leigh speaks from her identity as a woman with blue-collar roots and a middle-class adulthood, educated, feminist, and a non-practicing Protestant in the Calvinist tradition. Further, we engage each other in dialogue about these observations on disclosure. We also draw on the multiple voices of others who have conducted research in the area, using theoretical arguments, statistics, and previous research in communicating about incest and research about interviewing as communication practice.

The goal is to make available to the reader "many ways of knowing" and to give readers "layers of experience so they may fill in the spaces and construct an interpretation of the writers' narrative".

Telling: Disclosing the Secret

According to the Department of Health and Human Services, in 1996 child protective agencies across the United States identified almost 1million children as victims of substantiated or indicated abuse or neglect, an increase of approximately 18% since 1990. Of those one million children, about 12% or 120,000 children were sexually abused. Further, child protection agencies found that 77% of the perpetrators in all child maltreatment cases were parents and an additional 11% were other relatives of the victim. In nearly three quarters of sexual abuse cases the perpetrator was male.

These statistics reveal important understandings about the sexual abuse of children. First, the statistics suggest that while the public fears the stranger-child rapist, the far greater threat of sexual victimization lies within the web of family relationships.

Next, these statistics reveal that while women do abuse children sexually, the primary perpetrators are males, in particular fathers, brothers, stepfathers, uncles and/or male cousins. Finally, these statistics, derived from investigations conducted by child protection agencies into reported suspected abuse, likely represent only a portion of the actual incidence rates.

Some experts indicate that one in every three girls and one in every seven boys will experience some form of sexual abuse prior to their eighteenth birthday. The reality is that for many children their suffering will go unnoticed and unreported by adults and their voices will continue to be silenced through various strategies by the perpetrator.

Leigh: As I re-read the previous paragraph for at least the fiftieth time, I try to decide if I should delete it. Doesn't everybody know this by now? In some strange way these words flatly stated as a kind of mathematical formula minimize the horrifying reality of many children's daily existence. The very people who are charged with loving and protecting them violate their physical, psychological, and spiritual well being.

Then they threaten or co-opt the child into silence. In this instant I have changed my mind. I think I should re-write the preceding paragraph in BOLD CAPITAL LETTERS as a repeated disclosure of familial treachery and exposure of the stranger/child rapist myth. It can not be said often enough or loudly enough until it ENDS.

Robbin: Your reaction is so much more emotional than mine. I DO know this by now and have lived it, in addition to years of work as a rape crisis advocate. But I struggle to see myself as a statistic. I go numb reading them. They are not real in the same way as my story, or the stories I heard in group therapy, or from students in my office who somehow sense they can tell me their stories.

A reviewer comments: It's obviously necessary to highlight the particular vulnerability of women and girls in a patriarchal culture, but in a way that doesn't disregard male survivors or female perpetrators as unimportant exceptions by virtue of their being, so to speak "aberrant aberrations." I don't think the essay has to apologize for not dealing with men's experience of sexual abuse (or for masking it with the generic she when describing survivors), but neither should it feel compelled to justify that omission by a logic of "majority/minority," particularly given the appeal elsewhere to the rhetorical power of minoritization of survivors generally.

The stats, for example, suggest that something like only 25% of the perpetrators are women. This doesn't justify their exclusion from the discussion of perpetrators anymore than it would justify gender- specific language in the case of, say, "only" 25% of firefighters being women.

Leigh: As I reflected on these comments and our likely response to the reviewer in the revision, I asked Suzanne, the editor of WSIC, if the reviewer might let us include this comment within the layered account along with a reflection on the comment. He agreed. Further, he volunteered to challenge the public-private boundary in peer review of scholarship by revealing his identity to us and by giving us permission to identify him in publication. His name is Craig Gingrich-Philbrook.

Robbin: Bringing Craig, the reviewer, into this dialogue is a powerful transgression of the boundaries and silences that often exist within academic publishing. In my experience, reviewers often have a profound influence on the final chapter, and even in their praise sometimes manage to articulate what I'm/we're trying to do better than I/we have done.

Similarly, two of my significant male partners were also sexually abused as children (both by men). As I bring their names to the "Take Back the Night" candlelight vigil each year, I do not want to silence their experiences here. Leigh: When I first read these review comments from Craig I experienced that feeling of nausea that accompanies having "the wind knocked out of you." I wrote those paragraphs of "facts," trying to give some clarity to the realities of childhood sexual abuse.

In two small paragraphs from within my standpoint as a woman I had diminished the experiences of male survivors and inadvertently minimized the abusive activities of female perpetrators. After some time and reflection, Craig's comments reminded me of things I know to be true but failed to say. First, abuse is about the dialectic of power and powerlessness in a relationship.

Second, experiencing abuse teaches some people "to go and do likewise." As Ronai came to understand during her childhood sexual abuse by her father and mother, "I was learning the pecking order, biggers do it to littlers, smarters to dumbers, and this is how one found one's place in the scheme of things".

Third, in everyday conversation and in scholarly dialogue the silence of male survivors' voices is deafening. In this chapter Robbin and I speak from our standpoints and in that speaking we wish to validate the significance of individual incest experience through advancing a means for alternate accounts.

Through claiming a space for alternate accounts, we can open the dialogue about survivorship. We can acknowledge that men and women who have survived incest, whether at the hand of a male or female perpetrator, may face different challenges to disclosure, challenges created and perpetuated by a common hegemonic force, the patriarchal social and cultural system.

Robbin's interview: I was at home the following Christmas after Jacob Wetterling had been kidnapped. I remember it bugged me, I was like 'Aren't these kids just kidnapped by one of their parents?' because most missing kids are kidnapped by their parents Everybody in my family was sitting around the living room.

Everybody knows [about the incest], and everybody is talking about these poor kids that get kidnapped. 'God only knows what they're doing to them,' they'd say. I sat there getting madder at her [mother] and madder at her. Incest is an abusive act surrounded, supported, and enabled by secrecy. The secrecy is found in the relationship between the perpetrator and child, among the familial relations and extended kinship links, and within the community's social and cultural taboos against speaking out against the activity.

For the incestuously abused child, breaking the silence, telling the secret is important to the cessation of the abuse. However, such a disclosure usually is embedded within relationships with the perpetrator and/or family members. These relationships create significant communicative dilemmas.

Children may experience contradictions in feelings for the perpetrator and other family members, as these are the individuals to whom they are most likely to disclose the abuse initially. For example, children are often told that the family is at risk if they tell or that everyone will hate the child for telling. Sometimes children are threatened with death or the death of beloved others in the family. A child may also be told that she and only she is special to the perpetrator, that their relationship must be kept secret so others (usually mother and other daughters) won't feel sad or jealous.

Leigh: Fear, shame, love, hate, guilt, power, and powerlessness These are potent emotional forces in any family potentially toxic when accompanied by incest. We all likely have experienced these feelings but the source and intensity of such emotions, of course, is both quantitatively and qualitatively different for the survivor.

The interlocking relationships of families within and across generations are familiar to us as well, the "family ties that bind and gag," as Erma Bombeck, the humorist, used to say. For families experiencing incest, Bombeck's line is not a lighthearted play on words.

Instead, these words metaphorically describe everyday reality. Family members are bound together, often multigenerationally, tied by those emotions and the incest experience and gagged by the secret. When incestuously abused children do break the silence, their disclosure appears to be predicated on a set of rules or "logics" for disclosure.

In their study of sexual abuse disclosure by children, Petronio and her colleagues interviewed 38 children and adolescents who had voluntarily disclosed their abuse to peers, family members, and/or friends. The participants identified five categories of confidant characteristics: (1) credibility (trust and commonality); (2) supportiveness (feelings of love and understanding); (3) advocacy (act to stop the abuse); (4) strength (ability to handle emotionally the disclosure); and (5) protectiveness (free from negative repercussions).

As Petronio et al. argue, these children use their voices to recreate and rebuild trust, control, and safety. These logics may be complicated, however, by the child's contradictory experience of close relationships in which the parent-protector is simultaneously the perpetrator. Response to childhood disclosure of incest varies and telling the secret can result in both positive and negative consequences.

In the best case, disclosure may be followed by support

for and belief in the child and cessation of the abuse. On the other hand, disclosure may result in family dissolution and/or foster care placements of uncertain duration for the child. It is also possible that the child will be disbelieved and silenced, and may continue to experience abuse.

In such instances the silence often extends well into adulthood, and in both cases the child will suffer long-term effects of the abuse. The circumstances confronting adult survivors today reflect the "historical reinforcement of the cultural hegemony that has sustained the incest taboo".

As Ray has pointed out, the cultural prohibition against speaking out creates a false reality in which denial serves the interests of the individual perpetrator and maintains the patriarchally-dominated gender relations of the larger social and cultural system. Only in recent years have survivors been able to acknowledge their experiences and to have them validated. Dinsmore calls this denying of denial and naming of the act by the survivor, "telling myself."

Robbin's interview: I read an article in the newspaper that ironically my mother gave me So she gave me this chapter. It was the first time I ever saw what counted as incest. It was the first. I was 21-22 when I read this chapter, and I was like "oh, my god! That's what happened to me."

In their study of incest disclosures, Roesler and Wind found that while children were more likely to choose family members as initial disclosure targets, adult survivors selected therapists, partners, or friends as recipients of the initial disclosure. These adult initial disclosures occurred an average of 12 years after cessation of the abuse.

Survivors describe their reluctance to disclose as rooted in fears developed in childhood and linked to other emotions such as shame, guilt, sadness, and anger. In this initial disclosure the adult survivor risks further loss in the hope of release and empowerment.

Robbin: The first time is a brave miracle. I told Michael, the first boyfriend I shared both an intellectual and sexual intimacy with. He had a story of his own. What luck (or was it instinct?)! I'm not crazy. Someone understands. It [his experience] didn't seem to fuck him up as much as it [mine] did me. But he was supportive. Nevertheless, this "thing" that had happened to me still got inside this relationship which deteriorated sexually as intimacy deepened. Classic But the first telling for me was a positive telling. I don't think a lot of people can say that. Maybe for them a negative first telling experience can lead to greater victimization (from others and from oneself). I think this affects the choice to tell again and to whom and how.

Another kind of first telling that some survivors undertake is confrontational telling. The initial act of breaking the silence with the perpetrator and those who may be complicit in the silence, such as the other parent or other adult family members, holds both promise and threat. In most survivor experiences this telling is not the initial disclosure of the incest.

Indeed, in most cases the survivor has expended much effort in therapy and in working through supportive relationships with others before this kind of telling is even contemplated. Confrontational telling has significance in breaking the silence surrounding incest because of its potential effects on the survivor, the perpetrator, and the total family system.

Robbin's interview: So I brought the article (about incest) to dad and I had him read it. And I said, 'That's how I felt.' And he apologized not for doing it. He never said it was wrong to have done it. He apologized if he hurt me in any way because he loves me and he doesn't want to hurt me.

Robbin: I think this confrontational type telling is not just to the perpetrator, but can be to the other parent or to anyone whose nose it happened under, or who would have been somehow partially responsible to stop it. For me this would be confronting my dad, the perp, and my mom, the unwitting accomplice.

This is everything about Naming the Deed. Breaking the silence within the system that supported the silence. The end of denial. Confronting my dad was generally unsatisfying. In some ways, it accomplished what it should: naming, breaking silence, ending denial, marking a new truth to our relationship.

But I guess I always expected more of my dad, who of course taught me to expect more! When confronting my mom, the first telling was very unsatisfying despite having broken the silence, etc.

She was verbally supportive but not for long enough, and not emotionally enough present with ME. I felt it was a repeat of her absentee mom act, she didn't notice then, and she couldn't deal with it now. Wasn't quite ready to fess up to her own failure in this, so she focused on ways my dad also abused her.

True, but not my problem. I was a little girl. She was the mom. She was an adult. She can blame the fact that she wasn't skilled enough to make good decisions or to protect her kids on her mom, I guess. At the second telling reminding her that worrying about kids on TV wasn't going to fly with me, here I felt she finally got what I was saying, was more emotionally present for me.

Leigh: Robbin, this part of your disclosure story is always hard for me to hear. Your mother's responses to your telling create contradictions in me that I cannot seem to manage. As a single mother and a feminist, I am personally sensitive to and defensive about charges that accrue against mothers in the patriarchal culture.

Lempert describes mothers of incested daughters as being cast in violation of the cultural narrative of the "good mother." In this cultural narrative, mothers of incest families at minimum are blamed for ignoring the abuse and at times are accused of collusion and facilitation. I know there is evidence that in some cases the mother's participation in the family dynamic does lead to these conclusions.

At the same time, by focusing attention on the mother, it seems to minimize the attention toward and deflect responsibility from the father/male figure who committed the incest. As Lempert has said, once again patriarchy, hierarchy, and sexism win.

But as a mother, I ask myself, "How could she not know

what was going on? How could any mother not know?" Perhaps this is my way of placing myself within the "good mother" cultural narrative. I want to convince myself that I am the kind of mother who would have known.

I am the kind of mother who would have believed my child and saved my child. I am the kind of mother who would but I don't know for certain that I am that kind of mother. And you are right you were a little girl someone should have been watching out for you.

Robbin: Leigh, I share your concern about mother blaming. I worked at a radio station in the 1980s and I produced a show about a book called "Don't Blame Mother." It was the first time I realized the extent to which so much of the psychological industry does this. In my own healing, I have tried to manage this tension between my own little girl anger, which I feel is justified and the expression of which is central to my healing, and my feminist struggle against mother blaming. I know that within my family system, my mother was also victimized. I do want and need her to hear my voice as her child. But I also want to acknowledge the ways she took control of her own life, and made choices that took us both out of an abusive system. It's still a struggle for me to allow my feminism to let my mom off the hook. I continue to experience this process as a dialectical tension between living my emotional life and engaging my intellectual understanding of families as systems. I need to do BOTH.

The survivor literature on confrontation emphasizes that the importance of confrontation lies in the relief it gives to the confronter/survivor. In a sense, the survivor approaches confrontation with the certain expectation that she will be changed as a result of the encounter. She may hope for but should not expect change in the perpetrator or within other family participants. Of all the possible disclosure scenarios, confrontation is the riskiest. Here the risks are "mostly unknown and largely unpredictable".

Robbin: Confrontation has an important role in healing since it's a lot about breaking the patterns in a dysfunctional system. Maybe some people break ties after unsuccessful confrontations. I was lucky, I didn't have to. My family-mom, dad, siblings-has evolved with me, and I am grateful for that (No one calls me "Dad's favourite" anymore, that's for sure.)

Leigh: I admire your persistence in seeking redefinition and resolution within yourself and within your familial ties. How difficult this confrontational telling must be for the survivor, to nurture hope while guarding against the possibility of denial, disbelief, and dismissal. As a listener to the stories of your confrontations, I found myself, despite knowing the outcome, feeling some of that tension between hope and dread, wishing so that all would be well and wondering if in this telling it would not be so.

Robbin: As my father ages and now finds himself alone (his partner of 18 years has ended what all believed was a strong relationship and what I believed would be secure through old age), I find a new fear emerging. Will I be called on to nurture the man who abused me? Will my brother and sister empathize with my unwillingness to become a caretaker for my dad if and when that time comes? You are right, Leigh; despite knowing what now feels like an "outcome," there remains a very strong tension between hope and dread, between genuine love and unrelenting pain.

Hegde writes that "the control of another's communicative choices and options is a pivotal mechanism in sustaining power-based hierarchies". When women choose to disclose to break the silence to tell the secret to make the private public to tell the truth about their lives distinctly individualistic and highly personal communicative acts simultaneously empower individuals and resist the power-based hierarchy and cultural mythology of American family life.

RETELLING: DISCLOSING THE STORY

For adult survivors, the disclosure of the incest experience is an ongoing part of their personal relations and their healing as they attempt to make sense of their lives and experiences. In these retellings the incest narrative emerges, and with each effort to voice the incest narrative, the adult survivor engages in the sensemaking process. Lempert describes women's narratives of domestic abuse as "linguistic tools that serve to order experiences, construct reality, and creatively make sense of their violent intimate relationships". For adult survivors of incest, the narrative form functions similarly. In these retellings, survivors present a retrospective reconstruction of their experiences.

The narrative reconstruction may include but is not limited to several characteristic themes: assessments of the actions of the self, the perpetrator, other family members or adults; reflections on circumstances and motivations of those involved in the secret; consequences to self and others because of the sexual abuse and the violations of boundaries that accompany incest; explanations and interpretations of the incest experiences as influenced by time and the evolutions of life experiences, including strategic lying or changing the story.

Through these narratives adult survivors contextualize their childhood experiences of past abuse in the present, constructing explanations for others but, perhaps more importantly, for themselves. Further, in some of these re-tellings a particular meta-narrative form emerges: tales of incest disclosures and the responses to these disclosures become important themes of the re-telling disclosure form.

We wish to make clear that this process does not result in a single narrative, nor in a narrative for which a set of criteria must be applied and by which we can judge its rightness. As storyteller, the incest survivor retells the narrative based on her current understandings of her past and present, and of the "flashbacks, after-images, dream sequences, faces merging into one another, masks dropping and new masks being put on" that she experiences as she negotiates her life.

While the essential core of the narrative centralizes incest survivorship in each re-telling, the particular version told reflects different nuances and emphases. Thus, in some sense the incest narrative is new in each re-telling and in the re-telling the survivor communicatively creates a context in which to interpret those events. Robbin: Retellings are the repeats to various people, at various times, for various purposes, in a variety of ways.

Usually I retell to promote deeper intimacy and understanding in relationships with people who are new in my life. Certainly the retelling to friends contemporaneously to therapy (as part of therapy, and to people in the therapy group, including newcomers) is part of retelling. One of the things I realized is that nobody who is important to me can know me if they don't know this. Leigh: I try to remember where we were and when it was that you told me.

In some ways this narrative seems intrinsically and seamlessly linked to the ongoing narrative that is our friendship. On the other hand, sometimes I think I can't remember for other reasons, reasons that make me less than proud. Maybe I can't remember because I could not manage the weight of this knowledge at that moment. I sometimes fear that I was not present to hear your tale, as I was trying to process this information and simultaneously manage my own emotions. I know that can happen to receivers of survivor stories, despite survivors' best efforts to select their disclosure targets with care. My only certain knowledge is that we cried. My hope is that I did listen. I acknowledge the faith one must place in the other when telling this tale. Such revelations are not for the faint-hearted, either as speaker or as listener. Despite an inability to recall the details of this disclosure, this re-telling changed our relationship and changed me.

The knowledge is now mine, too, and the knowledge makes me accountable, not just to you and to our friendship, but also to myself and to the community. I cannot just sit idly by and let others engage an issue of both personal and political importance. Robbin: Not all retellings are motivated by the desire to develop more authentic interpersonal relationships, however. What I call "fucked-up telling" is telling for the wrong reasons.

This is telling from a victim place. Telling to shock or to scare people away. For me I played the "hard chick" who was too tough to care in some re-tellings (or pretended not to care). Or used re-telling as an emotional weapon to scare people into thinking I was too messed up to care about.

These re-tellings can be inappropriate in terms of time, place, person, circumstance, relational development, etc. They lack self-reflection and I think they can lead to perpetual status as a victim, as well as continued victimization.

Identifying oneself as a victim is like an invitation to the perpetrators of the world. Leigh: Acknowledging this kind of re-telling is important.

It reminds me of recent efforts by colleagues committed to studying the darker aspects of interpersonal communication.

In self-confession discourse, we hold a bias toward disclosure and to view all such tellings as motivated by the desire to heal, to move forward in some way.

You have described these "fucked— up retellings" as potentially perpetuating victimization. I think they may also be another way to have control, a way to manage relationships that your intuition tells you may not be good for you or may bring on unwanted intimacies.

Further, it strikes me that we seem to emphasize planned, purposeful, thoughtful re-tellings in research, even the disclosures we are emphasizing here.

You and other survivors from our interviews have described many disclosures as spontaneous, fragmented, and occurring with less than thoughtful expression.

The notion of "fucked-up tellings" reminds us that confession and disclosure are contextualized by relational and social power dynamics. In her discussion of confession, Mandziuk, like Foucault, argues that confession, while ostensibly a liberating act, often represents or evokes a further retrenchment of rules and strictures that prohibit disclosure of sexually-related experiences.

In this sense, sometimes telling about incest can produce silencing reactions, create an environment where new abuse becomes normative, or otherwise operates within a discursive power relationship that can be negative or oppressive for the incest victim/survivor. In her discussion of "coming out" as gay or lesbian, Dow concurs that the liberating aspect of confession may be reduced since prevailing power relationships can create a hegemonic effect even when disclosure seeks to disrupt the dominant order.

Robbin: Telling in new serious romantic relationships is also an issue. For incest survivors, this is especially true for sexually intimate relationships. This fact is crucially important to tell in each new relationship. The ability to do it well, manage it successfully within the relationship (which depends a lot on your partner), and deepen intimacy in the relationship is a sign of surviving.

Disclosure can lead to the partner feeling too much displaced guilt, anger, or fear of hurting you. This is not productive and, if unvoiced by the partner, can be quite destructive. The partner needs skills to co-survive. In some ways, being with an incest survivor means that the incest also "happened" to the partner. It is now in their life too. I think somewhere in here is also an increased willingness to own my anger and to articulate it when necessary.

There are also feelings of being so overwhelmingly damaged, always having to dredge this shit up each time there is a new dear friend or a new intimate partner. It has been easier for me in the lesbian community where there seems to be greater awareness about sexual abuse. Even if lesbians have not been abused or raped, they endure assault based on sexual identity every day.

This creates a deep wound in the community, but also a deep sense of commonality. Maybe that's one reason why I have always felt so good in this community. It has always been very SAFE as far as my incest experience goes. Leigh: When I read your reflections on re-telling, I continue to think about them within the dialectical framework, as we suggested in the study that was the origin of our present dialogue.

In that piece we proposed that the dialectic of secrecy-disclosure is the primary contradiction for incest survivors and the dialectic from which all other communicative contradictions arise. In each re-telling a survivor makes efforts to manage the dialectical tensions of relationships and the communicative contradictions of disclosure. Your narratives and reflections make me even more aware of the complexities of the context, of the actors involved, and of the relationships within which these contradictions are experienced. I am also moved by the very self consciousness (or rather the consciousness of self) that you bring to these reflections.

Viewing yourself as subject across time requires managing other dialectical tensions, not the least of which is the secrecy-disclosure contradiction within our relationships as friends, as interviewer and participant, and as co-participants in this dialogue. I am gratified that our scholarly discipline gives us the vocabulary and that our commitment to this subject gives us the will to continue this reflective process.

Robbin: Another dynamic in re-telling is becoming the one who reciprocally discloses. Perhaps by instinct, perhaps by sheer volume of occurrence, incest survivors become people who are disclosed TO. This discloser/recipient role happens with friends old and new. When someone discloses (and sometimes it happened to their mom or daughter or sister instead of them), the ability to be a supportive listener to them-someone who believes them and who understands-creates another level of healing.

It also creates an amazing bond. A place to go or to come to after a nightmare or some other setback, and to know and share the linkages-emotionally, psychologically, sexually. With friends, we need a place to talk about ongoing relationship issues where the groundwork is laid and where the assumptions are shared.

This kind of telling and being told is all about a process of surviving. Building relationships that are safe and supportive. This is also relevant as an advocate, especially working as a volunteer supporting other survivors of sexual assault. Here I have chosen to be someone who gets told the survivor story. This is taking on the responsibility often of being the first one told, for example at the hospital on a crisis call. It's huge, but feels great to be the one who believes, who supports, who understands deeply, who has resources to share, including reciprocating with my own disclosure and meta-narratives about when/how/why I have disclosed.

We began this journey because we desired to be the authors of our own lives. To describe the disclosure experience in our own voices, not in the distanced voice of traditional scholarship, is one form of authoring. We wanted to write this piece as advocates and activists.

We believe that the elimination of incest and all sexual violence, especially violence directed toward women, requires the radical revisioning of gendered relationships. And we both are committed to the notion that removing the stigma of incest is fundamentally linked to communication issues.

Removing the stigmatization of incest is clearly rooted in issues of communication. It is a process of negating messages told to the child by the perpetrator, significant others, and society. It is a process of changing the self-destructive messages victims tell themselves. It is a process of breaking the silence by telling the secret. It is a process of ending the isolation by sharing memories of the abuse with others. It is a process of stating the truth as the truth and a lie as a lie. It is the process of ensuring that legislation is passed and enacted to hold perpetrators, not mothers or children, responsible for incest. It is a process of passing laws and then imposing severe penalties for those convicted of incest. It is a process of becoming vocal advocates for "others." It is the process of forcing the public to hear the individual and collective voices of adult survivors that can end stigmatization and disenfranchisement for adult incest survivors. It is these last two disclosure processes described by Ray that are now our concern. From our advocacy standpoint we want to examine talking about the incest experience in the research interview, an interview contextualized by our relationship as friends. We also want to engage in dialogue about our present authoring of the interview experience as we talk about telling.

We have agreed that these advocacy activities resemble a kind of "coming out." In this instance, coming out forces us to experience the personal and professional, rational and emotional, objective and subjective, and public and private domains not as oppositional forces but as dialectical tensions, fundamentally unresolvable. In this talking about telling we have abandoned pretensions of getting it "right" in favour of getting it out.

Robbin: As a rape crisis advocate and sexual assault prevention educator and trainer, I use my experience to help others learn to identify sexual abuse themes and symptoms, and to teach them to help victims/survivors in their process. Some advocates are also victims/survivors. This creates a certain synergy, although this can also be dangerous (e.g., for advocates if they are still more victims than survivors, not to mention for clients). I consider this activist work. Also, in my role as professor, students often come to me. I recognize the signs. I create the safe place they can come. If it's safe for me, I mutually disclose, without the details of my story, of course, but to provide a role model of support and survival. I think this is an important aspect of becoming an activist. Becoming willing to share in ways that help others. It is also about offering hope and feeling a sense of purpose. At least this is a unique service I can provide at the university! HA!

As both a survivor and a communication professor, I can also help people learn to manage their own telling processes. I think these are two aspects of disclosure that have not been identified in the communication literature, though feminists have identified these issues. I also wonder how much this is consistent with experiences of disclosing other stigmatized information, such as sexual identity, or HIV status?

The notion that speaking and hearing survivor stories can be personally transformative for other survivors as well as the survivor storyteller herself has been well documented. Further, speaking out in public contexts serves the activist survivors' movement with its potential for societal and cultural transformation. Within an activist, social justice agenda then, participation by incest survivors in academic research is yet another strategy for resisting the dominant patriarchal discourse and the resultant stigmatization of the survivor.

Participants in these interviews frequently describe their motivations as more about helping others than themselves and express hope that social change may result from the publication of their experiences. While the research interview can become a disclosure space for locating voice, it also becomes a site within which the public-private boundary is contested and the tension between these domains managed.

Robbin: For me, talking about telling began with the decision to be interviewed for your study, Leigh. I thought this would bring my story to analysis and maybe to public discourse on these matters. I consider this to be a survivor move and an activist move, though it could have remained an anonymous interview, and I think activism is public. I did this same thing with a sexual harassment research project that happened in the field several years ago.

But then the authors did not change any of the identifying details of my story and people knew it was me. No consequences came down on me, that I know of, but it felt icky since it wasn't my choice to be de-anonymized. It was a violation of my trust, though I'm still glad I participated in the research. Now, with your study, and with the much more sensitive issue of incest, it was a very trusting situation. You are not only a colleague, Leigh, but a good friend, and you did the interview. You had gone through [rape crisis centre] training, so I knew you were emotionally prepared to do the interview, and that you knew a lot. I also trusted in our friendship implicitly. This was the first time I told you the whole story, I think, and it felt good, safe (even though I got very emotional), and like my stories were in good hands.

Leigh: At first, I was glad that you volunteered to participate in the interview. To me your willingness to participate symbolized two things. First, you valued the project as a survivor and, second, you trusted me as a researcher and as a friend to care for you and for the process. But as the interview time we had chosen grew closer, I admit to feeling some anxiety. I had never heard the totality of your story and while the interview questions only asked for "the details you wish to share and feel comfortable sharing," I knew that this would be a much more intimate disclosure of your experience than we had ever previously undertaken. I had been through the La Pinon [our community sexual assault recovery services organization] 40-hour training and had served on the Board for several years so I did not experience any trepidation about being able to be sensitive to the issues. Ironically, I felt only minimal anxiety in all the other interviews I conducted with other survivors, strangers to me and people with whom I needed to build a rapport before we could proceed. I think most of my anxiety came from a fear that this change in roles might somehow affect our relationship negatively. As I look back on it now, I don't think the fear was realistic but I experienced the anxiety in real ways. I think that's why I wanted you to come to my house and why I wanted to cook for you, to prepare dinner after we talked.

To me the act of preparing a meal is all wrapped up in the memories of caring and security to be found in my mother's kitchen. If you were willing to cross this privacy boundary and trust me, my best gift to you would be this service. While I eventually found my anxiety easing through the process of conducting the actual interview, in the weeks that followed I felt a different sort of anxiety, arising from a need to understand this experience within my academic understandings of interviewing as a research method. This piece we are writing and my reading in preparation for it have helped me frame and understand that process.

The central contradiction of intensive interviewing in the social sciences has been the simultaneous desire for social scientific objectivity, which is (erroneously) assumed when the interview is an encounter between strangers, and the necessity of building interpersonal rapport in the encounter to secure valid interview responses from participants.

Reinharz calls this the "friend, stranger, neither, both" controversy. Generally, the distinction is made between the researcher as stranger mode and the researcher as a friend to the people being studied. In the latter case, typically the researcher befriends or lives/works in close relation to those studied, frequently with the expressed desire to study those she befriends. But, what happens when the "web group of affiliation", or our friends, become potential participants in our research? We know little about the consequences of intensive interviewing within friendship dyads, but it is likely both positive and negative outcomes could potentially arise and could exist in tension with one another.

Interviewing friends may lead to an intensification of rapport and an increase in validity, as rapport is rooted in understanding of the other's identity, an established understanding in the case of friends, easing the discussion of topics in terms of both breadth and depth.

Simultaneously, presumably intimate friends may become strangers during the interview, a process that results from the form and structure of the interview itself; for instance, the use of a recorder and an interview schedule disrupt the relational and communication norms.

Further, as co-participants the interviewer and the interviewee may struggle with the objective-subjective dichotomy, attempting to manage the boundary between their professional and personal roles within the interview. Ironically, these dynamics may result in even less freedom to disclose and less validity in the data, the very opposite of desired outcomes when interviewing intimates.

While research-based concerns are significant, interpersonal concerns within and beyond the interview context also have relevance. Harkess and Warren eloquently state, "Interviews in a web of group affiliation are both structured by, and the restructuring of, the flow of social relations between interviewer and respondent, sometimes in a way unanticipated by either. Interpretations, accounts, and feelings weave from the past into the interview and from the interview into the future". In other words, while the interview is shaped by the prior relationship of the participants, inevitably the relationship of the participants will be affected by the interview. Leigh: For me, Harkess and Warren's validity concerns when interviewing within web groups of affiliation reflect an interesting methodological dilemma, still largely unresolved. I guess reviewers, editors, and academic peers who read these submissions will continue to evaluate that validity issue within the ongoing dialogue within our discipline and other social sciences about what counts as knowledge. But I did have concerns about the future dynamics of our relationship. In my view our relationship post-interview resumed many of its familiar rhythms. The intensity of the interview certainly deepened the intimacy of our friendship in those moments, but we cannot live our daily lives with that level of interpersonal engagement.

Instead this level of disclosure, albeit significant, remains just one moment in the complexities, understandings, and shared meanings of our friendship. That night I did make a pledge to myself that I would do all I could to respect your story. While the privacy of all the interview participants was protected, I was especially cognizant that your identity be concealed as the research report would appear before our colleagues. (At that point, we had not even considered the kind of disclosure practice we now are undertaking. As I review those past decisions, this disclosure effort seems so daunting.) I would be unable to truly evaluate the relational consequences of our interview experience until the JACR article was in print. Your response to that publication would be my personal measure of validity. I was acutely conscious that the risks to personal and professional identity in this process were yours. The burden of the risks to our friendship was mine.

If I had betrayed your confidence and trust in any way, I would be accountable. For that reason I am gratified that you were unable to identify yourself within the chapter. Robbin: The first time I looked at the JACR article, I scanned for the excerpts, I guess looking for my voice. After all, I'd made the decision to be interviewed and wanted my experience to count for something. A legitimization of sorts. Another silence broken, perhaps, in bringing this aspect of my identity to my professional life. Colleagues in my field were now among those who "knew," even if only this group of researchers would know my identity. It was also a choice for me that the other authors know my identity. This was a new phase of "outness." And it brought me to an increased desire to want to break the silence that is perpetuated by the personal-professional dichotomy that I think is an unhealthy, complicitous ideology.

For god's sakes, Oprah did it years ago! The relative stigmatization has been incredibly reduced during my adult life. The bifurcation of personal-professional is the culprit here. And how well it serves the (mostly male and often workplace) perpetrator. Keep the personal out of the workplace. This must be a horrible story for women/adult survivors everywhere. But as I scanned the article, I couldn't distinguish, initially, between my voice and those of the others. All our stories are so similar in some ways, at the emotional level maybe. But words like "grandfather," words revealing small details of stories, tipped me off. "That's not me." And then there was the familiar practice of comparing that I have often caught myself doing in group therapy. "Oh, her experience was so much worse than mine." Still unable to acknowledge the pain and loss I endured when compared to stories filled with violence and torture.

I still have trouble identifying those things with my story. But maybe it's been my intellectual and communication skills that have brought me to this place. I feel like I have survived and thrived. My feminism and my academic discipline have brought me language with which to understand my experience and process it. But I'm still struggling to keep surviving. It never stops.

Participating in the original research and now reflecting on that research represent a new level of advocacy and a new level of disclosure for us both. We will be going public and truly blurring the personal-professional and private-public boundaries for ourselves and in our scholarship. We do not claim that blurring these boundaries is unproblematic either for ourselves or for other scholars, as responses to recent unconventional scholarship in communication cause us to anticipate potential controversy.

The irony, we recognize, is that in this act of personal-professional and private-public boundary-crossing we are focusing on incest, by definition characterized by inappropriate boundary-blurring. Will this chapter itself be viewed as inappropriate boundary-blurring? In the experience of incest the boundary is broken by the more powerful against the less powerful and the act of boundary breaking is meant to silence and destroy.

As women and feminist scholars, the blurring of the public-private, personal-professional boundaries is an act of resistance to disciplinary and socio-cultural hegemony. This boundary-blurring is an emancipatory project meant to give voice and illuminate. Leigh: It would be dishonest not to admit that at times I have struggled with my professional identity in doing this research.

This is a central problem for many women and persons of colour in academe, of course. The claim is that you study women's issues/minority issues because you are a woman/a member of a minority group. Allen, Orbe, and Olivas have engaged in dialogue about this and related issues eloquently and revealingly and I was moved to my own tears by their reflections.

When I studied the communication of support in the experience of breast cancer, participants in the study sought my experience. Did I have credentials as a breast cancer survivor myself? I could understand their need to know and disclosed my family experience. But colleagues also asked this question. Surely, my interest was personal first and professional second was the implication.

By the way, when a male researcher studies prostate cancer or heart disease and the communication practices surrounding those illnesses, I doubt he is asked those same personal questions. My disclosures to colleagues were frequently contextualized by the personal but then argued as relevant to the academic and theoretical realms, trying always to justify my interest, to grant myself professional, not personal, credentials.

Then I was a novice researcher learning about research during the rise of interpretive approaches within the discipline, often operating on intuition and a fundamental belief that the personal and the professional can be integrated. These many years later I have read more, talked more with others like you who have expanded my thinking and views of scholarship.

Now I can say that I study these issues because they are centrally communicative and give us insights into broader theoretical understandings of the lived communication experiences of all people. I study these issues because they are human issues, and, yes, I study these issues because they come from the lives and experiences of women.

Nonetheless, this project created more contradictions for me and I get angry with myself for my own ambivalence. How will I be identified? What attributions about my personal and professional identity will be made? Many who read this piece will assume I am an "in the closet" incest survivor.

Others, because we have used only your interview and experiences will assume that I am not a survivor or my experiences would have been part of this discussion as well. Some may even fault me for not disclosing my status in an essay about disclosure and blurring the boundaries between the personal and professional in scholarship.

Am I a survivor? The power of boundary-crossing rests on the freedom to choose, and I have exercised my choice. My participation in this layered account does not depend on an answer to that question. More importantly, as a scholar I need not provide a reason for my participation any more than those who study compliance-gaining or media effects or any of a myriad of interests that represent communication scholarship must provide their reasons. My reasons are my own.

Robbin: Leigh, I was always excited about the research project for JACR. And now that we are doing this chapter, being interviewed anonymously then seems so safe and tame by comparison. As I read this chapter for the first time after the integration of my interview excerpts, my written self-reflections, and our dialogues, I feel much trepidation. I still think, "Oh, what if my doctoral advisor reads this?" And this publication will be on my curriculum vitae! It all feels surreal. But it is necessary. Detached scholarship has never really been my thing, anyway. Now I am writing about telling, putting my name to the story.

Is this what Van Maanen had in mind as a "confessional tale?" Even months after deciding to do this, it is still tremulously approached. I feel it is important but scary. I want to go to the next logical level, and I'm a scholar, not a talk show host, a novelist, or whatever. So the next logical level for me is scholarly writing-my medium. I guess in Post-Traumatic Stress Disorder and incest, etc., the story is healing and is supposed to be trauma reducing. I am now wondering if this will still work as we up the ante. I worry that somehow this knowledge could damage MY professional credibility. Again, separate worlds. Divided identity. Sounds familiar. Isn't that what incest does to you in the first place? Maybe this last telling, this professional-talking and writing-about—telling, is the most unifying telling. Maybe. But still it's hard as hell! The control of another's communicative choices and options is a pivotal mechanism in sustaining power-based hierarchies. We purposefully wanted to repeat the quote from Hegde as we reflect on the private-public boundary within the personal-professional dialectic in this talking about telling. As we have participated in the primary dialogue about incest disclosure, we also have been holding a sidebar conversation about the appropriate choice of a publication outlet for this layered account we are presenting.

It is interesting that our discussion has centered not on the appropriate outlet due to the substance of the chapter as much as it has centered on an outlet more open to alternative expressions than traditional social science research reports. We have considered the various journal options within our own discipline. We also have considered trying to publish this work outside of communication, perhaps in sociology. In this conversation we have had to manage ongoing contradictions, as well.

We are communication scholars speaking and writing about communication practices but also concerned about our communication colleagues' reactions to our form of communication. Critiques of the conduct of research and the representation of knowledge have been offered in communication, but here we are, still debating the choice of the relatively few venues where this work would be both welcomed and legitimated.

We also have struggled with the presentation of this work as it might appear to our departmental and college colleagues. If this is published and becomes a part of our academic records at our respective institutions, how will it be received? The tensions surrounding the representation of knowledge are manifest in our own everyday lived experiences not simply in some abstract philosophical argument.

This experience parallels the experience of survivorship and disclosure in one respect. If we speak and speak in this form, will we be silenced? If we speak, in this form, will our knowledge claims be believed? In Ronai's layered account, sociology is compared to the abusive patriarch demanding silence of his children -sociologists- about what goes on in his household.

Her argument maintains that the traditional form of representation in sociology typified by article format requirements serves the interests of that patriarch as it preserves the illusion of science and rationality for a process that is eminently a social product, characterized by mistakes, leaps of faith, personal interests and motives, and sometimes luck and happenstance. This secret must be kept to support the facade of functionality and to keep the "family" together. It is a near perfect fit between the mythology of American family life and the mythology of American academe in the social sciences. Writ large in American consciousness, the cultural beliefs ascribed to in these mythologies are enacted on small everyday stages, in the kitchens, living rooms, and bedrooms of individual families, and in the offices, classrooms, and conference rooms of academic departments. In these enactments the negotiation continues the boundary between private and public is contested and the personal becomes political.

We are not sure how to conclude this writing about telling, re-telling and talking about telling in the incest experience. Within the traditional norms of what counts as good academic research writing, we would review our espoused goals for this project and try to assess whether we have achieved them. In that case we would say that we suggested that we had two goals: first, to bridge the tension in feminist standpoint theory between the need to develop commonalities among women's everyday experiences while also valuing the unique experience of individual women.

We argued that the layered account provided a means for that bridging and then we presented a layered account of the forms of incest disclosure as evidence. Through Robbin's experience we illuminated new details about the disclosure of stigmatizing information. The form of disclosive acts, telling, re-telling, and talking about telling, and the types of acts within those forms, emerged from this layered account.

Again, we emphasize that differences among survivors (including gender, race, class, sexual orientation, and religion) will produce distinctive layered accounts. Robbin's experiences and insights may differ substantially from those of other women. For example, Robbin notes that her academic discipline brought unique insights and a language to talk about her experience. And although Jewish women may face particular constraints on telling because of the Jewish cultural myth that "Jewish men do not abuse their children," her relative material advantage allowed her to become independent from her family at an early age. Further, this layered account is bounded by space and time and captures that single representation only. Much as the incest survivor's re-tellings can be viewed through the lens of today's experiences, knowledge and perspective, so too this layered account might become more nuanced, more finely detailed, differently structured, and so forth, if woven together now.

For example, the inclusion of the reviewer's comments within the account provided another occasion for reflexivity and another opportunity to challenge the professional-personal boundary. We have never met Craig and Suzanne.

Our relationship has been constrained by the boundaries of professional roles. Yet both Suzanne and Craig were willing to blur the boundary between the personal and professional and the public and private.

Through email "conversations" and a more open review process, we have again confronted the personal-professional boundary and enacted its blurring in the present account. Thus, the layered account presented here serves as an exemplar account and opens a space for dialogue on the power and potential of juxtaposing forms of representation.

As our second goal we suggested that this examination of disclosure forms would be reflective of how incest survivors manage the publicprivate boundary and negotiate meaning in their lives. We also found ourselves managing that same private-public boundary as friends, interviewer and interviewee, and as co-authors. As we conclude this account we confront our own limitations on our ability to reflect on ourselves as objects and to write about ourselves as subjects. We reflect on the possibility that in our ongoing struggle with the public-private boundary some unconscious or conscious monitor may have ruled in favour of privacy over intellectual or personal exploration of some idea or issue in our dialogue.

Further we anticipate that the publication of this chapter may produce an ongoing negotiation of these boundaries, as we encounter reactions to our findings and to our approach of reporting them. We reach this point then searching for another conclusion, literally and figuratively. In the literal sense we wish to end this work with the call to further action, first by encouraging further communication scholarship on issues that meet a social justice agenda, issues that are politically charged but personally involving. Second, we wish to join with others calling for and supporting alternative representations of knowledge in the social sciences.

Bibliography

Chomsky, N. and Herman, E. (2000) The Political Economy of Human Rights, Volumes 1 and 2. Boston: South End Press.

Comor, E.A. (2001) The re-tooling of American hegemony: US foreign communication policy from free flow to free trade. In A. Sreberny-Mohammadi, D. Winseck, J. McKenna and O. Boyd-Barrett (eds) Media in Global Context, A Reader. London: Edward Arnold.

Evans, H. (2004) Prometheus unbound. Iain Walker Memorial Lecture, Green College Oxford, May.

Golding, P. and Murdock, G. (2002) Ideology and the mass media: the question of determination. In M. Barrett, P. Corrigan, A. Kuhn and J. Wolff (eds) Ideology and Cultural Production. London: Croom Helm.

Herman, E. (2003) Media in the US political economy. In J. Downing, A. Mohammadi and A. Sreberny-Mohammadi (eds) Questioning the Media: A Critical Introduction, 2nd edn. London: Sage.

Hutchins, R. (2001) Commission on the freedom of the press: A Free and Responsible Press. Chicago: University of Chicago Press.

Kellner, D. (2000) The Persian Gulf TV War. Boulder, CO: Westview Press.

Murdock, G. (2004) Redrawing the map of the communication industries. In M. Ferguson (ed.) Public Communication. London: Sage.

Prentice, Eve-Ann (2004) My nights under fire in Pristina. Times, 22 May 1999.

Stevenson, N. (2002) Understanding Media Cultures: Social Theory and Mass Communication. London: Sage.

Index

E

F

G

H

I

J

L

M